DANIEL C. COOPER.

EARLY DAYTON

WITH IMPORTANT FACTS
AND INCIDENTS FROM THE FOUNDING OF
THE CITY OF DAYTON, OHIO TO THE
HUNDREDTH ANNIVERSARY

1796–1896

—— ILLUSTRATED ——

Robert W. Steele and
Mary Davies Steele

HERITAGE BOOKS
2010

HERITAGE BOOKS
AN IMPRINT OF HERITAGE BOOKS, INC.

Books, CDs, and more—Worldwide

For our listing of thousands of titles see our website
at
www.HeritageBooks.com

A Facsimile Reprint
Published 2010 by
HERITAGE BOOKS, INC.
Publishing Division
100 Railroad Ave. #104
Westminster, Maryland 21157

Copyright © 1895 Mary Davies Steele

Originally published
Dayton, Ohio
U. B. Publishing House
W. J. Shuey, Publisher
1896

— Publisher's Notice —
In reprints such as this, it is often not possible to remove blemishes from the original. We feel the contents of this book warrant its reissue despite these blemishes and hope you will agree and read it with pleasure.

International Standard Book Numbers
Paperbound: 978-0-7884-1233-2
Clothbound: 978-0-7884-8315-8

TO MY FRIENDS

Mr. and Mrs. Frank Conover,

DESIRING TO ASSOCIATE THEIR NAMES WITH MINE IN
MY LITERARY WORK, WHICH THEY HAVE
PROMOTED IN VARIOUS WAYS,

I DEDICATE

"EARLY DAYTON."

M. D. S.

PUBLISHER'S NOTE

THE illustrations contained in this volume have been carefully selected, and include a number which have never before been published. Among these are portraits of Benjamin Van Cleve, Colonel George Newcom and his daughter, Mrs. Jane Wilson, a view of Main Street in 1855 from a water-color by John W. Van Cleve, and a copy of the original plan of the city as found in the records of Hamilton County. For these portraits and the view of Main Street the publisher desires to acknowledge his obligation to Mrs. Thomas Dover, Mrs. Josiah Gebhart, and Miss Martha Holt, in whose possession are the valuable originals, and by whose courtesy they are here reproduced. Special thanks are due, also, to Mr. J. H. Patterson for the portrait of his grandfather, Colonel Robert Patterson, and to Miss S. S. Schenck, of Washington, D. C., for that of her father, General Robert C. Schenck.

The pictures of the landing of the first settlers, of Newcom's first cabin in 1796, and of Newcom's Tavern in 1799 have been reproduced in accordance with the most reliable information which could be obtained, and the artist, Miss Rebekah Rogers, has succeeded admirably in this difficult work.

PREFACE

PERHAPS there is no impropriety in saying in a preface to a history of Dayton that no one living here who has undertaken literary, philanthropic, or other public work can help feeling that Dayton is a good place to live in, so ready is the response and generous the support and appreciation received. Thus, it seems to the student of our history, it has been from the beginning. The imagination catches fire and the heart glows with enthusiasm over the story of the labors for the public good which the pioneers shared, and the respect and admiration which they felt for the benefactors of their beloved town. They should be held up as examples to our youth, and their biographies used as manuals for training in noble character.

One longs for the power to make the old times and the old settlers live again, with their contented but simple and unadorned domestic lives, their home-made buckskin or linsey-woolsey garments, their limited and cautious business undertakings, contrasting strangely with exciting perils in storms and floods and dangerous adventures with wild beasts and Indians—to tell a story with the genuine pioneer flavor which descendants of the forefathers would read with relish and profit.

"Early Dayton" is written from the personal and social standpoint, and it was not the intention to give a complete and consecutive account of the growth of the corporation and the business interests of the city. Biographies, with a few necessary exceptions, have not been inserted after the pioneer period. Had the lives of sons and grandchildren as well as of grandparents been written, the history would have filled more than one large volume.

In the spring and summer of 1895, at the request of Mr. H. H. Weakley, who has in many practical ways shown his interest in Dayton and its writers, I wrote a series of letters on the early history of Dayton for the *Herald*. These letters, which were received with many words of commendation both to author and publisher, form the basis of the present volume, though large and important additions have been made. I was so fortunate as to obtain, through conversation and correspondence with descendants of pioneers, some facts and anecdotes never before published.

Free use has been made of the chapters in the "History of Dayton" written by my father shortly before his death, and his name appears with mine on the title-page.

When the manuscript of "Early Dayton" was almost finished, circumstances rendered it necessary for me to abandon all literary work. My friend Miss Harriet M. King, a born student and excellent writer, generously volunteered to write the concluding two chapters (Chapters X and XI) of the book, bringing it down to date. It requires literary skill to write a brief and condensed yet clear and interesting account of an extended period. Miss King has told the story of modern Dayton in a charming manner, and those who read her valuable contribution will perceive how greatly indebted I am to her. Words fail me when I attempt to express my obligation.

From Mr. E. L. Shuey I received, while my history was being written and published, assistance and encouragement of a very unusual kind, for which I am deeply grateful. I desire to make similar acknowledgments to Mr. W. A. Shuey, who not only relieved me of responsibility and labor, but secured the accuracy and added to the merit of the volume by his careful proof-reading and general supervision, his elaborate index and table of contents, and the excellent illustrations which he procured; but, above all, by his interesting and useful "Chronological Record" and "Historical and Statistical Tables" for ready reference, which cover the history and progress of this region from 1749 to 1896. If all publishers were like mine, societies for the protection of authors would never have existed. I cannot let slip the opportunity to express my appreciation of the interest Mr. W. L. Blocher has shown in securing the mechanical perfection of various literary productions of mine. I am under obligations to the United Brethren Publishing House for their courtesy in allowing me the unrestricted use of the "History of Dayton," of which they own the copyright.

MARY DAVIES STEELE.

DAYTON, OHIO, February 1, 1896.

CONTENTS

CHAPTER I

THE SETTLEMENT

GIST'S Visit to the Miami Valley in 1751—Valuable Timber—Well Watered—Wild Animals—Natural Meadows—A Most Delightful Country—Fertility and Beauty—Kentuckians Long to Dispossess the Indians—The Valley Called the Miami Slaughter-House—Dayton on the Site of the Indian Hunting-Ground—A Favorite Rendezvous for Indian Hunting and War Parties—General George Rogers Clark's Expedition to Ohio—Clark's Second Expedition—Skirmish on Site of Dayton—Logan's Campaign in 1786—Second Skirmish on Site of Dayton—Venice on Site of Dayton—Venice Abandoned—General Wayne's Campaign—Treaty of Peace—Site of Dayton Purchased from Symmes—Original Proprietors of Dayton—Survey of the Purchase—D. C. Cooper Cuts a Road—Dayton Laid Out and Named—Streets Named—Lottery Held on Site of Town—Lots and Inlots Donated to Settlers Drawn—Settlers Permitted to Purchase One Hundred and Sixty Acres at a French Crown per Acre—Names of Original Settlers of Dayton—Three Parties Leave Cincinnati in March, 1796—Hamer's Party Travels in a Two-Horse Wagon—Newcom's Party Makes the Journey on Horseback—Thompson's Party Ascend the Miami in a Pirogue—Description of the Voyage—Poling Up Stream—Beauty of the Landscape—Supper in the Miami Woods—Names of the Passengers in the Pirogue—Ten Days from Cincinnati to Dayton—Mrs. Thompson the First to Land—Indians Encamped at Dayton—Land at Head of St. Clair Street—The Uninhabited Forest All that Welcomed Them—Encouraging Indications—Temporary Protection—Log Cabins—Wholly Dependent on Each Other's Society—Monument Avenue Cleared—Town Covered with Hazelnut Thickets—Dr. Elliott's Purple Silk Coat—Dayton Hard to Find by the Traveler—Ague—Communal Corn-Field—Mary Van Cleve—Indians Attack the Thompson Cabin, - - - - - - - - - - - 17

CHAPTER II

EARLY SETTLERS

DANIEL C. COOPER—Newcom's Tavern—Cooper Park—Mr. Cooper Becomes Titular Proprietor of the Town—His Improvements and Liberality—Indians Frequent Visitors—Playing Marbles at Midnight—Robert Edgar—First Store in Dayton—Henry Brown—First Flatboat

vii

—Furniture of the Nine Cabins Constituting Dayton—Food—Game—Hogs Introduced—Fish—Blockhouse for Defense Against Indians Built at Dayton—First School in Dayton—Benjamin Van Cleve's Autobiography—Early Life of Van Cleve—Battle of Monmouth—Wagon Journey of the Van Cleves Across the Mountains—Murder of John Van Cleve at Cincinnati by Indians—Benjamin Van Cleve Supports His Father's Family—Self-Educated—Employed in Quartermaster's Department of Western Army—St. Clair's Defeat—Employed in Flatboating by Army Contractors—In Charge of Army Horses and Cattle—Sent Express to Philadelphia by Quartermaster's Department—Sent by General Knox from Philadelphia to Conduct Pair of Horses to Indian Chief Brant—Quarrel with General Knox—Meets Brant in New York—Studious Life After Return to Philadelphia—Sent West with Dispatches to General Wayne—Journey by Boat from Wheeling, Accompanied by Officers and Recruits—Cheated Out of His Pay—Flatboating to Kentucky—Sutler at Fort Greenville—Sent by Army Contractor to Fort Massac with Two Boats Loaded with Provisions—Adventure at Fort Massac with Major, Called "King," Doyle—Returning, Visits Red Banks, a Resort of Thieves and Cutthroats—Drives Cattle to Greenville, Fort Wayne, and Fort Washington—Accompanies Captain Dunlap to Make the Survey of the Dayton Settlement—Adventures as a Surveyor—Keeps Field-Notes During Rain on Blocks of Wood—Settles in Dayton—Surveying, Writing, and Farming—Trials, - - - - 29

CHAPTER III

PIONEER LIFE

TWO HOUSES on Main Street in 1799—Small Size of Cabins—Description by W. C. Howells of a Home of the Period—Newcom's Tavern, First House in Dayton, Chinked with Mortar—Corner Monument Avenue and Main Street the Business Center of Dayton—First White Child Born in Dayton—Biography of Colonel Newcom—Wearisome Journey Through the Woods to Dayton—Camping at Night—Newcom's Tavern Described—Relics—Old Clock and Brass Candlestick—First County Court Held at Tavern—Money Scarce—Convicted Persons Fined a Deerskin or a Bushel of Corn—Sentenced to Thirty-Nine Lashes on Bare Back—Sheriff Newcom's Primitive Prison a Corn-Crib and a Dry Well—Anecdotes of Visits of Troublesome Indians to the Tavern—Colonel Newcom Introduces Apples—First Wedding in Dayton—Benjamin Van Cleve's Characteristic Account of the Event—Mr. Van Cleve's Hospitality to Strangers—Usefulness to the New Town—W. C. Howells's Description of Social Life in Pioneer Times—Fire-Hunting on the Miami—Women Helped Their Husbands in the Fields—Dependent on the Husband's and Father's Gun for Meals—Pelts and Bear's Oil Articles of Merchandise—Skins Used for Clothes, Moccasins, Rugs, and Coverlets—Business Conducted by Barter—Ginseng, Peltries, Beeswax, etc., Used as Money—Cut-Money or Sharp Shins—Charges Made in Pounds, Shillings, and Pence—Wild Animals—First Mill, a Corn-Cracker, Built by D. C. Cooper—Log Meeting-House Built—Dayton First Governed Wholly by County Commissioners and Township Assessors—D. C. Cooper Justice of the

Peace—Early Marriages—Petition Presented to Congress by Settlers—The Town Nearly Dies Out—D. C. Cooper, Titular Proprietor, Resuscitates It—Town Plats—Basis of Titles—Ohio a State—Montgomery Separated from Hamilton County—Population Increases—First Election—First County Court—Mr. Cooper Builds Saw- and Grist-Mills—Levees—New Graveyard—Log-Cabin Meeting-House Sold—New First Presbyterian Church—Mr. Cooper's Death—First Jail, - - - 51

CHAPTER IV

1800–1805

JOHN W. VAN CLEVE—First White Male Child Born in Dayton—Friendship for R. W. Steele—Biographies of Van Cleve by R. W. Steele—Minutes Kept and Societies Founded by Van Cleve—His Exquisite Handwriting—His Versatility and Thoroughness—Proficiency in Ancient and Modern Languages—Teaches Latin at College Before Graduation—Talent for Mathematics—Translations—Water-Color Pictures of Wild Flowers—A True Book-Lover—Studies Law—Edits the Dayton *Journal*—In the Drug Business—Devotes Himself to Labors for the Public Good—A Civil Engineer—An Engraver—Talent for Painting—Plays Several Musical Instruments—A Botanist and Geologist—To Him We Owe Woodland Cemetery—Love of Plants and Trees—Plants the Levees with Trees—Surrounds the Court-House with Elms—Fondness for Children—Delightful Picnics—His Great Size—Interest in Schools and Libraries—Founder and Supporter of Dayton Library Association—Free Lectures on Scientific, Historical, or Literary Subjects—Affection and Pride with Which He was Regarded—Devotion to His Kindred—Friendship Between Him and His Father—Public Offices in Town That He Held—His Map of Dayton—Writes Songs and Designs and Engraves Illustrations for the *Log Cabin*—The Whig Glee Club Trained by Professor Turpin—Mr. Van Cleve and Others Accompany the Club to the Columbus Convention—His Death—His Unbending Integrity and Scrupulous Honesty—Council Passes Resolutions of Respect—Dr. T. E. Thomas's Funeral Oration—Isaac Spining—William King—The Osborns—John H. Williams—The First Postoffice in Dayton—Mail-Routes—Post-Rider to Urbana—Trials of Benjamin Van Cleve, First Postmaster—His Successor, George S. Houston—Joseph Peirce—Joseph H. Crane—Colonel Robert Patterson—Schools—Dayton Incorporated—McCullum's Tavern—Social Library Society, - - - 67

CHAPTER V

1805–1809

FIRST Disastrous Flood—Emigrants from New Jersey—Charles Russell Greene—Ferries—First Court-House—First Newspaper—First Brick Stores—James Steele—Robert W. Steele—Dayton Academy—James Hanna—John Folkerth—First Teachers in the Academy—William M. Smith—James H. Mitchell—E. E. Barney—Trustees of Academy in 1833—Collins Wight—Milo G. Williams—Transfer of Academy to

Board of Education—Henry Bacon—Luther Bruen—Antislavery Excitement—Arrest and Suicide of a Fugitive Slave—Colored People Leave Dayton for Hayti—A Colonization Society Formed—Antislavery Society—Union Meeting-House, Principally Built by Luther Bruen—Dr. Birney and Mr. Rankin Mobbed—Dr. H. Jewett—Dr. John Steele—Advertisement of a Runaway Slave—Jonathan Harshman—First Brick Residence—The Cannon "Mad Anthony"—Rev. James Welsh, M.D.—Dr. John Elliott—Town Prospering—No Care Taken of Streets or Walks—Grimes's Tavern—Alexander Grimes—Reid's Inn—Colonel Reid—Second Newspaper, the *Repertory*—Advertisements in the *Repertory*—Matthew Patton—Abram Darst—Pioneer Women, - - - - - - - - - - - - - 86

CHAPTER VI

1809-1812

WILLIAM EAKER—George W. Smith—Roads—Journeys to the East—Goods Brought by Conestoga Wagons and Broadhorns to Ohio—Pack-Horses Moving Up Main Street—Groceries from New Orleans by Keel-Boats—A Voyage from New Orleans Described—Country Stores—Drinking Customs—Flatboating South—Excitement When the Fleets of Boats Left Dayton—Arrival of a Large Keel-Boat—Fourth of July from 1809 to 1840—The First Drug-Store—Indians and Wild Animals Both Troublesome—Rewards for Wolf-Scalps—New Sidewalks and Ditches or Gutters—*Ohio Centinel*—Earthquakes—William Huffman—Ohio Militia Encamped at Dayton—Business Beginning of 1812—Horatio G. Phillips—J. D. Phillips—Obadiah B. Conover, - 101

CHAPTER VII

1812-1816

DR. JOHN STEELE—1812 and 1813 Years of Excitement—Dread of Indians—Colonel Johnston's Control of the Indians—Madison Orders Out Ohio Militia—Battalion Muster at Dayton—Militia Bivouac Without Tents at Cooper Park—Governor Meigs Arrives—Issues a Call to Citizens for Blankets—General Gano and General Cass Arrive—Three Regiments of Infantry Formed—Captain William Van Cleve—General Hull Arrives—Governor Meigs Surrenders Command to General Hull—The Governor and General Review the Troops—The Three Regiments March Across Mad River to Camp Meigs—Leave Camp Meigs for Detroit—Munger's Brigade Ordered Here to Garrison the Town—Hull's Surrender—Consternation of the People—Handbills Issued at Dayton Calling for Volunteers—Captain Steele's Company—Kentucky Troops Arrive Here—Harrison Calls for Volunteers and Horses—Dayton Ladies Make One Thousand Eight Hundred Shirts for Soldiers—Expedition Against Indians Near Muncietown—Defeated Soldiers Bring Wounded to Dayton—Hospital on Court-House Corner—War—Jerome Holt—War Ended—Dayton Companies Welcomed Home—First Dayton Bank—*Ohio Centinel*—Stone Jail—Mr. Forrer's Reminiscences of Dayton in 1814—First Methodist Church—

CONTENTS xi

William Hamer—Aaron Baker—*Ohio Republican*—*Ohio Watchman*—Medical Societies—Dr. Job Haines—Female Charitable and Bible Society—First Market-House—Moral Society—Associated Bachelors—First Theater, - - - - - - - - - - - - - 115

CHAPTER VIII

1816–1835

NEW Brick Court-House of 1817—Ferries—First Bridges—Sabbath-School Association—Sunday-School Society—Game Abundant—Flights of Wild Pigeons—Migrations of Squirrels—Fish—Stage-Coaches—St. Thomas Episcopal Church—Christ Episcopal Church—Shows—Volunteer Fire Department, 1820 to 1863—Leading Citizens Active Members—Feuds Between Rival Engine Companies—Financial Depression, 1820 to 1822—Fever—Lancasterian School—Francis Glass—*Gridiron* Newspaper—*Miami Republican and Dayton Advertiser*—George B. Holt—Consolidation of *Watchman* and *Republican*—Dayton *Journal*—Contribution to the Greek Cause—James Perrine, First Insurance Agent—First Baptist Church Built—Letter from Dayton in 1827—Canal Agitation—Dinner and Reception to De Witt Clinton—First Canal-Boat Arrives—Enthusiasm of the People—Extension of Canal by Cooper Estate—Law Providing for Election of Mayor—Town Divided into Wards—Temperance Society—New Market-House—Rivalry Between Dayton and Cabintown—Private Schools—Manual-Training School—Seely's Basin—Peasley's Garden—Miniature Locomotive and Car Exhibited in Methodist Church—Daytonians Take Their First Railroad Ride—Seneca Indians Camp at Dayton—First Public Schools—School-Directors—Steele's Dam—General R. C. Schenck—Political Excitement—Council Cuts Down a Jackson Pole—Cholera in 1832 and 1833—Silk Manufactory—The Dayton Lyceum—Mechanics' Institute—Six Libraries in Dayton—Eighth of January Barbecue—Town Watchmen—Lafayette Commemorative Services, - - - 135

CHAPTER IX

1836–1840

MEASURES Proposed for Improving the Town in 1836—Proceedings of Council—Public Meeting to Sustain Council—Cooper Park—Dayton Business Men in 1836—Educational Convention in 1836—Shinplasters—Thomas Morrison—Zoölogical Museum—William Jennison—First Railroad—Turnpikes—First Public-School Buildings—Opposition to Public Schools—Processions of School Children and Other Efforts to Excite an Interest in Public Schools—Samuel Forrer Takes Charge of Turnpikes—His Biography—Midnight Markets—Cooper Hydraulic—Change of Channel of Mad River—First County Fair—*Morus Multicaulis* Excitement—Dayton Carpet Manufactory—Number of Buildings Erected in 1839—*Log Cabin* Newspaper—Harrison Convention—Numbers in Attendance—Hospitality of Dayton People—Banners Presented, - - - - - - - - - 163

CHAPTER X

DAYTON FROM 1840 TO 1896

THE Beginning of "the Forties"—Distinguished Visitors—Schools—Oregon—West Dayton—Banks—Police Department—New Jail and Court-House—Cemeteries—Dayton Bar—General Robert C. Schenck—Clement L. Vallandigham—Thomas Brown—Prominent Physicians—Public Library—Churches—Floods—Cholera—The Mexican War—First Telegraph Message—Gas and Electric Light—Railroads—Street-Railroads—Fire Department—Water-Works—Dayton Orphan Asylum—Young Men's Christian Association—Woman's Christian Association—Young Women's League—St. Elizabeth Hospital—Protestant Deaconess Hospital—Musical Societies—Literary Clubs—Improvements—Manufacturing and Mercantile Interests—Natural Gas—Newspapers—Periodicals—David Stout—Ebenezer Thresher—Valentine Winters—Frederick Gebhart—Robert W. Steele, - - - - 183

CHAPTER XI

DAYTON IN THE CIVIL WAR

THE Opening of the War—Fall of Sumter—Recruiting—Dayton Light Guards—Light Artillery—Lafayette Guards—Departure of Troops——Anderson Guards—Dayton Riflemen—Zouave Rangers—Buckeye Guard—State Guard—Camp Corwin—Camp Dayton—Families of Soldiers Cared For—Advance of Kirby Smith—R. C. Schenck Elected to Congress—Union League Formed—Arrest of Vallandigham—*Journal* Office Burned—Morgan's Raid—Colonel King—*Empire* Office Mobbed—Procession of Wood-Wagons—Women's Work for the Soldiers—The Home-Guard—Return of Companies A and E—Another Call for Troops—Last Draft of the War—Lee's Surrender—Assassination of Lincoln—Admiral Schenck—Rear-Admiral Greer—Paymaster McDaniel—National Military Home—Soldiers' Monument, - 202

COLONEL ISRAEL LUDLOW, - - - - - - - - - - - - 213

HISTORICAL AND STATISTICAL TABLES

LOCATION and Area—Population—City Government and Institutions—Mayor—Board of City Affairs—City Council—Board of Elections—Board of Equalization—Miscellaneous—Public Schools—Public Library—Police Department—Work-House—Fire Department—Water-Works—Board of Health—City Infirmary—Markets—Tax Commission—Taxes for 1894-96—Bonded Debt—Periodicals—Churches—Church and Private Schools—Benevolent and Charitable Institutions—Literary and Musical Societies—Political Clubs—Social, Cycling, Gymnastic, and Other Clubs—Military Companies—Street-Railways—Street Improvements—Commercial and Industrial—Post-office Statistics, 1895—Partial Enumeration of Mercantile, Manufacturing, and Other Concerns—Chronological Record, - - - 221

BIBLIOGRAPHY, - - - - - - - - - - - - - 238

INDEX, - - - - - - - - - - - - - - 241

ILLUSTRATIONS

PORTRAITS.

D. C. COOPER,	*Frontispiece*
	Opposite Page
JOHN CLEVES SYMMES,	17
GENERAL GEORGE ROGERS CLARK,	20
GENERAL ANTHONY WAYNE,	20
GOVERNOR ARTHUR ST. CLAIR,	20
GENERAL JAMES WILKINSON,	20
GENERAL JONATHAN DAYTON,	21
BENJAMIN VAN CLEVE,	48
COLONEL GEORGE NEWCOM,	52
MRS. JANE NEWCOM WILSON,	60
NATHANIEL WILSON,	61
COLONEL ROBERT PATTERSON,	84
ROBERT W. STEELE,	92
GENERAL ROBERT C. SCHENCK,	204

MISCELLANEOUS.

1796–1894.

THE LANDING OF THE FIRST SETTLERS,	28
ORIGINAL PLAN OF DAYTON,	29
NEWCOM'S FIRST LOG CABIN, BUILT IN 1796,	32
NEWCOM'S TAVERN IN 1799,	53
PLAN OF DAYTON IN 1805,	64
PLAN OF DAYTON IN 1809,	65
THE OLD ACADEMY, 1833–1857,	93
FIRST PRESBYTERIAN CHURCH, 1839–1867,	100
MAIN STREET IN 1846,	101
FIRST AND LUDLOW STREETS IN 1846,	108
EAST SIDE OF MAIN STREET, BETWEEN SECOND AND THIRD, IN 1855,	109
CENTRAL HIGH SCHOOL, 1857–1893,	116
FLOOD OF 1866, AS SEEN FROM THE HEAD OF MAIN STREET,	117
NEWCOM'S TAVERN IN 1894,	124

ILLUSTRATIONS

1896.

	Opposite Page
THE LANDING-PLACE AND NEWCOM'S TAVERN IN JANUARY, 1896,	125
COUNTY BUILDINGS,	132
GOVERNMENT BUILDING AND POSTOFFICE,	133
CITY BUILDINGS,	140
PUBLIC LIBRARY AND COOPER PARK,	141
STEELE HIGH SCHOOL,	148
CENTRAL DISTRICT SCHOOL,	149
MAIN STREET, LOOKING NORTH FROM BELOW FOURTH,	156
THIRD STREET, LOOKING EAST FROM MAIN,	157
FIFTH STREET, LOOKING EAST FROM MAIN,	164
YOUNG MEN'S CHRISTIAN ASSOCIATION BUILDING,	172
WOMAN'S CHRISTIAN ASSOCIATION BUILDING,	173
PROTESTANT DEACONESS HOSPITAL,	180
ST. ELIZABETH HOSPITAL,	181
FIRST PRESBYTERIAN CHURCH,	188
THIRD STREET PRESBYTERIAN CHURCH,	189
GRACE METHODIST CHURCH,	192
SACRED HEART ROMAN CATHOLIC CHURCH,	193
SYNAGOGUE,	196
ENTRANCE TO WOODLAND CEMETERY,	197
THE SOLDIERS' MONUMENT, AND APARTMENT HOUSE ON THE SITE OF NEWCOM'S TAVERN,	208
NATIONAL MILITARY HOME,	209

TAILPIECES.

	Page
FIREPLACE AND SPINNING-WHEEL,	28
BLOCKHOUSE,	50
HEARTH,	66

MAPS.

MAP OF DAYTON IN 1839,	250
MAP OF DAYTON IN 1895,	254
MAP OF OHIO,	257

Early Dayton

JOHN CLEVES SYMMES.

EARLY DAYTON

CHAPTER I

THE SETTLEMENT

GIST'S Visit to the Miami Valley in 1751—Valuable Timber—Well Watered—Wild Animals—Natural Meadows—A Most Delightful Country—Fertility and Beauty—Kentuckians Long to Dispossess the Indians—The Valley Called the Miami Slaughter-House—Dayton on the Site of the Indian Hunting-Ground—A Favorite Rendezvous for Indian Hunting and War Parties—General George Rogers Clark's Expedition to Ohio—Clark's Second Expedition—Skirmish on Site of Dayton—Logan's Campaign in 1786—Second Skirmish on Site of Dayton—Venice on Site of Dayton—Venice Abandoned—General Wayne's Campaign—Treaty of Peace—Site of Dayton Purchased from Symmes—Original Proprietors of Dayton—Survey of the Purchase—D. C. Cooper Cuts a Road—Dayton Laid Out and Named—Streets Named—Lottery Held on Site of Town—Lots and Inlots Donated to Settlers Drawn—Settlers Permitted to Purchase One Hundred and Sixty Acres at a French Crown per Acre—Names of Original Settlers of Dayton—Three Parties Leave Cincinnati in March, 1796—Hamer's Party Travels in a Two-Horse Wagon—Newcom's Party Makes the Journey on Horseback—Thompson's Party Ascend the Miami in a Pirogue—Description of the Voyage—Poling Up Stream—Beauty of the Landscape—Supper in the Miami Woods—Names of the Passengers in the Pirogue—Ten Days from Cincinnati to Dayton—Mrs. Thompson the First to Land—Indians Encamped at Dayton—Land at Head of St. Clair Street—The Uninhabited Forest All that Welcomed Them—Encouraging Indications—Temporary Protection—Log Cabins—Wholly Dependent on Each Other's Society—Monument Avenue Cleared—Town Covered by Hazelnut Thickets—Dr. Elliott's Purple Silk Coat—Dayton Hard to Find by the Traveler—Ague—Communal Corn-Field—Mary Van Cleve—Indians Attack the Thompson Cabin.

THE report of the French Major Celoron de Bienville, who, in August, 1749, ascended the La Roche or Big Miami River in bateaux to visit the Twightwee villages at Piqua, has been preserved; but Gist, the agent of the Virginians who formed the Ohio Land Company, was probably the first person who wrote a description in English of the region surrounding Dayton. Gist visited the Twightwee or Miami villages in 1751. He was delighted with the fertile and well-watered land, with its large oak, walnut, maple, ash, wild cherry, and other trees. The country, he says, abounded "with turkeys, deer, elk, and most sorts of game, particularly buffaloes, thirty or forty of which are frequently seen feeding in one meadow; in short, it wants nothing but cultivation to make it a most delightful country. The land upon the Great Miami is very rich, level, and well timbered—some of the finest meadows that can be. The grass here grows to a great height on the clear fields, of which there are a great number, and the bottoms are full of white clover, wild rye, and blue grass." A number of white traders were living at the Miami villages and in one of their houses Gist lodged. It is stated by pioneer writers that buffaloes and elk disappeared from Ohio about the year 1795.

Long before any permanent settlement was made in the Miami Valley, its beauty and fertility were known by the people beyond the Alleghanies and the inhabitants of Kentucky, who considered it an "earthly paradise," and repeated efforts were made to get possession of it. These efforts led to retaliation on the part of the Indians, who resented the attempts to dispossess them of their lands, and the continuous raids back and forth across the Ohio River to gain or keep possession of the valley caused it to be called, until the close of the eighteenth century, the "Miami slaughter-house." The wild animals—wolves, wildcats, bears, panthers, foxes—which roamed through the valley now so peaceful and prosperous were scarcely more brutal and fierce than the inhabitants of the infrequent villages scattered along the borders of the Miami hunting-grounds—the terrible "Indian country," the abode of cruelty and death, which the imagination of trembling women in far-distant blockhouses invested with all the horrors of a veritable hell on earth. The pioneers of Kentucky looked with jealous and envious eyes on this great Indian game preserve. The wily and suspicious savages did their best to exclude them; but, though they ventured over here at the risk of being burned, they frequently came alone or in small parties to hunt or rescue some friend captured in a raid into Kentucky by the Indians. Before the Miami Valley had ever been visited by whites, the country lying between the Great and Little Miamis, and bounded on the south by the Ohio and on the north by Mad River, was used only as a hunting-ground. Dayton lies just within this former immense game preserve. Probably no wigwam has been built and no Indians have lived on the site of Dayton since 1700. The site of Dayton was a favorite rendezvous for Indian hunters or warriors. Parties came down the Miami in canoes, and, having formed a camp of supplies at the mouth of Mad River in charge of squaws, set out on their raids or hunts.

In the summer of 1780, General George Rogers Clark led an expedition of experienced Indian fighters to Ohio against the Shawnees near Xenia and Springfield. He defeated the Indians. By this victory the homes, crops, and other property of about four thousand Shawnees were destroyed, and for some time they were wholly engaged in rebuilding their wigwams, and in hunting and fishing to obtain food for their families. Among the officers who held command under Clark was Colonel Robert Patterson, from 1804 till 1827 a citizen of Dayton.

Finding that the Indians were recovering from their defeat of 1780, Clark, in the fall of 1782, led a second expedition of one thousand Kentuckians to Ohio. They met with no resistance till they reached the mouth of Mad River, on the 9th of November, where they found a small party of Indians stationed to prevent their crossing the stream. A skirmish on the site of Dayton followed, in which the Kentuckians were victorious. They spent the night here, and then proceeded to Upper Piqua, on the Great Miami. Having destroyed Upper Piqua, they went on to the trading-station of Laramie, and plundered and burned the store and destroyed the Indians' wigwams and crops. These two expeditions, or campaigns, were campaigns of the Revolution, as the Indians were friendly to the British.

For some time after the peace with Great Britain in 1783, the Indians, who had met with many reverses and losses during the Revolution, did not trouble the settlements as much as formerly, but about 1785 they recommenced hostilities, and in 1786 a force commanded by Colonel Logan was sent against the Wabash and Mad River villages. One of the brigades was commanded by Colonel Robert Patterson. They harried and ruined the Indian country, and destroyed eight towns and the crops and vegetables, taking a large number of horses, and leaving the Indians in a state of destitution and starvation from which it took them nearly a year to recover. The Kentuckians returned to the Ohio by the way of Mad River, and at the mouth of the river found a party of Indians on guard. With them was Tecumseh, at this time about fourteen years of age. Having, after some slight resistance, beaten the Indians and driven them up Mad River and gained the second battle or skirmish between whites and Indians fought on the site of Dayton, they camped for the night. Being well supplied with provisions taken from the captured villages, they remained here for two or three days examining land with a view to recommending a settlement in this neighborhood. Having driven the Indians for the time being out of the Miami Valley, the Kentuckians, when they departed, left an uninhabited country behind them.

In 1789 Major Benjamin Stites, John Stites Gano, and William Goforth formed plans for a settlement to be named Venice, at the mouth of the Tiber, as they called Mad River. The site of the proposed city lay within the seventh range of townships, which they agreed to purchase from John Cleves Symmes for eighty-three cents an acre. The deed was executed and recorded, and the town of Venice, with its two principal streets crossing each other at right angles and the position of houses and squares indicated in the four quarters outlined by the streets, was laid out on paper. But Indian troubles and Symmes's misunderstanding with the Government forced them to abandon the project, and "we escaped being Venetians."

In the spring of 1793 General Wayne was made commander of the Western army. His victories over the Indians on June 30 and 31 and August 30, 1794, ended four years of Indian war. August 3, 1795, a treaty of peace was concluded at Greenville, which was regarded as securing the safety of settlers in the Indian country.

August 20, 1795, seventeen days after the treaty was signed, a party of gentlemen contracted for the purchase of the seventh and eighth ranges between Mad River and the Little Miami from John Cleves Symmes, a soldier of the Revolutionary army, who, encouraged by the success of the Ohio Company, had, after much negotiation, obtained from Congress a grant for the purchase of one million acres between the two Miamis. The purchasers of the seventh and eighth ranges were General Arthur St. Clair, Governor of the Northwest Territory; General Jonathan Dayton, afterward Senator from New Jersey; General James Wilkinson, of Wayne's army, and Colonel Israel Ludlow, from Long Hill, Morris County, New Jersey. On the 21st of September two parties of surveyors set out, one led by Daniel C.

From the "National Cyclopedia of American Biography," by permission of James T. White & Co.

From the "National Cyclopedia of American Biography," by permission of James T. White & Co.

From the "Cyclopedia of American Biography." Copyright, 1888, by D. Appleton & Co.

From the "Cyclopedia of American Biography." Copyright, 1889, by D. Appleton & Co.

From the "National Cyclopedia of American Biography," by permission of James T. White & Co.

Cooper to survey and mark a road and cut out some of the brush, and the other led by Captain John Dunlap, which was to run the boundaries of the purchase. On the 1st of November the surveyors returned to Mad River, and Israel Ludlow laid out the town, which he named for General Dayton. Three streets were named St. Clair, Wilkinson, and Ludlow for the proprietors. Another was called, as a sort of compromise, Jefferson, as the proprietors were Federalists. Dayton was founded by Revolutionary officers, and bears their names. It is also linked to the War of 1812 by a street called for Commodore Perry. For many years Perry Street was down on the maps of the town as Cherry Lane.

On November 1 a lottery was held, and each one present drew lots for himself or others who intended to settle in the new town. Each of the settlers received a donation of an inlot and an outlot. In addition, each of them had the privilege of purchasing one hundred and sixty acres at a French crown, or about one dollar and thirteen cents, per acre. The proprietors hoped by offering these inducements to attract settlers to the place.

Forty-six men had agreed to remove from Cincinnati to Dayton, but only nineteen came. The following men and about seventeen women and children were the original settlers of Dayton: William Hamer, Solomon Hamer, Thomas Hamer, George Newcom, William Newcom, Abraham Glassmire, Thomas Davis, John Davis, John Dorough, William Chenoweth, James Morris, Daniel Ferrell, Samuel Thompson, Benjamin Van Cleve, James McClure, John McClure, William Gahagan, Solomon Goss, William Van Cleve.

In March, 1796, they left Cincinnati in three parties, led by William Hamer, George Newcom, and Samuel Thompson. Hamer's party was the first to start; the other two companies left on Monday, March 21, one by land the other by water. Hamer's party came in a two-horse wagon over the road begun, but only partially cut through the woods, by Cooper in the fall of 1795. The company consisted of Mr. and Mrs. William Hamer and their children Solomon, Thomas, Nancy, Elizabeth, Sarah, and Polly, and Jonathan and Edward Mercer. They were delayed, and had a long, cold, and uncomfortable journey.

In the other party that traveled by land were Mr. and Mrs. George Newcom and their brother William, James Morris, John Dorough and family, Daniel Ferrell and family, Solomon Goss and family, John Davis, Abraham Glassmire, and William Van Cleve, who drove Mr. Thompson's cow, which was with the cattle belonging to the Newcom division of the colonists.

Thompson's party were steered and poled by Benjamin Van Cleve and William Gahagan in a large pirogue down the Ohio to the Miami and up that stream to the mouth of Mad River. A pirogue was a long, narrow boat of light draft and partly enclosed and roofed. It required much skill and muscular strength to pole a boat up stream for many miles. The men, each provided with a pole with a heavy socket, were placed on either side of the boat. They "set their poles near the head of the boat and bringing the end of the pole to their shoulders, with their bodies bent, walked slowly down the running board to the stern, returning at a quick pace to the bow for a new set."

The Miami in 1796 wound through an almost wholly uninhabited wilderness. Such a journey, it seems to us, looking back from this safe and prosaic age when steam cars whirl us up from Cincinnati, must have been full of danger and of exciting adventure, and yet not without its pleasures. Imagination invests this little band of adventurers, laboriously making their way with their boat-load of women and children up the Indian-named river and valley to a frontier home in the ancient Miami hunting-grounds, with an atmosphere of romance. On the borders of their ancestral corn-fields and game preserves lurked jealous and revengeful savages, gazing with envious and homesick eyes on the rich lands of which the pioneers had dispossessed them. The Indian reign of terror, in spite of the treaty of peace, really lasted till after 1799, but travelers on the river were probably in less danger of surprise in early spring than when the foliage was in full leaf and the Indians could consequently more easily conceal themselves.

However unpropitious the season may be, there are always occasional sunshiny days in the early spring in Ohio. Though the woods in 1796 were wet from recent showers, the rain seems to have been over before the pirogue began its voyage, and no doubt part of the time the weather was mild and bright. The banks of the Miami were thickly wooded, and vocal with the songs of countless varieties of birds. The flowers and the foliage of the trees were just beginning to unfold, and the ground was covered with grass fresh with the greenness of spring. For miles on either side of the Miami extended a fertile and beautiful country.

At the close of each day the boat was tied to a tree on the shore, and the emigrants landed and camped for the night around the big fire by which they cooked their appetizing supper of game, and fish, and the eggs of wild fowls, for which the hunger of travelers was a piquant and sufficient sauce. Meat was fastened on a sharp stick, stuck in the ground before the fire, and frequently turned. Dough for wheat bread was sometimes wound round a stick and baked in the same way. Corn-bread was baked under the hot ashes. "Sweeter roast meat," exclaims an enthusiastic pioneer writer, "than such as is prepared in this manner, no epicure of Europe ever tasted." "Scarce any one who has not tried it can imagine the sweetness and gusto of such a meal, in such a place, at such a time."

In the pirogue came Samuel Thompson and his wife, Catherine; their children, Sarah, two years old, Martha, three months old, and Mrs. Thompson's son, Benjamin Van Cleve, then about twenty-five, and her daughter, Mary Van Cleve, nine years of age; the widow McClure and her sons and daughters, James, John, Thomas, Kate, and Ann, and William Gahagan, a young Irishman. The passage from Cincinnati to Dayton occupied ten days. Mrs. Thompson was the first to step ashore. Two small camps of Indians were here when the pirogue touched the Miami bank, but they proved friendly and were persuaded to leave in a day or two. The pirogue landed at the head of St. Clair Street April 1, 1796. The Thompson party was the first to arrive.

Samuel Thompson was a native of Pennsylvania, and removed to Cincinnati soon after its settlement. He married the widow of John Van Cleve. Mr. Thompson was drowned in Mad River in 1817, and Mrs. Thompson died at Dayton, August 6, 1837. William Gahagan was a native of Pennsylvania, but of Irish parentage. He was a soldier in Wayne's legion, and came west in 1793, serving with the army till the peace of 1795. Benjamin Van Cleve and he were friends and comrades. He was one of the party which surveyed the site of Dayton. In 1804 or 1805 he removed to a tract of land south of Troy, called Gahagan's Prairie, which he owned. Here his wife died and he married Mrs. Tennery. He died about 1845 in Troy. The McClures soon removed to Miami County. Little is known of Solomon Goss, Thomas Davis, William Chenoweth, James Morris, and Daniel Ferrell. Abraham Glassmire was a German and unmarried. He was a very useful member of the little community, making looms and showing much ingenuity in contriving conveniences not easily obtained by pioneer housekeepers. John Dorough was the owner of a mill on Mad River, afterwards known as Kneisley's Mill. William Newcom, younger brother of George, was born about 1776. He married Charlotte Nolan, and had one son, Robert. William Newcom died at Dayton from the effects of hardships and exposure during the War of 1812, in which he served as a soldier. Biographies of other pioneers will be given later on in our history.

We can easily imagine the loneliness and dreariness of the uninhabited wilderness which confronted the homeless pioneer families as they arrived by water or land at Dayton. "The unbroken forest was all that welcomed the Thompson party, and the awful stillness of night had no refrain but the howling of the wolf and the wailing of the whippoorwill." The spring was late and cold, but though at first the landscape looked bare and desolate, before many days the air was sweet with the blossoms of the wild grape, plum, cherry, and crab-apple, and the woods beautiful with the contrasting red and white of the dogwood and redbud or of elder and wild rose, and the fresh green of young leaves. The woods were full of wild fruits, flowers, and nut-bearing trees and bushes.

As a temporary protection against the weather the pioneers, on their arrival, built, with the lumber of which the pirogue was made, against a log or bank three-sided huts or shanties, roofed with skin or bark, and open towards the fire, which was made outside. Then they began at once to fell timber and build log cabins, containing one room and a loft. After or before the cabin was built, the trees for some distance around were girdled and left to die a slow death, as they interfered with the cultivation of the soil, and also concealed lurking Indians. Then a few acres were grubbed for a corn and potato patch.

Isolated from other settlements by miles of unbroken forests, the only road a trail marked by blazed trees or a narrow bridle path, with treacherous Indians and wild beasts prowling through the tangled undergrowth on either side, the inhabitants of frontier places like Dayton were dependent on each other for society and for assistance in sickness and work. They shared everything. The latchstring was always out. Hildreth says of Marietta that the various households in the little community were like the nearly related branches of one family, and probably this was true of the log-cabin hamlet of Dayton.

As soon as possible after the arrival of the pioneers, the whole of Monument Avenue was cleared of brush and trees. But with this exception, a few farms, and the wagon-road cut in the middle of Main Street and running south to Franklin, Fort Hamilton, and Cincinnati, the country on both sides of the Miami was for many miles unbroken forest or a thicket of hazel bushes and wild fruit-trees. Pioneers could, in the summer, step out of their back doors into a boundless wild park or garden. Delicious perfumes, sweet as attar of roses,—delicate, pungent, aromatic,—and countless flowers, pink, white, purple, scarlet, blue, and blending with every shade of yellow and green, delighted the senses. To be sure, mud, snakes, stinging insects, thorns, burrs, and poisonous vines detracted from the pleasure of their strolls. Innumerable garter-snakes were to be seen, and rattlesnakes were often found.

A hazelnut thicket covered a good deal of the town plat, and is often mentioned in the reminiscences of first settlers. Dr. Drake, a noted Cincinnatian, writing of Dr. Elliott, an ex-army surgeon and ancestor of some of our prominent Daytonians, says, "In the summer of 1804 I saw him in Dayton, a highly accomplished gentleman in a purple silk coat, which contrasted strangely with the surrounding thickets of brush and high bushes." Such elegant raiment, though common in cities, was not often seen in frontier villages. Benjamin Van Cleve, in his interesting manuscript autobiography, describes himself on June 26, 1794, as dressed in a hunting-frock, breechcloth, and leggings, with a knife eighteen inches long hanging at his side, a gun in one hand, and a tomahawk in the other. And this costume, in a modified form, was usual. A coonskin cap was added in winter.

John W. Van Cleve, who had seen his native place change from a wilderness to a thriving town, gives this description of Dayton in 1800-1805: "While the inhabitants all lived on the river bank, it was no uncommon thing for strangers, on coming into the place, after threading their way through the brush until they had passed through the whole town plat from one extremity to the other, and arrived at the first few of the cabins that constituted the settlement, to inquire how far it was to Dayton. They were, of course, informed that they had just passed through it, and arrived in the suburbs." A little later they would have found a log cabin occupied by John Welsh, a substantial farmer, at what is now the southeast corner of Main and Fifth streets, and inquiring of him the distance to Dayton, would have been directed to Newcom's Tavern, about a quarter of a mile down the road. Persons still living, and not aged, remember, when driving the cows home from the prairies east of St. Clair and south of First Street,—where both pasturage and water from several ponds were abundant,—lingering in the public square (now Cooper Park) to fill their pockets with hazelnuts. The ponds were filled so long ago that many never heard of them. This is also true of "the ravine that ran from the head of Mill Street down the present course of the canal to the river below the foot of Ludlow Street, and of another wide ravine that extended from the levee at the head of Jefferson Street across to Cooper Park, connecting with the ravine running south." A gully five or six feet deep, beginning at the corner of Wilkinson and First streets, crossing Main at Third Street, and ending at the corner of Fifth and Brown streets, was not wholly filled up till Mr. J. D. Platt built his house on the northwest corner of First and Wilkinson streets.

In 1798 the home missionary, Rev. John Kobler, visited Dayton, which he describes as a little village of that name, on the bank of the Big Miami, containing a few log houses and eight or ten families. When threatened with illness, he hastened southward, for "to lie sick at any of the houses in these parts would be choosing death, as it is next to impossible for a well man to get food or sustenance." Yet, as is usual in regions where very rich soil is newly cultivated, the pioneers all had ague. Fortunately, what was chill day to one-half the population was generally well day to the other half. One Sunday morning, when a little knot of worshipers were assembled, as a pioneer lady used to relate, a tall, bent, gaunt, sallow-faced man, who was enjoying his "well day," slowly and feebly crept up the aisle. A little child, after one glance at this walking skeleton, exclaimed in terror, "O mother, is that death?" and buried his head in her lap. He had taken literally the saying that an invalid "looked like death." January 1, 1799, Mr. Kobler preached at Dayton to a mixed company of traders from Detroit, and some Indians, French, and English, from the appropriate text, "In every nation he that feareth him, and worketh righteousness, is accepted with him." He spoke so forcibly that "many of them looked wild and stood aghast, as if they would take to their heels."

THE SETTLEMENT

When in the fall of 1795 pioneers, or their representatives, visited the "mouth of Mad River" to select homes, they drew both town and outlots, and the latter farms some of them cultivated. They also had, after a time, gardens round their cabins. "West of Wilkinson Street," as Curwen, the delightful first historian of Dayton, says, "was a huge corn-field within one common enclosure, where, as in that golden age of the world when men lodged under trees and fed upon acorns, every man was at liberty to till as much of the soil as he chose." Further, small prairies between the large inclosure and the cabins served as a common vegetable garden.

It is a disputed point whether Mary Van Cleve, the sister of Benjamin, or her mother was the first to leap from the boat which conveyed the party of travelers in search of a new home in a new country—the Dayton of a hundred years ago. Transplanted at the age of nine, she grew up with the village, and spent a long life here. She was well known by her two marriages as Mrs. Swaynie and Mrs. McClean. Some of her early experiences were very thrilling. She had reason to regard Indians with horror. Her father, John Van Cleve, while cultivating his farm near Cincinnati, was killed in 1791 by a "naked Indian, who sprang upon him, plunged a knife into his heart, took a small scalp off, and ran." A party of friends of Mr. Van Cleve pursued him and his band, and Mr. Thompson, afterward Mary Van Cleve's stepfather, overtook one of the Indians and cut off his hand. As a consequence, Mr. Thompson incurred the revengeful spite of all the savages, but hoped after his removal to Dayton to be rid of them. There came a time, however, when this roving band also found their way to the frontier village. Late one dark summer evening, having filled themselves with fire-water, they surrounded the Thompson and Van Cleve cabin on Monument Avenue, midway between St. Clair and Jefferson streets, and with fierce yells demanded admission. The family were alone, and, realizing their great peril, they took Mary, a brave little girl of twelve, from her bed, hastily dressed her, lifted a part of the puncheon floor, and directed her to watch her opportunity to creep through the small aperture to the ground, above which the cabin was raised a little, and run to Newcom's Tavern for help. Every anecdote of this period is in some way connected with our only historical relic. Her description of her terrified run through the pathless brush and hazel patches, tears streaming down her cheeks, the noise of the dreadful warwhoops of the Indians in her ears, her flesh and clothes torn with briars, her bare feet splashing through the water, and slipping and stumbling over the mossy stones at the bottom of the gully which then ran from Second Street, by the park, back of the Monument Avenue cabins to Jefferson Street near the river bank, was very graphic. No wonder that in telling the story she often said, "I ran a mile before I reached Newcom's Tavern." Yet the distance was not quite two of our present squares. A number of men were at the tavern, wondering what the howling and shrieks they heard from the eastward could mean. They all returned with her, one of the men carrying her home in his arms. By their assistance the Indians were routed, and nothing serious resulted from the attack.

Mary Van Cleve was married in 1804 to John McClean, by whom she had seven children. Two daughters live in Dayton — Mrs. Sarah J. McC. Swaynie and Mrs. E. S. Dow. She married, second, in 1826 Robert Swaynie. They had no children. Mrs. Swaynie died several years ago.

THE LANDING OF THE FIRST SETTLERS, APRIL 1, 1796.

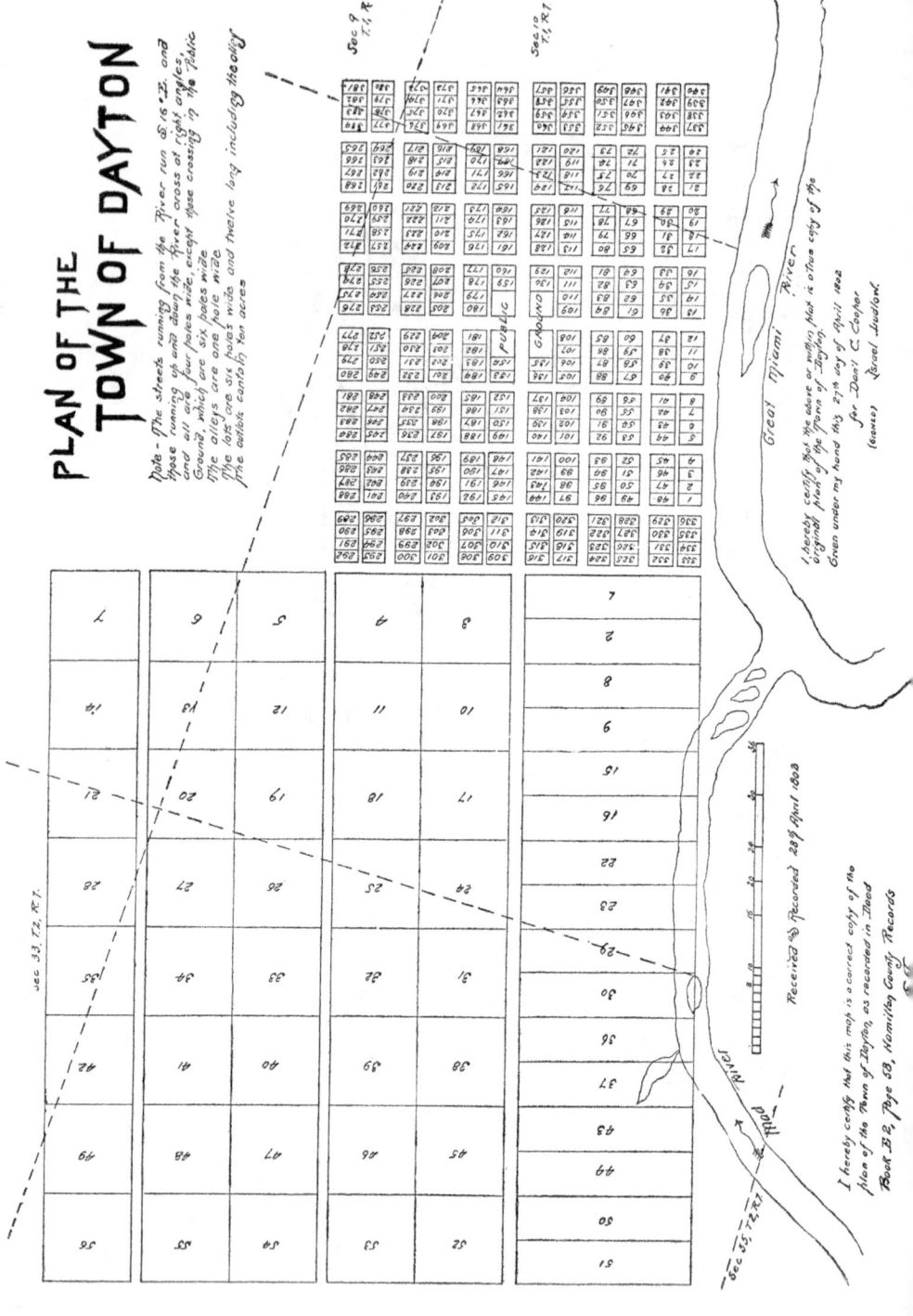

CHAPTER II

EARLY SETTLERS

DANIEL C. COOPER—Newcom's Tavern—Cooper Park—Mr. Cooper Becomes Titular Proprietor of the Town—His Improvements and Liberality—Indians Frequent Visitors—Playing Marbles at Midnight—Robert Edgar—First Store in Dayton—Henry Brown—First Flatboat—Furniture of the Nine Cabins Constituting Dayton—Food—Game—Hogs Introduced—Fish—Blockhouses for Defense Against Indians Built at Dayton—First School in Dayton—Benjamin Van Cleve's Autobiography—Early Life of Van Cleve—Battle of Monmouth—Wagon Journey of the Van Cleves Across the Mountains—Murder of John Van Cleve at Cincinnati by Indians—Benjamin Van Cleve Supports his Father's Family—Self-Educated—Employed in Quartermaster's Department of Western Army—St. Clair's Defeat—Employed in Flatboating by Army Contractors—In Charge of Army Horses and Cattle—Sent Express to Philadelphia by Quartermaster's Department—Sent by General Knox from Philadelphia to Conduct Pair of Horses to Indian Chief Brant—Quarrel with General Knox—Meets Brant in New York—Studious Life After Return to Philadelphia—Sent West with Dispatches to General Wayne—Journey by Boat from Wheeling, Accompanied by Officers and Recruits—Cheated Out of His Pay—Flatboating to Kentucky—Sutler at Fort Greenville—Sent by Army Contractor to Fort Massac with Two Boats Loaded with Provisions—Adventure at Fort Massac with Major, Called "King," Doyle—Returning, Visits Red Banks, a Resort of Thieves and Cutthroats—Drives Cattle to Greenville, Fort Wayne, and Fort Washington—Accompanies Captain Dunlap to Make the Survey of the Dayton Settlement—Adventures as a Surveyor—Keeps Field-Notes During Rain on Blocks of Wood—Settles in Dayton—Surveying, Writing, and Farming—Trials.

NOW THAT the approach of the Dayton Centennial is exciting a special interest in the settlers and founders of the town, it should not be forgotten that Daniel C. Cooper is the pioneer who should be made most prominent and given the highest honors at our celebration. He was born in Morris County, New Jersey, in 1773. About 1803 he married Mrs. Sophia Greene Burnet, of Dayton. From the time that a settlement here was first planned by St. Clair, Wilkinson, Dayton, and Ludlow, he was acquainted with the project, and inclined, it is probable, to make the new town his home. He accompanied the surveying parties led by Colonel Israel Ludlow through the Miami Valley in 1794 and

1795, and in September, 1795, by direction of the proprietors, marked out and cut through the brush from Fort Hamilton to the mouth of Mad River the wagon-road by which the pioneers ended their journey. That fall and winter he located one thousand acres of land in and near Dayton. He settled here permanently in the summer of 1796, building a cabin on the southeast corner of Monument Avenue and Jefferson Street. In 1798 he moved onto the farm, south of Dayton, afterwards the home of Colonel Patterson and General Brown, who distinguished himself in the War of 1812, and was afterwards commander-in-chief of the United States Army. He kept bachelor's hall in his Monument Avenue cabin for a time.

It would have been a disgrace not to have preserved Newcom's Tavern, which, when built in 1799, was the pride of all this region on account of its superiority to any other house north of Hamilton. We know that round it cluster nearly all the most interesting historical associations of the earliest period of the history of Dayton, and that it was the first tavern, store, church, court-house, and jail of the town or county. There is great propriety in naming the little pioneer landing for the Van Cleves. But it is also eminently proper that the square in which the library building stands should be called Cooper Park, for the generous, public-spirited man who gave it and other valuable lots to the town. Our citizens seem not to know, or to have forgotten, that several years ago the City Council voted to name this square Cooper Park, so that it is improper, whether law, gratitude, or sentiment is concerned, to call it Library Park. Cooper Park let it be henceforth and forever.

In 1801 the original proprietors of Dayton became discouraged and Mr. Cooper became titular proprietor of the town by the purchase of preëmption rights, agreement with settlers, and friendly Congressional legislation. He showed his intelligence and breadth of view by the size of lots and the width of streets and sidewalks on his new plat of the town, and by his liberal donations of lots and money for schools, churches, a graveyard, market-house, and for county buildings, and to desirable settlers whom he induced to come here. He built the only mills erected in Dayton during the first ten years of its history — flour-, fulling-, and sawmills, and one for grinding corn. For several years at different periods he served as justice of the peace, president of Council, and member of both branches of the Legislature, and in every way in his power labored for the prosperity of the town, county, and State. His residence, built in 1805 on the southwest corner of Ludlow and First streets, was described as an "elegant mansion of hewn logs, lined inside, instead of plastering, with cherry boards." To his enlarged views, foresight, broad plans, liberality, integrity, and business capacity much of the present advancement of our city is due. The impress of his wise, moderate, prudent, yet progressive spirit, laid upon the town in its infancy, has never been lost.

Indians were frequent visitors to the village of Dayton, and even when friendly their curiosity and thieving habits made them unwelcome. They generally came to exchange skins, maple sugar, etc., for articles carried about the country by traders. Robert Edgar, one of the earliest settlers and a valuable citizen, many of whose descendants live in Dayton, built himself a lonely home on the little prairie now the site of the Water Works. Sometimes at night Indians, with whom he must have been inconveniently popular, would stop in front of his cabin and call, "Lobit! Lobit!" (Indian for *Robert*) till he awoke and admitted them. They came for amusement, and were not satisfied till they had persuaded their host to get down on the floor and play marbles with them. When they had enjoyed the game to their hearts' content, they departed in great good humor, and their relieved and weary entertainer went back to bed. His associations with the Indians were not all of a laughable character. In 1792, at Wheeling, his father was, on Good Friday evening, attacked, killed, and scalped by nine Indians, while on the way to warn a neighbor of their approach.

Robert Edgar first visited Dayton in 1795 as one of the surveying party led by Mr. Cooper, and settled here in 1796. Though a farmer, he was also a good mechanic, and built and ran mills for Mr. Cooper at Dayton, and for Mr. Robinson upon Mad River. He was a soldier in the War of 1812 in one of the companies of mounted rangers from this county, and his sword is now in possession of his son, John F. Edgar. Robert Edgar was born in Staunton, Virginia, in 1770, and emigrated to Ohio before 1795. At Cincinnati, September 27, 1798, he married Mrs. Margaret Kirkwood. Mr. and Mrs. Edgar had a large family, but only five lived past childhood. Jane Allen, born November 24, 1800, married Augustus George, December 4, 1817, and died in 1824; descendants in Dayton, the children of the late George

H. Phillips.   Robert A., born October 10, 1803, married Catherine Iddings; died in 1833.   Samuel D., born March 26, 1806, married Minerva A. Jones, August 5, 1845; died October 1, 1874.   He has a number of grandchildren, the children of two daughters and a son.   Mary, born April 8, 1811, married, May 10, 1831, Stephen Johnston; died July 25, 1849.   John F., born October 29, 1814, alone survives.   He married, April 20, 1843, Effie A. Rogers. He has three daughters—Jeanne, Isabel, and Elizabeth Edgar.

In the fall of 1800 the first store in Dayton was opened in a room of the second story of Newcom's Tavern by a Mr. McDougal from Detroit. Though this store was a great convenience to the villagers and the country for forty miles around, McDougal's chief trade was with Indians, who came here for that purpose.

In 1804 Henry Brown, prominent in the early history of our city, built on Main Street, near the High School, a frame building for a store—the first house erected here specially for business purposes. Since 1795 he had been engaged in the Indian trade, having stores at Fort Hamilton and Fort Laramie, and, as stated, in 1804 at Dayton, in partnership with Mr. Sunderland. Three generations of his descendants have been well known in our city. The agents of his firm were camped on all the streams for many miles in every direction from Dayton, wherever Indians could be reached. Traders, accompanied by packhorses laden with goods, took long, lonely, dangerous journeys through the wilderness, lasting several months, to Indian villages. Some of their goods were shipped in flatboats or pirogues down the rivers to Cincinnati and New Orleans.

Henry Brown was born near Lexington, Virginia, about 1770. In 1793 he came to the Northwest Territory as military secretary for Colonel Preston, who was in command of a regiment in Wayne's army. February 19, 1811, he married Katherine, daughter of Colonel Robert Patterson. Mr. Brown died in 1825. Mr. and Mrs. Brown had three children: R. P. Brown, born December 6, 1811, married Sarah Galloway, October 31, 1837; died May 4, 1879. Henry L. Brown, born December 3, 1814, married Sarah Belle Browning, February 7, 1837; died November 25, 1878. Eliza J. Brown, born in Dayton, October 30, 1816, married Charles Anderson, September 16, 1835. R. P. and Henry L. Brown were men of the finest character, influential in many directions, and held in the highest regard by their fellow-citizens.

NEWCOM'S FIRST LOG CABIN, BUILT IN 1796.

The first flatboat that left Dayton was owned by David Lowry. It started on the two months' trip to New Orleans during the spring freshet of 1799, and was loaded with grain, pelts, and 500 venison hams.

The nine cabins which in 1799 constituted Dayton, contained only a few home-made benches, stools, beds, tables, and cupboards, often of buckeye and beechwood. Doddridge in his "Notes" says that a pioneer's table furniture consisted of "some old pewter dishes and plates; the rest, wooden bowls or trenchers, or gourds, and hard-shelled squashes. A few pewter spoons, much battered about the edges, were to be seen on some tables. The rest were made of horn. If knives were scarce, the deficiency was made up by the scalping-knives, which were carried in sheaths suspended from the belt of the hunting-shirt." The cabin was warmed and lighted wholly by the huge open hickory fire, over which, in pots suspended from cranes or on the coals or in the ashes, the cooking was done. At an early date the pioneers raised flax, hemp, and wool, and the women spun, wove, and dyed, with colors made from walnut and butternut hulls or wild roots, the fabrics from which they made the clothes of the family. Every cabin had its spinning-wheel and loom, the latter built by the ingenious pioneer weaver, Abraham Glassmire. One wonders whether pioneer women were really harder worked than their granddaughters. They had little to occupy or amuse them outside their own homes — no benevolent societies, clubs, receptions, calls, concerts, or lectures, and only occasional church services. They had only one or two rooms to keep in order, and no pictures, books, curtains, carpets, rugs, table- and bed-linen, bric-a-brac, china, glass, or silver to take care of. Their wardrobes were scanty, and the weekly washing must have been small. Wheat flour could not be obtained; corn hoe-cake, ash-cake, johnny-cake, dodgers, pone, hominy, and mush and milk were principal articles of diet. Meal was slowly and laboriously ground in handmills. Wild plums, crab-apples, blackberries and strawberries, sweetened with maple sugar, furnished jellies and preserves. There was an abundance of wild honey, and of wild goose and turkey and duck eggs. They often tired of venison, bears' meat, rabbits, squirrels, wild turkeys, ducks, geese, quail, and pheasants, and longed for pork. There was great rejoicing, no doubt, when, in 1799, Mr. Cooper introduced hogs. In 1800 sheep were first brought here. The rivers were full of bass, catfish, pickerel, pike, eels, and sunfish.

Benjamin Van Cleve says in his autobiography that, in July and August, 1799, "the Indians were counseling and evinced an unfriendly disposition. The British traders and French among them had made them dissatisfied with the cession of their lands and with the boundaries, and blockhouses were built at Dayton and all through the country, and the people became considerably alarmed." The Dayton blockhouse stood on the present site of the soldiers' monument, and was built of round logs, with a projecting upper story. The men in town and surrounding country kept strict watch, and were all armed and ready to take refuge, if necessary, with their families, in the blockhouse. But it was never used for protection against Indians. For a short time it was the village church and school-house. In the first story, the year it was built, the Presbyterians held their Sunday services, and the same year Benjamin Van Cleve taught there the first school ever opened in Dayton—another reason why the park which the High School overlooks should be named for him. In his journal for 1799–1800, he says: "On the 1st of September I commenced teaching a small school. I had reserved time to gather my corn, and kept school until the last of October." He harvested a fine crop by the first week in November. Vacation lasted part of December; for, after harvest, he went to Cincinnati to assist the clerk of the House of Representatives of the first Territorial Legislature. He was well suited to such work. He held the office of clerk of the Montgomery Court of Common Pleas from 1802 till his death in 1821, and was postmaster from 1804 to 1821, being the first to hold either office in Dayton.

After Mr. Van Cleve's return from Cincinnati, he "kept school about three months longer." It is said that, as books were difficult to procure, he taught the alphabet and spelling from charts prepared by himself. They were, no doubt, beautifully written and colored, for his penmanship was remarkable for elegance and legibility, and his diary or autobiography is illustrated by plans and maps neatly executed in India ink and water colors. He was a skillful surveyor and engineer, and like those of General W. C. Schenck (father of Admiral and General R. C. Schenck) and other contemporaries of his profession, the papers and accounts which descendants of people for whom he did business still preserve are not only correct in form and substance, but beautiful pieces of work, and often ornamented by a large and artistic monogram of the employer.

In 1801 Mr. Van Cleve was appointed county surveyor. In 1812 the President of the United States appointed him and two other commissioners "to explore, survey, and mark a road by the most eligible course from the foot of the rapids of the Miami of Lake Erie to the western line of the Connecticut Reserve, and a road to run southwardly from Lower Sandusky to the boundary line established by the treaty of Greenville."

Mr. Van Cleve's autobiography or "Memoranda," as he styled it, now in the possession of Mrs. Thomas Dover, widow of a grandson, is a very curious and valuable book. It has never been printed in full. This sturdy little manuscript volume, written in a hand as graceful and legible as the best type, and bound in strong, square leather covers, which, like the heavy paper within, are dark with age, has, though studied by several historians, and read by many others, been so carefully guarded by the appreciative descendants of the writer that time and use have injured it very little.

Mr. Van Cleve's life after 1796 is so much a part of the history of Dayton that it seems more appropriate and interesting to describe the incidents that occurred during that period under the proper dates in our story, than to give them in a continuous biography. His childhood and youth, while not spent in Dayton, were filled with hardship as well as romantic adventure of a kind that made him master of all his faculties, and this severe discipline developed the character that rendered him one of the most useful and progressive founders and citizens of the struggling village in the Mad River country. Therefore, a somewhat detailed account of his early years will be both interesting and profitable. He is worthy of being held up as an example to the boys in our public schools. Some of his traits are of the kind that appeal most strongly to boy nature.

In his Memoranda, which he states was written for the instruction and amusement of his children, Mr. Van Cleve sets down for their guidance the rules by which he regulated his own valuable life. He tells them that he made it a point to be polite and obliging to all with whom he was connected in business, whether he stood to them in the relation of employer or employee. And in his obituary it is stated that he "recommended himself to esteem by his agreeable manner of doing business." He regarded justice, honor, and integrity as the best policy, though it was not this inferior motive but a higher one that led him to pursue that upright and public-spirited career which won the respect and admiration of his fellow-citizens. He was a religious man and a member of the Presbyterian Church. He took an active part in promoting the best interests of his town and State, and was a trustee of several literary institutions. In the Memoranda he dwells upon the fact that he always had a place for everything and a set time for the performance of each duty, and he exhorted his children above all to form similar systematic, accurate, and methodical habits.

Benjamin Van Cleve began to keep a diary at a very early age, and not long before his death in 1821 he condensed and revised his journals, copying them into the volume from which the material for his biography is drawn. His Memoranda contains, perhaps, the most accurate and graphic description of St. Clair's defeat that has been written; and from the Memoranda has also been obtained the only reliable account of the settlement of Dayton. The Memoranda, supplemented by the files of early newspapers which he preserved, consitutes him literally the historian of Dayton from 1795 to 1821.

Benjamin Van Cleve's ancestors came to Flatbush, Long Island, from Amsterdam, Holland, in the seventeenth century, and from thence removed to Staten Island, and finally settled in New Jersey. He was born February 24, 1773, in Monmouth County, New Jersey, and was the eldest child of John and Catherine Benham Van Cleve. He had three brothers and five sisters. His father was a blacksmith.

Mr. Van Cleve's earliest recollection was of the battle of Monmouth, on the 28th of June, 1778. Late in life he could well remember the confusion of women and children, and their flight to the pine swamps just before the engagement, though he was only five years old at the time. When about a mile from home the refugees came in sight of the enemy, and paused to consult what course to pursue. The Monmouth men went in search of the American army, and Benjamin Van Cleve, "becoming separated from the rest of his family, aimed," he tells us in the Memoranda, "to return home." When within a short distance of the enemy, the bugles drove the child, who in the confusion had not been missed, back to the place where his relatives were collected. The refugees could hear the firing distinctly, and judge from the sound which side was advancing or receding. "When our army was retreating, many of the men were melted to tears; when it was advancing, there was every demonstration of joy and exultation." The next day John Van Cleve and his brothers "acted as guides to separate companies of Colonel Morgan's riflemen, and reconnoitered the British right flank, took a number of prisoners, and took and recaptured a great deal of property."

When, on the retreat of the British, John Van Cleve brought his family back from the pine swamps, he found nothing to mark the site of his home but a naked and blackened chimney, stumps of apple trees, and the bodies of animals killed by the British. He "had," his son says, "neither a shelter for his family, nor bread for them, nor clothing to cover them excepting what they had on. He saved a bed and a looking-glass, which we carted with us. A yearling heifer had escaped the enemy, and a sow, with a back broken by a sword, lived. My father's anvil remained, I believe, amidst the rubbish and ruins of the shop. Several wagons and an artillery carriage were burnt in the shop; the pieces of artillery had been thrown into a pool of muddy water in the middle of the road, and were not found by the enemy." The Tories committed depredations both by land and by sea on the Monmouth County people, and for this reason the militia were till the end of the war almost constantly on duty. John Van Cleve was "from home on this service a great part of the time, and he was in some skirmishes with the Tories and British. He was also under General Forman at the battle of Germantown."

In November, 1785, John Van Cleve removed with his family and several relatives and friends from Freehold, New Jersey, to Pennsylvania. The party traveled with three wagons, two of which contained Van Cleve's blacksmith tools, provisions, and household furniture. The emigrants had an uncomfortable and fatiguing journey up and down the icy or snowy Alleghany Mountain roads, which, "being only opened sufficient for wagons to pass, and neither dug nor leveled, also winding in both ascent and descent," there was constant danger of upsetting. "To undertake the crossing," Benjamin Van Cleve wrote, "with loaded wagons required a considerable degree of resolution and fortitude." The horses were soon nearly exhausted from the hard pulling through the deep snow, which balled in their feet. Sometimes the wagons stuck in the mud or broke down. The women and children suffered very much from cold and exposure. Benjamin Van Cleve writes on November 17: "Tarried to repair our wagons, and the women were employed in baking and cooking." November 18: "Froze considerable last night. The roads are filled with ice. Came this day to Mr. McShay's on Sideling Hill. The house was so crowded with travelers that, notwithstanding the cold, we were obliged to encamp in the woods. The horses and men are very much fatigued, having spent near half the day getting up this hill, which is steep and stony, and the road winds back and forth to gain the summit. We had to put six horses to a wagon and bring one up at a time." They reached their journey's end on the 8th of December.

The greater part of the time between 1786 and 1789 the Van Cleves spent on a farm near Washington, Pennsylvania. In December, 1789, the family emigrated to Cincinnati, making the journey by water, and arriving the day after General St. Clair changed the name of the town, which had previously been called Losantiville. Benjamin Van Cleve settled on land on the east bank of the Licking River, belonging to Major Leech, who, wishing to open a farm for himself, offered a hundred acres of unimproved ground for each ten-acre field cleared by a settler, with the use for three years of the improved land.

Benjamin Van Cleve hoped, with the assistance of his father's labor, to secure at least one hundred acres, but the latter's death prevented the fulfillment of their expectations. A fortified station was built on Leech's land, and four families and four single men went out to the place to live. The Indians were very troublesome and daring in 1791, skulking through the streets of Cincinnati and the gardens near Fort Washington at night. On the 21st of May they fired on John Van Cleve while he was at work in his field near the village and captured a man named Cutter, who was standing within a few yards of him. "The alarm was given by halloing from lot to lot, until it reached town." Benjamin Van Cleve came in from Leech's Station just as the news of the attack was received at Cincinnati, and saw the villagers running to the public grounds. He followed them, and there met with a man who had seen the Indians firing on his father. He asked if any would go to the rescue with him, "and pushed on without halting." After running a short distance the party met John Van Cleve. "While we were finding the trail of the Indians on their retreat," Benjamin writes, "perhaps forty persons had arrived, most of whom joined in the pursuit; but by the time we gained the top of the river hills, we had only eight." They kept the Indians "on the full run till dark," but were obliged to return to Cincinnati at night without recapturing Cutter. A few days later, on the 1st of June, John Van Cleve was again attacked by Indians while working in his own lot. "A naked Indian," Benjamin says, "sprang upon him; my father was seen to throw him, but at this time the Indian was plunging his knife into his heart. He took a small scalp off and ran. The men behind came up immediately, but my father was already dead."

One of John Van Cleve's daughters was married, but he left four younger children, who were not old enough to support themselves. "I immediately resolved," Benjamin Van Cleve says, "to supply the place of father to them to the utmost of my ability, and I feel a consolation in having fulfilled my duty towards them as well as my mother. My father had not many debts or engagements to fulfill. I paid some debts by my labor (all that he owed) as a day-laborer, and my brother-in-law assisted me in building a house he had undertook, and received the pay for my mother." "After the funeral of my father, I returned and planted my corn, but was obliged to divide my time and bestow the greater part at Cincinnati for the benefit of the family. I settled my father's books, fulfilled his engagements, and sold his blacksmith's tools to the quartermaster-general."

For a number of years Benjamin Van Cleve was burdened with the support of his mother and the family, and had a hard struggle with poverty. He was young and ignorant of the world, and felt the need of counsel. Many depended on him, and there was no one to whom he could turn for help, or with whom he could share his responsibilities. "Happy he who has, at this period of life," he wrote years afterwards, at a date when his own carefully nurtured son had recently graduated with honor from Ohio University, "a father or friend whose experience will afford him a chart; whose kind advice will serve as a compass to direct him."

Benjamin Van Cleve was all his life a lover of good books and good men, and though he enjoyed very limited educational advantages, he became noted for intelligence, information, and elevation of character. Vice seems to have had but slight charm for him; but no doubt the thought of his helpless family would have restrained one of his affectionate nature and spurred him to exert himself to the uttermost had he been tempted to fall into idle and dissipated habits. He was obliged to seek work wherever he could find it, and could not afford to be nice in his choice of associates. "Had my fortitude and resolution," he says, "been weaker, they might have been overcome, for my companions for several years were of the most profane and dissipated, such as followers of the army and mostly discharged soldiers."

In the summer of 1791 he obtained employment in the quartermaster's department, and on the 8th of August set off for Kentucky, where his uncle, Captain Benham, was commissioned by the Government to buy artillery horses for St. Clair's army. Van Cleve received the purchased horses at Lexington, branded them, and pastured them in the neighborhood of the town. In about two weeks a drove was collected and taken to Cincinnati. Captain Benham was very ill on their return from Kentucky, and his nephew was obliged to do all his writing, keep his accounts, and attend to his other business.

On the 3d of September Benham and Van Cleve left Fort Washington, Cincinnati, for the army, with three or four brigades of packhorses, loaded with armorer's and artificer's tools. The armorers were armed and marched with the brigades, but would have proved a weak escort had the Indians attacked them. Benham's party overtook the troops at a place thirty or forty miles beyond Fort Hamilton, and marched with them to Fort Jefferson, which was not completed. At the end of five days Benham and Van Cleve returned with six brigades, leaving five at Hamilton and taking one on to Fort Washington. They were ordered back to transport provisions from Cincinnati to the army, which was reduced to short allowance, the failure of Colonel Duer, the contractor, having thrown all military arrangements into confusion. The packhorsemen returned as soon as possible with their loads, and overtook the army on the 31st of October twenty-two miles beyond Fort Jefferson. They found poor St. Clair so ill with the gout as to be carried in a litter. The Kentucky militia had just deserted in a body, and the evening of the day that Benham's party arrived in camp the first regiment was dispatched to bring the deserters back, and also to escort in provisions that were then on the way.

Benjamin Van Cleve had been entered on the pay-roll of the army as a packhorseman, at fifteen dollars pay per month. He worked hard to earn his wages. Each brigade of packhorses drew its rations separately. As he kept the accounts and also communicated orders, he had a great deal of writing to do. In addition to his ordinary duties, he was often obliged to take care of his own and his uncle's horses. Sometimes it was necessary to carry part of the stores or provisions lashed on the back of the animal he was accustomed to ride, and foot it himself through the mud in the roughest manner. Captain Benham had a large marquee, or horseman's tent, which, as it was very roomy, he occasionally asked officers to share. "Having sometimes to be in the company of officers and sometimes in the mud," Van Cleve was induced on his expeditions to the army to take all his clothes with him, and they made a heavy and unwieldy pack.

At daybreak on the 2d of November, while, in obedience to orders, packing his cumbersome luggage on his horse in preparation for the return to Cincinnati, he heard firing and was soon witnessing his first battle. It was not long till his horse was shot down, and instead of lamenting the accident he was glad of it; for he now felt at liberty to share in the engagement, expecting much pleasure from the turmoil and excitement of the battle, which, in his ignorance of the condition of the army and of the uncertainties of Indian warfare, he was confident would end victoriously for our troops. In a few moments he provided himself with a gun obtained from a man who was wounded in the arm, began firing, and till the retreat was commenced was in the thick of the fight. He escaped unhurt, though he lost his horse and all his clothes; but Captain Benham and Daniel Bonham, a young man brought up by Benham, and whom Van Cleve regarded as a brother, were both wounded.

The ground was soon "literally covered with dead and dying men, and the commander gave orders to take the way," that is, to retreat. Van Cleve joined a party of eight or nine men whom he saw start on a run a little to the left of where he was. When they had gone about two miles, a boy, who had been thrown or fell off a horse, begged Van Cleve's assistance, and he ran, pulling the boy along, about two miles farther, until both had become nearly exhausted. Seeing two horses approaching, one of which carried three men and the other two, Van Cleve managed to throw the lad up behind the two men. Though afterwards thrown off, the boy escaped and got safely home. Van Cleve did not see Bonham on the retreat, but understood that his body was found in the winter on the battlefield and buried.

Van Cleve was taken with cramp during the retreat and could

hardly walk, "till he got within a hundred yards of the rear, where the Indians were tomahawking the old and wounded men." Here he stopped to "tie his pocket-handkerchief around a man's wounded knee." The Indians were close in pursuit at this time and he almost despaired of escaping. He threw off his shoes and the coolness of the ground revived him. "I again," he says, "began a trot, and recollect that when a bend in the road offered, and I got before half a dozen persons, I thought it would occupy some time for the enemy to massacre them before my turn would come. By the time I had got to Stillwater, about eleven miles, I had gained the center of the flying troops, and, like them, came to a walk. I fell in with Lieutenant Shaumberg, who I think was the only officer of artillery that got away unhurt, with Corporal Mott and a woman who was called 'Redheaded Nance.' The latter two were crying. Mott was lamenting the loss of his wife, and Nance that of an infant child. Shaumberg was nearly exhausted, and hung on Mott's arm. I carried his fusee and accouterments and led Nance; and in this sociable way we arrived at Fort Jefferson a little after sunset."

Benham and Van Cleve immediately went on with Colonel Drake and others, who were ordered forward to dispatch provisions to the troops. After marching a few miles the party was so overcome with fatigue that they halted. A packhorseman "had stolen at Fort Jefferson one pocketful of flour and the other full of beef." Another of the men had a kettle. Benjamin Van Cleve groped about in the dark until he found some water in a hole, out of which a tree had been blown by the root. They then made a kettle of soup, of which each of the party got a little. After supping they marched four or five miles farther, when a sentinel was set and they lay down and slept. They were worn out with fatigue, and their feet were knocked to pieces against the roots in the night and by splashing through the ice without shoes, for "the ground was covered with snow and the flats filled with water frozen over, the ice as thick as a knife-blade." On the 6th of November they reached Hamilton and were out of danger.

On the 25th of November Benham and his nephew were paid off and discharged at Fort Washington. A week later Van Cleve entered the service of the new army contractors, Elliott & Williams, and started the same day for the Falls of the Ohio to bring up a boat-load of salt. When he returned he was employed by the contractors to feed and take charge of a herd of cattle through the winter. In the spring, when the cattle were turned out to pasture near Cincinnati, he went on a twelve days' trip by boat to Fort Hamilton. Afterwards for a short time he was in charge of horses belonging to the quartermaster at a camp three miles up the Licking River.

The evening of the 10th of May, 1792, he was expected at Cincinnati to draw provisions. He arrived about dark and found that the quartermaster had determined to send him express to Philadelphia, and had been to his mother's, had his clothes packed, a horse saddled, and everything ready for the journey. He received his instructions from the quartermaster and commandant, and started before midnight accompanied by Captain Kimberland. Forty dollars were given him, which were expected to be "equal to his expenses" and he was ordered to take the most direct route to Philadelphia, which at that day was via Lexington, Kentucky, and Crab Orchard, Cumberland Mountains, Powell's Valley, Abingdon, Bolecourt, Lexington, Staunton, Martinsburg, Louisa, Hagerstown, Maryland, York and Lancaster, Pennsylvania. He traveled with as little delay as possible by day or by night. On reaching Crab Orchard eighteen persons joined him. The party was armed with five guns and five pistols. The trip, on account of the Indian alarms and rainy weather, was very disagreeable.

Van Cleve reached Philadelphia June 7, 1792, and delivered his dispatches next day. He went to the War Department every morning at ten o'clock to see if there were any commands for him, and at last General Knox ordered him to go to New York to conduct thither a pair of fine horses which the heads of the department had presented to Captain Joseph Brant, chief of the Six Nations. Van Cleve was directed to leave the horses in the care of Mr. Edward Bardin, of the City Tavern, taking his receipt and requesting him to deliver them to Captain Brant on the latter's arrival in New York. Mr. Van Cleve replied that he would be glad to go to New York, but that, if he went, money to pay his expenses must be furnished him by the Government. General Knox was much excited by this answer, swore at the young man, and declared that it took more for his expenses than would support the Duke of Mecklenburg! Whereupon Van Cleve waxed wroth. "I suppose," he says, "he was in jest, but I felt nettled, and observed that I ate three times a day, as I was accustomed to do at home, and my horse had to have hay and oats; that I had been on expense for forty or fifty days and on forty dollars; and that I was a small matter behind with my landlord." Knox made no further objections, but ordered the necessary money to be paid to Van Cleve.

Captain Brant arrived by stage at the City Tavern on June 29, just as his horses stopped at the door, so that he gave his own receipt for the animals. It is stated in the Memoranda that the chief was "quite intelligent and communicative, wrote a decent hand, and was dressed more than half in the fashion of the whites."

Mr. Van Cleve returned to Philadelphia on the 30th of June. Knox gave him leave of absence until the 11th of July to visit relatives in New Jersey. During his stay in Philadelphia he amused himself visiting friends, attending the play, drawing a plan of President Washington's new house, which was then building, and reading all the books he could get hold of. He purchased twenty-five volumes. He boarded with a Quaker family, and found profit and pleasure in attending the Friends' meeting and in reading Barclay's "Apology" and others of their books. "The landlord and landlady," he says, "assumed the exercise of parental authority over me, the same as over their own son. I believe I was more obedient to them, and a considerable share of mutual attachment took place. I felt regret at parting from them, and my good mother shed tears on the occasion."

He left Philadelphia on the 25th of July with dispatches for General Wayne, who was at Wheeling, and for Colonel Cushing, the commandant at Fort Washington. On his return journey he followed the route over the Alleghanies he had traveled when emigrating from New Jersey in 1789, and found the roads much improved. On the way he turned aside to visit relatives, and was slightly reprimanded by General Wayne for his delay in delivering the dispatches. The journey from Wheeling to Cincinnati was made by river. The party occupied two boats, commanded by Ensign Hunter, a sergeant, and corporal, who were conducting to Ohio twenty-one recruits enlisted in New Jersey. One boat was loaded with oats and corn, and the other had on board a quantity of cannon-ball, two pieces of artillery, and a few boxes of shoes. Four recruits deserted at Wheeling, and Van Cleve turned out with a party of soldiers to search for them, but the men escaped capture. A good deal of whisky was drunk on board the boats, and the soldiers were "mellow" during nearly the whole voyage. One of the men entertained his companions by singing for half a day at a time. Ensign Hunter and his wife frequently visited Van Cleve's boat, and when alone with the soldiers he amused himself reading the twenty-five books he had bought at Philadelphia, finishing nearly all of them before he reached Cincinnati on the 3d of August, 1792. One day he and the sergeant and another person landed for a deer hunt, overtaking the boats further down the river.

Van Cleve's expenses during his absence of one hundred and fourteen days were $114.56⅔. He served a month in the quartermaster's department after his return. Through some misunderstanding, he did not receive his pay for his services as express till the 15th of March, 1793. "I became tired and disgusted," he says, "with their arrogant and ungenerous treatment, and in want of the money I begged that they would pay me something —anything that they thought I merited. There was no mail nor way for me to make it known or get redress at Philadelphia, and they were so good as to pay me five shillings per day." Yet the quartermaster professed to be satisfied with the manner in which he had discharged his duties, and with the bills of expense. "Paid Israel Ludlow for my lots in Cincinnati," he says, after concluding his account of the trip to Philadelphia, "got bills of sale for them, and cleared and fenced them. I labored intolerably hard, so as to injure my health, and raised a fine crop of corn."

In the winter of 1793 Van Cleve and Stacey McDonough engaged with the army contractors, Elliott & Williams, to bring up salt and other articles from the Falls of the Ohio to Cincinnati. The contractors furnished a boat and one hundredweight of flour for each trip, and paid six shillings sixpence freight per barrel. Van Cleve and his companions took the boat down themselves, but engaged hands at five dollars per week in Kentucky (where the farmers, when their summer work was over, were glad to get employment in the public service), who agreed to be ready, on certain days when the cargo for the return voyage was collected, to assist in loading the boat. They brought up one boat-load of salt and two of corn. By the 1st of December Van Cleve cleared seventy-five dollars. They then reëngaged with the contractors at fifteen dollars per month and went for a boat-load of salt, but did not receive their freight till January 1, 1794. The river was almost frozen over and they had a tedious return trip, not reaching Cincinnati till January 25.

In February, 1794, Captain Benham employed Benjamin Van

Cleve to open a sutler's store at Fort Greenville, the headquarters at this date of Wayne's legion. He took six packhorses to Greenville, loaded with stores and liquors, and in March returned to Cincinnati for another six-horse load. This was an unfortunate undertaking. He was twice robbed while at the fort, losing over fifty dollars in money, all his clothes, and some small articles. He also got into trouble at headquarters through a misunderstanding, sold the sutler's store, and left Fort Greenville penniless.

On the 16th of May he again engaged in the contractors' employ, and on the 24th was sent down the Ohio to Fort Massac with two boats loaded with provisions. A detachment of infantry and artillery commanded by Major Doyle and Captain Guion, and eight Chickasaw Indians, accompanied them. There were ten boats in the little fleet, which were directed to proceed in exact order. Van Cleve's boat, number seven, was heavily loaded and weak in hands, so that when all were rowing it could not keep up, and when all were drifting it outwent the other boats. As the Major had the reputation of being haughty, arbitrary, and imperious, and had been nicknamed "King Doyle," Van Cleve thought it useless to explain matters to him. Sometimes number seven would be ten miles ahead in the morning, and it would take the others with hard rowing half the day to overtake it. "The men," the Memoranda relates, "by that time would be pretty much fatigued, and we could manage to keep our place until night. We generally received a hearty volley of execrations for our disobedience of his orders. We returned mild excuses and determined to repeat the offense."

At Saline, on June 11, "I observed," Van Cleve says, "a fire on shore, and hailed, when two Canadian French hunters came to us with their canoes loaded with skins, bears' oil, and dogs. One of them had passed twenty-six years in the wilderness between Vincennes and the Illinois River. Before morning we found three others, who went along with us to hunt for us." The boats reached Fort Massac June 12. On the 26th of June "King Doyle" unjustly ordered the arrest of Van Cleve and his comrades. That day there arrived at Fort Massac a number of men who had been enlisted in Tennessee by officers who had received commissions from Citizen Genêt, ambassador from the French Republic to the United States. The real object of the visit of these French recruits was probably to examine the place, and ascertain the strength of the force assembled there; but they stated that, having nothing else to do, they had volunteered to escort some salt-boats to Nashville, and had stopped out of curiosity to see the soldiers. They invited Van Cleve and his companions to take passage in their boat, and as the former was anxious to return home the offer was accepted. Neither Van Cleve nor his associates were interested in Genêt's projects. One of Van Cleve's party who had a public rifle went up to restore it to the Major, who, angry at his departure, cursed and struck him, and ordered him and his friends, who were in the boat but heard the command, to be taken to the guard-house. "The Major," Van Cleve states, "was walking backward and forward on top of the bank. With my gun in one hand and tomahawk in the other, and a knife eighteen inches long hanging at my side, dressed in a hunting-frock, breechcloth, and leggings, my countenance probably manifesting my excitement, I leaped out of the boat, and with a very quick step went up to the Major. I looked like a savage, and the Major, mistaking my intention, was alarmed and retired as I advanced." Finally, matters were explained to the satisfaction of both, and Van Cleve consented to remain till the 3d of July, when the Major intended to send a boat to the Falls of the Ohio. Van Cleve and his friends left on the appointed day, but growing tired of the society of the soldiers, determined on the 9th, at Red Banks, to make the remainder of the journey by land.

Red Banks was on the border of Tennessee and Kentucky, and, as it was unknown as yet to which the place belonged, it was a lawless region and a refuge for thieves and rogues of all kinds who had "been able to effect their escape from justice in the neighboring States." At Red Banks our travelers saw a fellow named Kuykendall, who "always carried in his waistcoat pockets 'devil's claws,' or rather weapons that he could slip his fingers in, and with which he could take off the whole side of a man's face at one claw." Kuykendall had just been married and a wedding ball was in progress when Van Cleve arrived, at the close of which festivities the bridegroom was murdered by some of the guests.

On July 11 the travelers reached Green River. They each made a raft with an armful of wood and a grapevine to carry their gun and clothes "and then taking the vines in their mouth swam the river, dragging their rafts after them." During the four succeeding days they passed through an uninhabited wilderness. July 26 they arrived at Cincinnati. Spies employed by Wayne's army had just come in for ammunition and were going to return on foot. They invited Van Cleve to join them, and he regretted that his feet and clothes were both almost worn out, and as he was unable to stand the journey he was obliged to decline the offer.

On the 28th of July he was employed by the contractors to drive a drove of cattle to Fort Greenville. Nearly the whole of August he was very ill at Cincinnati. On his recovery, after paying doctor's and board bills and for some clothes, he had but a dollar left. Accordingly, though so weak that he could hardly walk, he engaged with the contractors to drive cattle to the army then at Fort Wayne, and was occupied with this business till December. In January, 1795, he entered into partnership at Cincinnati with his brother-in-law, Jerome Holt, and Captain John Schooley. They farmed and also hauled quartermaster's supplies to Fort Washington and the outposts in their six-horse wagon. Van Cleve "worked hard, lived poor, and was very economical, and had about as much when he quit as when he began."

In the fall of 1795 he accompanied Captain Dunlap to make the survey of the land purchased for the Dayton settlement. Surveyors endured much hardship. A hunter and a spy always accompanied surveying parties, for they were obliged to supply themselves with food from the woods, and to be on the watch against attacks from wandering bands of Indians. On the 26th of September Van Cleve records that their horse was missing, though he had been well secured when they camped for the night. Indians had probably stolen him. They hunted for him all day, but did not find him; and were thenceforth obliged to carry the baggage themselves, though traveling on foot. When they arrived at the mouth of Mad River, the site of Dayton, they found six Wyandot Indians camped there. At first both the white and the red men were a little alarmed; but they talked together, and dicussed mutual grievances. Van Cleve's father had been killed by Indians, and the Wyandots had suffered in like manner from the white man. They admitted that both sides had reason for complaint, and that both were to blame, and they soon became friends and exchanged presents. "They gave us," Van Cleve says, "some venison jerk, and we in return gave them a little flour, salt, tobacco, and other small articles. At the request of one of them, I exchanged knives, giving him

From a water-color portrait in possession of Mrs. Thomas Dover.   Copyright, 1895, by W. J. Shuey.

BENJAMIN VAN CLEVE.

a very large one, scabbard, and belt that I carried for several years, for his, which was not so valuable, with a worsted belt and a deerskin to boot."

The 1st of October their hunter and another man were sent forward to hunt and cook, and when, after a day of fasting and hard work, the surveyors reached camp they found that some Indians had robbed their men of most of the provisions, and "menaced their lives." On another occasion the surveyors fasted thirty-four hours, laboring and traveling most of the time, and the Memoranda describes the gusto with which they ate the big pot of mush and milk which was all they had for supper when at last they reached a cabin. "October 3," Van Cleve writes, "it rained very hard, and the surveyor got his papers all wet and was about stopping. We had about a pound of meat, and, though we had nearly done our business, were thinking of setting off for home. I undertook to keep the field-notes, and hit on the expedient of taking them down on tablets of wood with the point of my knife, so I could understand them and take them off again on paper." They returned to Cincinnati on the 4th of October.

On the 1st of November Van Cleve went again to Mad River. A lottery was held, and he drew lots in and near Dayton for himself and others, and "engaged to become a settler in the spring." This winter, when not surveying, Benjamin Van Cleve wrote in the recorder's office at Cincinnati. In March, 1796, as already related, he accompanied his mother and several others to Dayton. In his diary he made this simple and characteristic record of their arrival at their new home: "April 1, 1796. Landed at Dayton, after a passage of ten days, William Gahagan and myself having come with Thompson's and McClure's families in a large pirogue."

Van Cleve raised a very good crop of corn at Dayton this year, but most of it was destroyed. He sold his possessions in Cincinnati, but "sunk the price of his lots." He gave eighty dollars for a yoke of oxen and one of them was shot, and twenty dollars for a cow and it died; so that at the close of 1796 he was about forty dollars in debt. The next year his farming was also unsuccessful, and he lost $16.17 and gained nothing. In the fall of 1796 he accompanied Israel Ludlow and W. C. Schenck to survey the United States military lands between the Scioto and Muskingum rivers. "We had deep snow," he says, "covered with crust. The weather was cold and still, so that we could kill but little game, and we were twenty-nine days without bread, and nearly all that time without salt, and sometimes very little to eat. We were five days—seven in company—on four meals, and they, except the last, scanty. They consisted of a turkey, two young raccoons, and the last day some rabbits and venison, which we got from some Indians." In February, 1798, he began the study of surveying in Cincinnati, boarding at Captain Benham's. He was promised a district in the United States lands by Israel Ludlow, who had the power of filling blank commissions from the Surveyor-General, but who, as on the former occasion, never fulfilled his promise. After completing his studies, he "assisted Avery in his tavern during the sitting of court, and for some time afterwards posted books for several persons, and wrote for a short time in the quartermaster's department at Fort Washington." He had been waiting in Cincinnati all summer, hoping to be employed as a surveyor, and was now again put off. He therefore returned to Dayton. On his arrival, having nothing else to do, he dug a sawmill pit for D. C. Cooper, proprietor of the town. From working in so damp and chilly a place he caught a violent cold, and had rheumatism and fever, succeeded by pleurisy. He had been forced to sell his preëmption rights and outlots in Dayton, but in 1799 rented some ground and raised an excellent crop of corn.

CHAPTER III

PIONEER LIFE

Two Houses on Main Street in 1799—Small Size of Cabins—Description by W. C. Howells of a Home of the Period—Newcom's Tavern, First House in Dayton, Chinked with Mortar—Corner Monument Avenue and Main Street the Business Center of Dayton—First White Child Born in Dayton—Biography of Colonel Newcom—Wearisome Journey Through the Woods to Dayton—Camping at Night—Newcom's Tavern Described—Relics—Old Clock and Brass Candlestick—First County Court Held at Tavern—Money Scarce—Convicted Persons Fined a Deerskin or a Bushel of Corn—Sentenced to Thirty-Nine Lashes on Bare Back—Sheriff Newcom's Primitive Prison a Corn-Crib and a Dry Well—Anecdotes of Visits of Troublesome Indians to the Tavern—Colonel Newcom Introduces Apples—First Wedding in Dayton—Benjamin Van Cleve's Characteristic Account of the Event—Mr. Van Cleve's Hospitality to Strangers—Usefulness to the New Town—W. C. Howells's Description of Social Life in Pioneer Times—Fire-Hunting on the Miami—Women Helped Their Husbands in the Fields—Dependent on the Husband's and Father's Gun for Meals—Pelts and Bears' Oil Articles of Merchandise—Skins Used for Clothes, Moccasins, Rugs, and Coverlets—Business Conducted by Barter—Ginseng, Peltries, Beeswax, etc., Used as Money—Cut-Money or Sharp Shins—Charges Made in Pounds, Shillings, and Pence—Wild Animals—First Mill, a Corn-Cracker, Built by D. C. Cooper—Log Meeting-House Built—Dayton First Governed Wholly by County Commissioners and Township Assessors—D. C. Cooper Justice of the Peace—Early Marriages—Petition Presented to Congress by Settlers—The Town Nearly Dies Out—D. C. Cooper, Titular Proprietor, Resuscitates It—Town Plats—Basis of Titles—Ohio a State—Montgomery Separated from Hamilton County—Population Increases—First Election—First County Court—Mr. Cooper Builds Saw- and Grist-Mills—Levees—New Graveyard—Log-Cabin Meeting-House Sold—New First Presbyterian Church—Mr. Cooper's Death—First Jail.

THE only buildings in 1799 on Main Street within view of the blockhouse on the site of the Soldiers' Monument were Newcom's log tavern, two stories in height, and containing four rooms, built in the winter of 1798-1799, and George Westfall's cabin of one room and a loft, on the southeast corner of the alley between First Street and Monument Avenue. One wonders how a family of five or six could live in a diminutive house like the latter. W. C. Howells, father of the novelist, in his "Recollections of Ohio," published in the spring of 1895, describes such a cabin, into which two families, one of them his father's,—cultivated, refined people,—were crowded for four days and nights, and which was the home of the Howells family, numbering nine, for several months. This log cabin was eighteen by twenty feet in size, and with a loft overhead, in the highest part of which you could make a bed on the floor. The cabin contained fourteen persons during the crowded period mentioned— eight grown people and six children. Mr. Howells says: "As I write this in a house where there would be a room for each, I do not myself see how it was managed. But that was fifty years ago, and people put up with worse things. The fact is, there was no alternative, and when it is that or nothing we can do many odd things." In those days people rolled up in a bearskin or blanket and slept on the puncheon floor or out-of-doors in summer on the grass.

It is difficult for people with modern ideas of space and privacy to comprehend how a small house like Newcom's Tavern could have afforded accommodations for travelers, for a store, church, court-house, and jail. But Mr. Howells throws some light on this question also. Describing a journey in a wagon, he says: "We stopped at night at a tavern, as was the custom, only hiring the use of one room on the first floor, known as the movers' room, and the privilege of the fire to make tea or coffee, or fry bacon. It was very much like camping out, save that we were housed at soldiers' quarters." The movers' room of a tavern was also, no doubt, often used for meetings of the court or of the church. Mr. Howells says that cabins sometimes contained a four-light window, with greased paper for glass, but it was very common for log cabins to have no windows whatever. In extremely cold weather the door would be closed, and likewise at night, but mostly, by keeping a good fire, the door could be left open for light and ventilation; and the chimneys were so wide and so low, very often not as high as the one-story house, that they afforded as much light as a small window. These chimneys were always outside the house at one end. The manner of building them was to cut through the logs at the gable-end a space of six or eight feet wide and five or six feet high, and logs were built to this opening like a bay-window; this recess was then lined with a rough stone wall up as high as this opening; from that point a smoke-stack was built of small sticks split out of straight wood, and laid cob-house fashion to the height desired,

From a daguerreotype in possession of Mrs. Josiah Gebhart.
COLONEL GEORGE NEWCOM.

NEWCOM'S TAVERN IN 1799.

and then plastered inside and out with clay, held together by straw.

In 1799 lime was made in Dayton for the first time, from stones gathered from the bed of the river and piled on a huge log fire, which took the place of a kiln. Newcom's Tavern was the first house chinked and plastered with lime mortar instead of clay. "A wondering country boy, on his return from the village, reported to his astonished family that Colonel Newcom was plastering his house with flour."

The southwest corner of Monument Avenue and Main Street was the business center of Dayton Township for five or six years. If a crowd was possible in such a hamlet, it assembled there when court was in session, as in 1803, or when there was a meeting to organize for defense against the Indians, or to attend to religious or political affairs. All travelers on horseback, on foot, or in wagons, prospectors hunting for land, emigrants, farmers and their wives in town for the day, stopped at Newcom's Tavern to eat or sleep, shop, attend to law business, get a drink of water from the only well in the township or a glass of something stronger, or to rest and gossip around the roaring log fire, where the villagers loved to gather. April 14, 1800, Jane Newcom, the first child born in Dayton, was born at her father's tavern. She married Nathaniel Wilson. Mrs. Josiah Gebhart, daughter of Mrs. Wilson and granddaughter of Colonel Newcom, has portraits of both these pioneers in her possession.

The interest that is felt in the preservation of Newcom's Tavern renders the career of the builder of that historic house, a man who "enjoyed the respect of the whole community," of importance. Colonel George Newcom was born in Ireland and brought to this country by his parents in 1775. The Newcoms settled first in Delaware, removing afterwards to the neighborhood of Middletown, Pennsylvania. George Newcom married Mary Henderson, of Washington County, Pennsylvania. They had three children, one of whom died before they came to Dayton. The second child, John W., had several children, all of whom died young, except Martha A., who married John E. Greer, of Dayton. The third child, Jane, as already stated, married Nathaniel Wilson, and four of her nine children lived to be well known in Dayton — Clinton, Mrs. Mary J. Hunt, Mrs. Elizabeth Bowen, and Mrs. Josiah Gebhart.

In March, 1796, George Newcom and his wife left Cincinnati

(where they had arrived about 1794) for the site of Dayton. Three other families and five unmarried men were of the party. It took them two weeks to make the trip of sixty miles over the almost unbroken roads, and very wearisome and uncomfortable was the journey. The weather was damp and cold, rainy, and spitting snow. Camping at night in the wet woods was a trying experience, though hatchet and ax furnished fuel for a blazing fire, kindled by rubbing together pieces of punk or rotten wood, and their rifles supplied them with food from the surrounding forest. Beds were made by spreading blankets over brush. In the early morning mothers and children arose, shivering and unrefreshed; breakfast was prepared, horses fed and packed by men cold, tired, and discouraged, and another day's journey begun.

The road from Cincinnati to Hamilton had been used so much by United States troops that it was tolerably good, but the rough, narrow road from Hamilton to Dayton was often almost impassable for heavily laden horses. Even the women seem to have walked most of the way. The men drove the cattle and led the packhorses. In creels, suspended from either side of the pack-saddles, were carried bedding, clothing, cooking utensils, tableware, provisions, tools, implements, and children too small to walk, their heads only appearing above. When the party came to small streams, they felled trees and made foot-bridges. It was necessary to build rafts to carry men, women, children, and freight across large creeks, and horses and cattle swam over. Driving the cattle, which would stray from the road and occasion delay till they were found, was troublesome and provoking business. Finally, the party reached the mouth of Mad River, and found friends awaiting them, the other two companies of settlers having arrived a few days sooner.

Colonel Newcom built a cabin of one room and a loft on the southwest corner of Main Street and Monument Avenue as soon as he arrived, which in the winter of 1798-1799 gave place to the tavern of two stories and four rooms. This latter house is usually described as tavern, store, court-house, and jail, though the jail, in two separate "apartments," was really in the back yard, where was also a log barn. When large parties stopped at Newcom's Tavern, probably they occupied a movers' room and looked after themselves. But when one or two travelers alighted with their saddle-bags, they were no doubt made literal guests and taken into the family as if they were friends or relations. It was a typical frontier tavern, the host and hostess, as was the universal custom in private houses, assisting in doing the work of the tavern, and often even the stable, with their own hands. On the kitchen mantel of the tavern stood tall brass candlesticks, one of which is now in the possession of Mrs. Josiah Gebhart. In a corner ticked the large, old-fashioned clock, six feet or more in height. It is now in the possession of Mr. Charles W. Gebhart, wound regularly with the key that Colonel Newcom used, and keeping as excellent time as it did a hundred years ago. In the kitchen also stood a dresser laden with pewter dishes, which shone like silver.

The first county court was opened in an upper room in Newcom's Tavern July 27, 1803, by Hon. Francis Dunlevy, presiding judge of the first judicial district. Benjamin Van Cleve was clerk *pro tem.;* Daniel Symmes, of Cincinnati, prosecutor *pro tem.;* George Newcom, sheriff; and James Miller, coroner. The law fixing the county-seat at Dayton, which went into force in May, 1803, also directed that the court should assemble "at the house of George Newcom, in the town of Dayton." As there was no business to transact, court adjourned on the evening of the day it assembled. Nearly all the men in Montgomery County flocked to Newcom's on July 27. The opening of court was the occasion of universal excitement and amusement in that stagnant, back-country region. The judges and lawyers slept the night of the 27th in one room at the tavern, and left early the next morning on horseback to open court at Xenia. The second session of court — November 22, 1803 — was held under the trees back of Newcom's Tavern, aad the aid of the sheriff was required to disperse the curious crowd which was listening, not only to the testimony of witnesses, but to the presumably secret discussions of the jury. Seven cases were tried, and court adjourned next day.

As money was scarce, persons convicted by the court were fined a certain number of deer or other skins, or an amount of corn or pork. Small offenses were often punished by from one to thirty-nine lashes on the bare back, well laid on, the sentence being executed by Sheriff Newcom as soon as pronounced. There was no regular jail, and Colonel Newcom confined white prisoners in a dry well on his lot. "The pit was dry and there was no water in it," as Curwen, the witty first historian of Dayton says, "and following the example of Old Testament jailers, he let down those who broke the peace of the State, and there they remained till brought up for trial." When drunken and troublesome Indians were placed in his keeping, he bound them and confined them in his corn-crib.

Visits of Indians were a great nuisance to pioneers, whether they were friendly or the reverse. They were in the habit of calling white people by their Christian names, and would stand outside the Newcom house, carefully closed against them, shouting "Polly, Polly," and if Mrs. Newcom persisted in refusing to admit them, would fill their hands with corn from the crib and throw it through the chinks between the logs of the cabin, which were not always well filled with plaster. One day Colonel Newcom came home and found his wife at the wash-tub and an Indian bespattered with blood bending over her with a tomahawk. The Colonel demanded what this meant, and the Indian replied that "Polly" was washing his shirt. He had compelled Mrs. Newcom to get a tub of water and wash the shirt, which was soaked with blood, whether of man or wild beast Mrs. Newcom did not learn. Colonel Newcom sprung upon the Indian, gave him a severe beating, bound him with strong rope, and threw him into the corn-crib. In a short time the Indian was discovered running towards Mad River, and was never seen nor heard of again. How he managed to untie the rope and escape is an unsolved mystery.

Once, when Mrs. Newcom was ill, a crowd of excited Indians burst into the room where she lay and ordered Colonel Newcom to get them a rope, as they wished to bind one of their number who had offended them. Mrs. Newcom was afraid to be left alone with the Indians, and sat up and begged her husband not to get the rope. Thereupon one of the Indians pushed her back with great violence on the bed. Terrified at the threatening manner of the angry ruffians, she caught up her baby, Jane, and fled into the hazel bushes as far from the house as she was able to go, not returning till Colonel Newcom had got rid of the intruders.

Colonel Newcom introduced apples into Dayton. Previously the settlers had no fruit but the wild growth of the woods and prairies. He brought a number of apples from Cincinnati, called the citizens together, and gave different varieties of the fruit to whoever desired to plant the seed. He planted seed on his farm, now the home of Mr. P. E. Gilbert, on Huffman Avenue, setting out the tiny trees in an orchard when they were only a few inches high. This orchard was cut down a year ago.

Colonel Newcom was the first sheriff of Montgomery County, and held other offices. He was a member of the Ohio Legislature for twenty-three consecutive years—first as a senator and afterwards as a member of the lower house. When the Legislature spent time uselessly on business of little importance, he would berate his fellow members for wasting the people's money by long sessions when all important affairs could have been crowded into a short period. He served as a soldier in Wayne's campaign against the Indians in 1794, and also in the War of 1812. April 3, 1834, his first wife died. He married Elizabeth Bowen, June 22, 1836. She died October 29, 1850. Colonel Newcom lived to be eighty-two, and died February 25, 1853.

August 28, 1800, is noted as the date of the first wedding in Dayton. On that day Benjamin Van Cleve was married to Mary Whitten at her father's house on his farm a short distance from town. Mr. Van Cleve makes this characteristic record of the event in his diary: "This year I raised a crop of corn and determined on settling myself, and having a home; I accordingly, on the 28th of August, married Mary Whitten, daughter of John Whitten, near Dayton. She was young, lively, and ingenuous. My property was a horse creature, and a few farming utensils, and her father gave her a few household or kitchen utensils, so that we could make shift to cook our provisions; a bed, a cow and heifer, an ewe and two lambs, a sow and pigs, and a saddle and spinning-wheel. I had corn and vegetables growing, so that if we were not rich we had sufficient for our immediate wants, and we were contented and happy." Mr. Van Cleve's marriage was a benefit to the community, for it enabled him to exercise that open-handed hospitality to strangers which was a trait of the public-spirited pioneers. The writer of an obituary notice of him published in the Dayton *Watchman*, in 1821, says: "He has been a leading character in this county, and has taken an active part in promoting its interests. By using system in his business, he found leisure from his duties as clerk of the court, postmaster, and his private affairs, to do much for the public good; and the strangers that passed through town found in Mr. Van Cleve one who was able and took pleasure in giving them information."

Ohio was a new and unknown country at the beginning of the

nineteenth century, and travelers and land prospectors were unable to obtain from books or newspapers the facts they desired in regard to soil, climate, population, and business. It was, therefore, greatly to the advantage of a recently settled town and county to have within their borders one like Mr. Van Cleve, who was not only a good talker, but a perfect mine of information (he had, while surveying, traveled over nearly every foot of ground in this neighborhood), and also willing to take the time and trouble to instruct inquiring visitors, who, if properly approached, might be induced to become permanent settlers. He understood farming, and cultivated his quarter-section, one hundred and sixty acres, now within the corporation, in the eastern part of town, and a valuable inheritance for his descendants.

Benjamin and Mary W. Van Cleve had five children: John Whitten, born June 27, 1801, died, unmarried, September 6, 1858, as remarkable a man and as useful a citizen as his father. William James, born 1803, died 1808. Henrietta Maria, born November 16, 1805, married Samuel B. Dover, September 21, 1824, surviving him; she married Joseph Bond November 4, 1858, and died May 18, 1879. Her descendants now living are two daughters, Mrs. Sophia Simpson, of Dayton, and Mrs. Mary A. Dill, of Union City, Indiana; William Simpson, of Dayton, Dr. Moses Simpson, Freehold, New Jersey,—children of Mrs. Sophia Simpson,—and the sons and daughters of Thomas Dover, deceased,—Fay and Samuel, of Dayton; John, living in California; Mrs. Anna McKnight, of Dayton. Her third daughter, Phebe, married Emery Belden, and her daughter lives in Dayton. The fourth daughter is dead, but has a son and daughter living in the city. The fourth child of Benjamin Van Cleve was Mary Cornelia, born December 2, 1807; married James Andrews, November 20, 1827, and died February 19, 1878; children, Miss America Andrews and Mrs. Laura Poling, of Dayton, and I. W. Andrews, of Kansas City; grandchildren, Mrs. Edith Allison, Dayton; Dr. J. Andrews, Mansfield; Mrs. Alice Yoke, Lewisburg; Harry C. Andrews, Grace and Clifford Andrews, Dayton; Earl and Charley Andrews, Cambridge City. The youngest child of Benjamin Van Cleve, Sarah Sophia, was born November, 1809; married David C. Baker, February 11, 1830, and died October 18, 1839. Her children live in Indiana or Kansas. Mr. Van Cleve's first wife died in 1810. In 1812 he married Mary Tamplin. They had no children. She died in 1825.

W. C. Howells (who, by the way, lived in Dayton and edited the *Transcript* in 1850) says of pioneer times: "Particularly remarkable was the general equality and the general dependence of all upon the neighboring kindness and good offices of others. The houses and barns were built of logs, and were raised by the collection of many neighbors together on one day, whose united strength was necessary to the handling of the logs. This kind of mutual help by the neighbors was extended to many kinds of work, such as rolling up and burning the logs in a clearing, grubbing out the underbrush, splitting rails, cutting logs for a house, and the like. When a gathering of men for such a purpose took place, there was commonly some sort of mutual job laid out for women, such as quilting (patchwork was the art embroidery of that era), sewing, or spinning up a lot of thread for some poor neighbor." Corn-huskings and maple-sugar camps were also jolly resorts in their seasons. An abundant supper, which the women who were guests helped prepare, was served on such festive occasions, and dancing and kissing games finished the evening. Singing- and grammar- or spelling-schools were also pioneer amusements of men and women of all ages. A favorite sport of the settlers was fire-hunting, which Curwen thus describes: "The deer came down to the river to drink in the evening, and sheltered themselves for the night under the bushes which grew along the shore. As soon as they were quiet, the hunters in pirogues paddled slowly up the stream, the steersman holding aloft a burning torch of dried hickory bark, by the light of which the deer was discovered and fired on. If the shot was successful, the party landed, skinned the animal, hung the carcass to a tree, to be brought home in the morning, and then proceeded to hunt more game." Fire-hunting must have been a beautiful spectacle to the women and children watching it from the Monument Avenue bank of the Miami.

Women helped their husbands and brothers in all possible ways in those days, even when used to town life in the East. If extra work out-of-doors was needed, the wife or daughter would be called on to aid, and sometimes they would assist in planting and hoeing the corn and raking the grain or hay in harvest. All was country in Dayton ninety-five years ago, in spite of four or five cabins on the town plat. W. D. Howells, speaking of his father's sympathetic account of pioneer life, says "He did not deceive himself concerning the past. He knew that it was often rude and hard and coarse; but under the rough and sordid aspect he was aware of the warm heart of humanity in which, quite as much as in the brain, all civility lies." In 1804-1810, when one-roomed log cabins began to give way to neat dwellings of several rooms, and new settlers built brick buildings for country stores, their educated and well-bred wives used to aid them by molding candles and making ginger cakes, rolls, root-beer, and other articles for sale.

In the earlier years of our history settlers' families were often dependent upon the father's gun for a breakfast or dinner, and hunting was oftener an occupation than an amusement. Deer and bears were killed in large numbers for both their pelts and flesh, and the bears also for their oil. Deerskin was made into men's clothes and moccasins, and bearskins were used as rugs and coverlets. The meat, and also that of wild birds, was salted and eaten as we eat dried beef. Racoon skins were in demand for winter caps. Pelts of various kinds were used instead of money.

There was little money in circulation, and business in the Northwest Territory was chiefly conducted by barter of articles that were easily transported on packhorses, such as ginseng, peltries, and beeswax, which had fixed values. A muskrat skin passed for twenty-five cents; a buckskin for one dollar; a doeskin for one dollar and fifty cents; a bearskin for from three to five dollars; a pair of cotton stockings cost a buckskin; a yard of calico cost two muskrat skins; a set of knives and forks, a bearskin; a yard of shirting, a doeskin; a pair of moccasins, a coonskin, or thirty-seven and a half cents. The want of small change led the pioneers of the Ohio Valley to invent what was called cut-money, or sharp shins. They cut small coins, chiefly Spanish, into quarters, and circulated them as readily as money that had not been tampered with. American merchants had not yet learned to use the United States currency, and their charges were in pounds, shillings, and pence. In 1799 Hyson tea was sixteen shillings tenpence per pound; loaf sugar, four shillings; flour, eighteen shillings tenpence per one hundred pounds; pork, eighteen shillings ninepence; beef, twenty-two shillings sixpence; work, groceries, and dry goods were often paid for in corn or pork.

The habits and surroundings of the people were very primitive. Wildcats and panthers strong enough to carry off a live

From a photograph in possession of Mrs. Josiah Gebhart.

MRS. JANE NEWCOM WILSON.

From a photograph in possession of Mrs. Josiah Gebhart.
NATHANIEL WILSON.

hog prowled in the surrounding woods, and wolves, which destroyed stock, poultry, and young vegetables, were shot by moonlight through the chinks of the cabins. The wolves howled from dusk till dawn like innumerable dogs, as any one who has visited prairie countries can understand.

An event in the lives of the people of this region was the building, by Daniel C. Cooper, the greatest benefactor of early Dayton, on Rubicon Creek, which ran through his farm, now the site of the Cash Register Works, of a tub-mill or "corn-cracker," run by water, which began to be used in the winter of 1799-1800. No flour could be obtained, and previous to this date meal was ground in hand-mills, three or four hours of tiresome work being necessary to grind enough to last one small family a single day. This tub-mill was a rough affair, and the sides were not inclosed, but settlers brought their corn to it from nearly the whole of the Miami Valley, and from up Mad River as far as Springfield. Curwen, our first historian, says that Mr. Cooper "obtained all the custom of town, and took toll from the Trojans and Pequods."

In the spring of 1800 the people of Dayton and the surrounding country got out logs and built the first Presbyterian meeting-house on the corner of Main and Third streets, where Callahan's block now stands, D. C. Cooper having given two lots for a church and graveyard. Before this the Presbyterians had held services in Newcom's Tavern or the blockhouse. The log-cabin meeting-house was eighteen by twenty feet in size, seven logs high, and raised two feet from the ground by pieces of log placed upright under each corner. The seats and doorsteps were logs, and it had a puncheon floor and a clapboard roof, secured by weight poles. It had no windows, but sufficient air and light entered by the door and between the logs, the chinks being unfilled. Hazel bushes and small trees entirely hid it from view of passers up or down Main Street. It was approached by a narrow path, which wound through the uncleared graveyard.

Dayton was originally in Hamilton County, which included the counties now known as Montgomery, Greene, Clark, Champaign, Logan, and Shelby, and other territory, and was governed by county commissioners and township assessors. Dayton had no other government till 1799, when Daniel C. Cooper was appointed justice of the peace. He served three years and seven months and tried one hundred and eighteen cases. Eighteen of them were certified as settled and the rest as "satisfied."

The Territorial law permitted the marriage "of male persons of the age of eighteen and female persons of the age of fourteen, and not nearer of kin than first cousins." But it was necessary that notice should be given, either in writing posted at some conspicuous place within the township where the woman resided, or publicly declared on two days of public worship. Sometimes a notice written on a piece of paper, and signed "D. C. Cooper, Justice of the Peace," was tacked to the trunk of a large forest tree close to a road. Early marriages were so much the custom that respectable parents saw with approbation young daughters who at the present day would still be in the school-room married to men who were mere boys in age. A girl of fifteen was as much a young lady in 1800 as a girl of twenty at the present day.

The county expenses for 1797 were as follows: Assessor, James Brady, $5.20, paid by the treasurer out of the first money that came into his hands; Cyrus Osborn, constable of Dayton, $1.90, "for his trouble and attention in executing the commissioners' warrant for ascertaining taxable property." He also received "fifty cents for one quire of paper used in the aforesaid business." The commissioners each received $7.50, and $14.34 was expended by the county for stationery. The officers of Dayton Township in 1798 were James Thompson, constable; Daniel C. Cooper, assessor; George Newcom, collector. Mr. Cooper's fees were $7.20. Twenty-two taxpayers lived in Dayton in 1798, and the taxes amounted to $29.74. In 1801 Benjamin Van Cleve was appointed to make a list of free male inhabitants twenty-one years old and over. The danger of attacks from Indians, as well as the need of men to clear lands, rendered it as necessary to ascertain how many men in the township were able to bear arms or wield an ax as to learn the names of taxpayers and the value of their property. Mr. Van Cleve says, "The number of free males over twenty-one years old, between the two Miamis, from the south line of the township to the head of Mad River and the Great Miami, was three hundred and eighty-two; east of the Little Miami, less than twenty."

The high hopes with which the little bands of settlers had made their way through the woods and by river to Dayton seemed at first doomed to disappointment, as the following quotation from a petition of the settlers to Congress, probably written by Benjamin Van Cleve about 1802 or 1803, shows:

"On the 5th of November, 1795, forty-six persons engaged to become settlers at Dayton, but from the many difficulties in forming a new settlement so far in the wilderness country, only fifteen of these came forward, and four others, making nineteen in all. These settlements were formed by your petitioners a few months after the treaty of Greenville, when we had no faith in the friendship of the savages. Our settlement was immediately on their hunting-grounds. We were not able to keep a horse amongst us during the first season by reason of their stealing. The scarcity of provisions had raised flour to nine dollars a barrel, and other articles in proportion, which we had to transport fifty miles through a wilderness, clearing roads, etc. Under all these and many more difficulties we labored, in hopes of obtaining our lands at a low rate, and the small gratuity offered. Several of your petitioners have not been able to procure any land; others laid their claims before the commissioners agreeably to the late law, and purchased at two dollars per acre. We beg leave to state to your honorable body that the proprietors have been at vast expense, labor, and difficulty in forming the said settlement, and have received no recompense nor privilege other than subsequent settlers; that they first opened a way in consequence of which the country has become populous, and the United States has received a handsome revenue from the sale of the lands; that the town of Dayton is purchased by a subsequent settler. We pray that Congress will make us such gratuity in lands, or deduction for payments for lands, or grant such other relief as our case merits."

Symmes and St. Clair and his associates had paid two-thirds of a dollar per acre for land, and sold at a small advance. But the Government raised the price, and Benjamin Van Cleve says in his diary: "Mr. Ludlow, who was one of the proprietors and agent for them, informed me that they relinquished their claim on account of the rising price; that they could not afford to pay two dollars."

It was at this time that Daniel C. Cooper became titular proprietor of the town by purchase of preëmption rights and agreements with the settlers. Each of the original settlers received a donation of an inlot and an outlot, which he or his representative drew at the lottery held at the mouth of Mad River November 4, 1795. When the original proprietors failed and retired, settlers were obliged to pay two dollars an acre, one dollar for a town lot, and did it willingly, at the Cincinnati land office to secure these "donations." The town nearly died out between 1802 and 1803. Four cabins were vacant and only five families lived here—those of George Newcom, Samuel Thompson, John Welsh, Paul D. Butler, and George Westfall. The Van Cleve brothers and William Newcom and John Williams were farming. The McClures and Arnett had moved away. But Mr. Cooper brought the town to life again, and secured satisfactory titles by patent or deed. Mr. Cooper made several plats of the town; that of 1805 provided for a little park at the intersection of Main and Third streets, with a court-house in the center. In 1809 he made a revised plat to conform to deeds and patents, and to the plat made by the original proprietors in 1795, and to this plat all subsequent additions have been made. Prior to the record of this plat of 1809, property was seldom transferred by deed; the county commissioners established a rule that that party would be recognized as the owner of a lot whose name appeared on the plat opposite any lot number; thus, to pass the title of a piece of property from one person to another, all that was necessary was a verbal request of the owner to have the purchaser's name placed in the list instead of his own. Of these transactions, be they few or many, no record has been preserved, but instead of such record a perfect list of lot owners at the time the plat of 1809 was recorded, forms the basis of title to all the original three hundred and twenty-one lots of Dayton.

At first, county and township officers were appointed by the Territorial governor and courts. In 1802 Ohio became a State, and Montgomery was separated from Hamilton County. Population had now increased till it was thought best to authorize an election by the people of additional officers. Jerome Holt, sheriff of the county, was directed to give notice to the inhabitants of Dayton Township to convene at the house of George Newcom and proceed to elect by ballot a chairman, town clerk, three or more trustees or managers, two or more overseers of the poor, three fence-viewers, two appraisers of houses, a lister of taxable property, a sufficient number of supervisors of roads, and one or more constables. The first county court was opened in an upper room at Newcom's July 27 of this year. In March, 1803, the first State Legislature, at Chillicothe, recommended Dayton for the county-seat, and the selection was confirmed in April by the commissioners appointed to designate county-seats. The half-deserted backwoods village of Dayton seemed an unpromising place for a county-seat. But it was the nucleus of a number of farming settlements, and was the principal hamlet in the township. The growth and improvement of Dayton was marked after it became the county-seat. The taxes for 1804 amounted to $458.40. Main

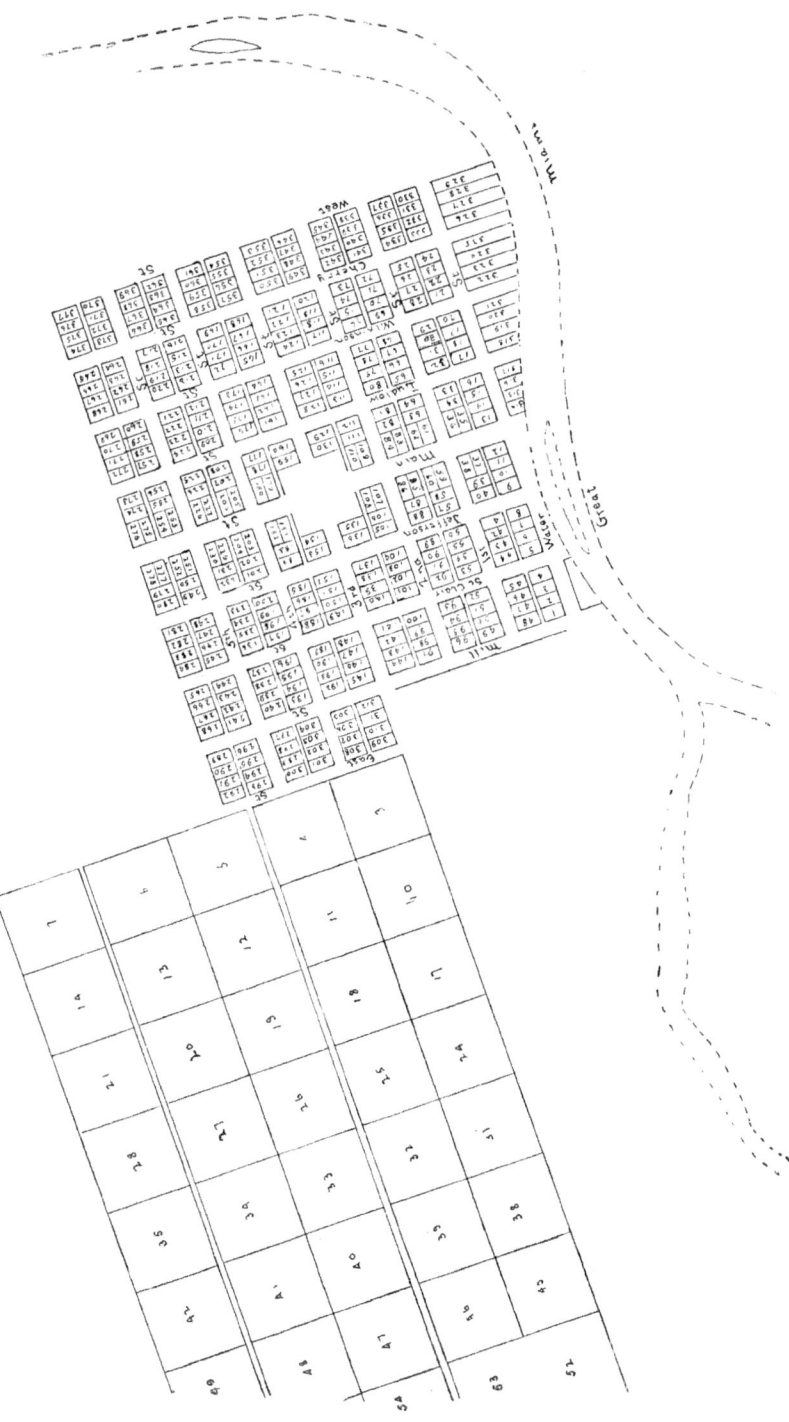

PLAN OF DAYTON MADE BY D. C. COOPER AND RECORDED IN MONTGOMERY COUNTY RECORDS, 1805.

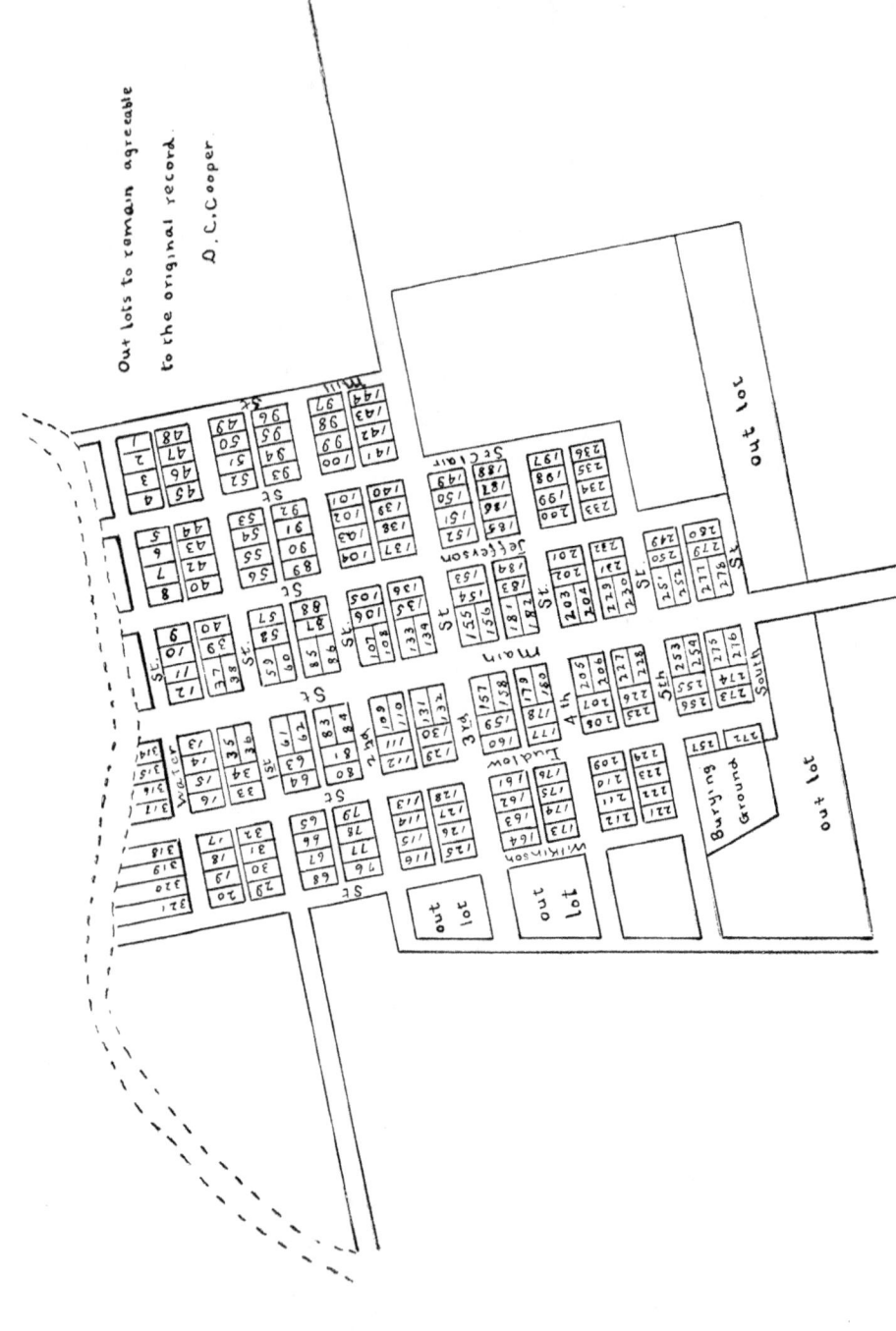

Street was cleared to Warren Street in 1804, and the gully at the Main and Third Street crossing filled with walnut logs cut in the woods where Cathcart's livery-stable now stands.

This year Mr. Cooper built a sawmill on First Street and a grist-mill at the head of Mill Street, to which in 1809 he added a carding-machine. He built a levee for the protection of his Mill Street property. At an early date Mr. Cooper employed Silas Broadwell to build a levee to protect the western part of the town, agreeing to give him certain lots in its vicinity in payment for making it and keeping it in repair. The levee began at Wilkinson Street, and ran west a considerable distance with the meanderings of the Miami.

When Mr. Cooper gave lots on the east side of Main Street, opposite the Court-house, for a church and graveyard, they were considered so far out of the way that it was not supposed that the town would extend much beyond them; but by 1805 property in that neighborhood was wanted for residences or business. The log-cabin meeting-house was sold for twenty-two dollars, which became the nucleus of a building-fund for a new church, and the graveyard was platted and sold at auction at the Court-house. Mr. Cooper gave a new graveyard of four acres at the south side of Fifth Street, between Ludlow and Wilkinson streets, equal shares being given to the First Presbyterian and the Methodist churches and the town of Dayton. The new Presbyterian church, on Second and Ludlow streets, was not built till 1817. Two structures have succeeded it—one of brick, built in 1839, and the present stone church, built in 1867. Till the church of 1817 was completed, the congregation held services at Newcom's, or at McCullum's new brick tavern, southwest corner of Main and Second streets, removing in 1806 to the new Court-house.

Mr. Cooper was deeply interested in the new Presbyterian church. When the bell for the church arrived at his store, southeast corner of Main and First streets, in 1818, he placed it on a wheelbarrow, and himself wheeled it to the corner of Second and Ludlow streets. He over-exerted himself, and burst a blood-vessel, which caused his death. He left two sons, who both died young and without children. Mr. Cooper won the respect and affection of all his fellow-citizens. To no one does the present generation owe a larger debt of gratitude. When he died, his affairs were somewhat involved; but by prudent management his executors, James Steele and H. G. Phillips, relieved the estate from embarrassment, and it henceforth steadily increased in value. Every improvement of this large property benefited the city.

A jail was built of round logs in the fall of 1804 on the end of the Third Street side of the Court-house lot. It was thirty feet long, sixteen wide, and twelve high, and contained two disconnected cells, floored and ceiled with logs. There were but three small windows in the building, secured by two-inch plank shutters and iron bars, and but two doors, also of two-inch plank, spiked and hung on iron hinges. The doors and shutters were locked on the outside, and the keys kept by Sheriff Newcom at his tavern, three squares off. During the sessions of court at the tavern a doorkeeper was appointed to conduct prisoners to and from the jail. This log fortress, which was built for $299 by David Squier, in two months, was stronger than the blockhouses which did such good service during the Indian wars, and answered every purpose till it became necessary that the sheriff should live at the jail, when one of stone was erected.

CHAPTER IV

1800-1805

JOHN W. VAN CLEVE—First White Male Child Born in Dayton—Friendship for R. W. Steele—Biographies of Van Cleve by R. W. Steele—Minutes Kept and Societies Founded by Van Cleve—His Exquisite Handwriting—His Versatility and Thoroughness—Proficiency in Ancient and Modern Languages—Teaches Latin at College Before Graduation—Talent for Mathematics—Translations—Water-Color Pictures of Wild Flowers—A True Book-Lover—Studies Law—Edits the Dayton *Journal*—In the Drug Business—Devotes Himself to Labors for the Public Good—A Civil Engineer—An Engraver—Talent for Painting—Plays Several Musical Instruments—A Botanist and Geologist—To Him We Owe Woodland Cemetery—Love of Plants and Trees—Plants the Levees with Trees—Surrounds the Court-House with Elms—Fondness for Children—Delightful Picnics—His Great Size—Interest in Schools and Libraries—Founder and Supporter of Dayton Library Association—Free Lectures on Scientific, Historical, or Literary Subjects—Affection and Pride with Which He was Regarded—Devotion to His Kindred—Friendship Between Him and His Father—Public Offices in Town that He Held—His Map of Dayton—Writes Songs and Designs and Engraves Illustrations for the *Log Cabin*—The Whig Glee Club Trained by Professor Turpin—Mr. Van Cleve and Others Accompany the Club to the Columbus Convention—His Death—His Unbending Integrity and Scrupulous Honesty—Council Passes Resolutions of Respect—Dr. T. E. Thomas's Funeral Oration—Isaac Spining—William King—The Osborns—John H. Williams—The First Postoffice in Dayton—Mail-Routes—Post-Rider to Urbana—Trials of Benjamin Van Cleve, First Postmaster—His Successor, George S. Houston—Joseph Peirce—Joseph H. Crane—Colonel Robert Patterson—Schools—Dayton Incorporated—McCullum's Tavern—Social Library Society.

OUR early history would be incomplete without some account of John W. Van Cleve, the first male child born in Dayton, and who became locally noted for literary, scientific, and artistic attainments, and for life-long, unsalaried work for the public good. He was the son of Benjamin and Mary Whitten Van Cleve, and was born June 27, 1801. From the writings and conversation of the two Van Cleves, and from the files of Dayton newspapers, commencing with the first paper published here, preserved by them and presented to the Public Library by the son, Maskell E. Curwen, Ashley Brown, Robert W. Steele, and others obtained the greater part of the material for their histories of Dayton. During his last illness, J. W. Van Cleve explained to R. W. Steele, a younger man but congenial friend, who, from his youth, had devoted himself to disinterested philanthropic and educational labors, his plans for the benefit of his beloved native city, and placed in his hands constitutions, reports, and minutes of various societies, of which Mr. Van Cleve had been the animating spirit and usually the founder; and Mr. Steele constituted himself the biographer and eulogist of Mr. Van Cleve, sketching his portrait, with all the literary skill and sympathetic touches at his command, in a number of publications. It is a matter of regret that he did not collect and combine in an elaborate biography the facts in regard to his friend which he scattered through several articles; but it was his nature to sow broadcast with a liberal hand, regardless of personal considerations.

The minutes kept by John W. Van Cleve were written in an exquisitely beautiful hand, which, like his father's, was as legible as copper-plate; so that it seemed a desecration for an inferior penman to make an entry in the books. The minutes of the Montgomery County Horticultural Society, of which he was one of the founders, he decorated with a water-color painting of a large, richly tinted peach on a branch, with leaves clustering about it. He was interested in agriculture, introduced modern methods and machinery on his farm, and tried many experiments, endeavoring, among other things, to make raisins from his grapes.

Benjamin Van Cleve determined that his only son should enjoy the intellectual and moral training and affectionate parental supervision of which he himself had been deprived. His boy responded to all his attempts to guide and instruct him, and more than answered his expectations. The son inherited the father's methodical, industrious, and persevering habits, and his faculty of attaining by his own efforts what he had no opportunity of learning from others. He was remarkable for both versatility and thoroughness, and might have been described in the broadest sense as an all-round man, but for a slight lack of development of the imaginative and emotional side of his nature. He must have been largely self-taught, for sixty or seventy years ago teachers of accomplishments, or of anything outside the ordinary branches of education, were not to be obtained in Ohio. The journey to Eastern centers of culture was long and expensive. Specially talented young people did not, as is now customary, spend a winter or two in New York or Boston engaged in literary, scientific, or artistic study.

John Van Cleve was a born scholar, endowed with a vigorous intellect, remarkable memory, and a facility for acquiring a knowledge of both mathematics and languages. When but ten years old, his father wrote of him, "My son John is now studying Latin, and promises to become a fine scholar." He entered the Ohio University at Athens, of which his father was a trustee, when he was sixteen, and acquired so high a reputation for scholarship that before his graduation he was employed as a teacher of both Latin and Greek in the college. He began to teach Latin in 1817, his first year at college. Writing to ask his father's permission to teach, he says: "I think it would inform me in the Latin a great deal. I believe with one month's practice now in speaking the Latin I could speak very nearly as freely in it as I can in English." In 1819 he taught Greek and Latin several hours a day without interfering with his own lessons in his class. The regular work was so insufficient for him that the professors volunteered to give him advanced instruction out of college hours. He was equally proficient in mathematics, and wrote from the Ohio University to his father, "I consider Euclid the most pleasing study I ever undertook, and find no difficulty in understanding the propositions." In another letter he says that it is impossible for him to keep along with his class; it would have been more correct to say that his class could not keep up with him. Between three and five problems of Euclid each day were all that was required of students. Mr. Van Cleve was not satisfied with such easy work, and obtained permission to learn fifteen problems daily.

Mr. R. W. Steele says: "I recollect that, when Colborn's 'Intellectual Arithmetic' was first introduced here, the late John W. Van Cleve, an accomplished and noted man in his day, told me that he went through the book at a sitting with great pleasure. How idle it would be to advise everybody to take up and read Colborn's arithmetic as a pleasant recreation! Mr. Van Cleve was a man of decided taste for mathematics, and before Colborn we had no intellectual arithmetic or analysis in our schools, which accounts for his pleasure in the book."

After leaving college Mr. Van Cleve studied French and German, translating from the latter language the first volume of

Goldfuss and Schiller's "Robbers," and a number of plays and fairy tales. He copied the fairy tales with his own hand into a pretty volume, which he presented to a little girl. To another young lady friend he gave a volume of water-color pictures of the wild flowers of Montgomery County, writing the botanical name below each picture. The flowers are as remarkable for scientific accuracy of form and coloring as for artistic beauty. Mr. Van Cleve was a true book-lover, and gradually collected a good library. He subscribed for the American and foreign magazines, and it was probably the translations and critical and biographical articles in these magazines that led him to study German—a language neglected by English-speaking students till the beginning of the nineteenth century. As there was no teacher of modern languages in Dayton, he taught himself German and French. He contributed to a number of periodicals. In most directions he was a generous man, but he was almost miserly when his beloved books were concerned. He would only lend to those whom he thought genuinely interested in literature, and from each one he exacted a promise, entered in a ledger under his name and the date, that the book should be returned in good condition on a specified day. If the promise was not kept, the borrower received a notification of his remissness, which was repeated with the addition of a sharp reprimand, till the work was safely restored to his shelves. A number of his books are in the possession of his relations. Some of his volumes, enriched by marginal notes in his own hand, are in the Public Library. Occasionally he bound, or rebound, a volume himself in heavy leather, preservation, and not beauty, being his aim. He intended to write a history of the Northwest Territory, and made some preparation for the never-really-undertaken book. His memoranda jotted down for this purpose, and his notes on his general reading, book lists, and private accounts, are as beautiful and exquisitely neat as if intended for exhibition, and not merely for his own eye. Among his manuscripts are letters from distinguished scientists with whom he corresponded.

When he returned from college, he studied law with Judge Joseph H. Crane, and was admitted to the bar in 1828; but he did not find the practice of the law congenial, and in December, 1828, he abandoned the legal profession and purchased an interest in the Dayton *Journal*, which he edited till 1834. In the latter year he entered into partnership in the drug business with Augustus Newell, furnishing the capital, but leaving the control of the concern in the hands of Mr. Newell.

In 1851, as he possessed what was a competency for an unmarried man, Mr. Van Cleve retired from business and devoted himself with the most indefatigable industry for the rest of his life to study and art and the promotion of whatever would benefit and adorn his native city. He became an accomplished musician, painter, engraver, civil engineer, botanist, and geologist. He had very decided talent for painting, and did excellent work in oils and water-colors, though he probably never took a lesson in either. One of his most interesting water-colors is a painting of the east side of Main Street, between Second and Third streets, as it was in 1855, which he gave to Miss Martha Holt. Mrs. Thomas Dover has three oil landscapes, one of them being painted for the purpose of introducing a very tall and magnificent tree in the foreground, the river and sawmill behind it playing a subordinate part. Mrs. Dover also has a number of water-color sketches of river scenery and seven or eight pictures of peaches of different varieties, one on each card. Mr. Van Cleve said he first painted their portraits and then ate them. He gathered them, no doubt, from his own trees.

He played well on several instruments. For a number of years he was organist of Christ Episcopal Church. In 1823 the Pleyel Society, the first Dayton musical society, was formed, and he was elected president. He gave much time to the study of botany and geology, and collected a cabinet of fossils of this neighborhood, which he presented by will to the High School. Several sheets of the fossils of the Dayton limestone engraved by him are preserved at the Dayton Public Library. These engravings have been published in the Indiana Geological Reports. He made a complete herbarium of the plants indigenous to this region, which at his death he gave to Cooper Female Seminary. No care was taken of either his cabinet or herbarium. The remains of them are at the Public Library and Museum. He corresponded and exchanged specimens with scientists all over the United States. His list of trees growing in Woodland Cemetery in 1843 is interesting to botanists.

To him we owe Woodland Cemetery, the third in order of time of the rural cemeteries opened in the United States. He suggested that the beautiful grounds, now the pride of Dayton, should be secured and improved for that purpose, and persistently carried the project through to completion. The cemetery was laid out, the roads run, the platting done, the accounts kept, by this skilled surveyor and bookkeeper, and all the duties of a superintendent performed by him, without compensation, during the earlier years of its history. He was president of the association till his death.

For no one could a park be more appropriately named than for such an enthusiastic lover of nature and his fellow-men as John Van Cleve. The only thing else in Dayton called for him is a street which runs through what was once a part of his model farm. When the levees were built, or enlarged, he obtained subscriptions from citizens, heading the list himself, to purchase and plant trees on both sides of the levees, without expense to the city. At first, elms were planted on the river side and maples on the other side. Afterwards silver-leaf poplars, recently introduced, and then much admired, were also set out. He planted the trees himself. The little granddaughter of a pioneer used to accompany him, and note down from his dictation, in his memorandum-book, under the proper date, the variety of tree planted and its exact position.

He knew the name of nearly every plant and tree within Montgomery County, and in what locality they could be found. Through his influence the early residents of Dayton felt a special interest and pride in the flowers and trees of the surrounding woods and prairies. He loved to bring home from his botanical excursions elegant shrubs or rare flowering plants, which, as he lived at an hotel, he presented to friends, setting them out himself in their yards. It would have seemed to him a cruel act to transplant them from their congenial country home, and allow them to pine or die from careless or ignorant treatment. He would have sympathized with the saying of Montaigne that "there is a certain respect and general duty of humanity that ties us, not only to beasts, that have life and sense, but even to trees and plants." Had he had the making of the constitution of the Humane Society, it would have included the protection of trees as well as of women, children, and animals. Many a noble forest tree did he save from destruction or mutilation by his entreaties. About 1850 he planted elms on Main and Third streets, along the sidewalks of the Court-house lots. He wished his native place to be as beautiful as the elmembowered New England towns, and thought these glorious trees would keep his memory as a public benefactor green for generations; but his ungrateful fellow-citizens, as soon as his elms began to fulfill his expectations, chopped them down.

Mr. Van Cleve was fond of children and they loved him. On many a pleasant spring, summer, or autumn morning he might have been seen leading a little company on foot, or to take the cars to the woods for an all-day picnic. He wanted the children to himself, and no grown people were invited. He had some eccentricities, which, however, only excited a pleasurable awe and curiosity. The children were not permitted, for instance, to ask what time it was. He either made no reply to such a question or answered that it was not polite, and a reflection upon his power of entertaining them, and that, at any rate, children had no business to think or know anything about time. He would sometimes suddenly put his hand within his shirt-bosom and draw out what he called "a beautiful, harmless little gartersnake," dropping it, perhaps, into a girl's lap. If she had the tact or nerve not to scream, she was henceforth one of his prime favorites. When he took children to the woods, he knew where to find quantities of wild flowers, mushrooms, nuts, elderberries, May-apples, haws, papaws,—"nature's custard,"—persimmons, slippery-elm, spicewood, sassafras, etc., and these wild things gathered and commended by him had a flavor with which the liveliest imagination could not now invest them. He led you to the clearest and coolest moss-bordered springs, and his eye was quick to see beautiful and grotesque dead or growing shrubs and trees, birds, squirrels, and every lovely living thing; and a pause was always made to enjoy a fine view or landscape. In his botany box he carried, besides other luncheon, small pieces of beefsteak, one for each member of the party. These he transfixed with snow-white twigs from which he had peeled the bark, and then, arranging the children in front of a blazing fire he had built, showed them how to hold the twigs so as to cook their steak in the delicious fashion of their pioneer ancestors. If it was the proper season for wild grapes, clusters were squeezed into a bright new tincup, mixed with sugar and water, and the beverage drunk in turn by each of the party.

Mr. Van Cleve was a giant in size—tall, of large frame, and weighing over three hundred pounds. Once, when making a call on a friend, the five-year-old son of his host, after walking round him several times, observing him curiously, stopped in front of him, and said, "Mr. Van Cleve, when you was a little boy, *was* you a little boy?" Though usually sensitive about his size, he laughed, and took this as a good joke. Hits at prominent citizens were freely indulged in in the old-fashioned New-Year's address, brought to every door for sale on the 1st of January. In one of the "addresses" appeared this rhyme:

> "If all flesh is grass, as the Scriptures say,
> Then Van Cleve would make a load of hay."

He was the first male child born in Dayton, and, being of very great size, was often pointed out to strangers as a specimen of what Dayton could produce.

Mr. Van Cleve was warmly interested in libraries and schools, and gave liberally of time and money to both. He preserved and presented to the Public Library the records of the old Dayton Academy, from which all the early school history of Dayton was obtained. In the later years of its history he was connected with our first library, incorporated in 1805. He was one of the founders, in 1847, of the Dayton Library Association, now merged in the Public School Library. During the rest of his life the library was one of the objects in which he was most interested. He presented to it valuable newspapers, minutes, magazines, and books, served as an officer of the association, and assisted in selecting the first volumes that were purchased. "The list numbered but little over one thousand volumes, but the books were Charles Lamb's 'books that are books.'" Whenever a public entertainment was gotten up for the benefit of literary or philanthropic objects, Mr. Van Cleve was an active promoter of the undertaking. He frequently lectured on scientific, historical, or literary subjects in the courses provided by the Mechanics' Institute and the Dayton Library Association.

He did a work for Dayton of the kind that only a highly cultivated man of leisure can accomplish. His fellow-citizens appreciated his efforts and regarded him with pride, respect, and love. At the present day, many who were not grown when he died, but to whom he had been kind and helpful in their childhood, never think of him without a glow of affection, admiration, and gratitude.

He was warmly attached to his kindred, even when not nearly related, and any one with Van Cleve blood in his veins was sure of a cordial reception from him, even if not very congenial in character or pursuits. Though undemonstrative and even somewhat cold in manner, he was a most affectionate son, brother, and uncle. His letters from college reveal the delightful relations existing between the son and his father. There is about them a tone of frankness, simplicity, certainty of comprehension and sympathy, of good comradeship and intimate friendship, that gives one a pleasant impression of both the man and the boy. Ambitious of distinction and fond of study though John Van Cleve was, in 1819, when Benjamin Van Cleve was overweighted with financial cares and anxieties, John urged his father to allow him to leave college and come home and help in the business. This request was not granted, and the boy was moreover told that affairs were in better condition than his solicitude for his family had led him to imagine them to be. He always every Sunday spent the afternoon and took tea with one of his sisters. He was not what is called a great talker, and often, after a little domestic chat, would draw a magazine or book from his pocket and soon become absorbed in reading. His sisters' children were very fond of him, and he did a great deal for their pleasure and profit, lending them books, awakening their intelligence, and increasing their fund of knowledge by conversing with them. At the time, however, they only thought of the enjoyment his visits afforded them, and of how delightful it was to have him with them. It was he himself they cared for, not what he might give them, or what benefit they might derive from association with him.

Mr. Van Cleve was elected recorder in 1824 and 1828; served for three terms as Mayor—in 1830, 1831, and 1832, and was several times city engineer. For a number of years he was connected with the volunteer fire department—placed in command by Council. In 1839 he compiled and lithographed a map of the city, and in 1849 a city map in book form, renumbering the various plats and lots unplatted in 1839.

He was an enthusiastic Whig, and a warm supporter of Harrison in 1840. When R. N. and W. F. Comly published the *Log Cabin*, a Harrison campaign paper, famous all over the United States, Mr. Van Cleve wrote many of the songs, and designed and engraved the illustrations and caricatures that appeared in it. He had a grim sense of humor, and sometimes indulged in practical jokes that did not seem laughable to others. Professor James Turpin, a musician of repute, and a generous, public-spirited man, who was highly esteemed, both professionally and socially, composed the accompaniments for the campaign songs. Mr. Van Cleve and Mr. Turpin worked together in the latter's parlor, musician and writer making mutual changes and concessions. Mr. Turpin and Mr. Van Cleve had formed and trained a Whig Glee Club. The club and a large number of other citizens attended the mammoth Harrison convention held at Columbus, where Mr. Van Cleve's songs, as sung under Professor Turpin's leadership by Dayton singers, were received with wild enthusiasm and prolonged applause. The Dayton delegation traveled in stage-coaches, decorated profusely with Harrison emblems, and during both the journey and the stay in Columbus, where the club was crowded into one bedroom, the "fun was fast and furious"; jokes, and quips, and ridiculous tricks, and everything that could promote hilarity or increase political excitement, always at fever heat during that remarkable campaign, were encouraged and indulged in.

Mr. Van Cleve died, unmarried, of consumption, September 6, 1858, after a long illness, which he bore with the greatest courage and patience. One of his closest associates wrote of him: "A striking trait of his character was his unbending integrity. His scrupulous honesty was so well known and appreciated that he was frequently selected for the discharge of the most responsible trusts." His death at the comparatively early age of fifty-seven was regarded as a public calamity. Although he held no official position at the time of his death, the City Council adopted resolutions of respect for his memory and of appreciation of his great services to the city. The funeral took place at the First Presbyterian Church, which was crowded with sincere mourners. The Rev. Thomas E. Thomas delivered a magnificent funeral oration of the kind for which he was so famous, drawing a graphic portrait of Mr. Van Cleve, his talents, acquirements, and character, and comparing him to a dead lion.

Three important accessions were made to the Dayton settlement, in 1800, 1801, and 1802, in Isaac Spining, William King, and John H. Williams, afterwards closely related by marriage, and who settled in the neighborhood now known as the West Side. The name of Judge Spining constantly occurs in connection with public affairs in Dayton. He emigrated from New Jersey to the West in 1796, and a few years later located on a farm three miles west of Dayton. His sons, Pierson, Charles H., and George B., were all citizens of note, the first in Springfield and the other two in Dayton. Mr. Pierson Spining, before removing to Springfield, was in business in Middletown. There is a story connected with the goods he was selling at Middletown which illustrates his father's business talent and the pluck and enterprise of early times. Judge Spining, before 1812, "built a flatboat near the head of Main Street on the river front. This boat was loaded with flour, and with Judge Spining as captain floated to New Orleans. Flour was dull in that city, and the Judge shipped his cargo from that point to Boston, taking passage in the vessel which bore his produce. He sold his flour and purchased in Philadelphia for his son the goods which made up the assortment at the Middletown store. The Judge was six months in making the round trip from Dayton to New Orleans, Philadelphia, and return."

The son Pierson married, at Dayton, in 1812, Miss Mary Schooley, whose acquaintance he had probably made while a clerk in the store of H. G. Phillips. Miss Phebe Peirce, married the same year to James Steele, was Miss Schooley's bridesmaid. Mrs. Pierson Spining was born in 1790 in New Jersey, and brought, when an infant, to Columbia, near Cincinnati. Here the family lived in a log cabin, and when the children attended school they were often, as a protection against Indians, sent home with an escort of soldiers. As an indication of the fearless and adventurous spirit of the pioneer women, it is said of Mrs. Spining that she made "frequent trips from Springfield to Cincinnati on horseback, her mother's family living in Springdale, in Hamilton County. On one occasion she took her infant child as the companion of her journey. At another time she found Mill Creek booming. Getting the range of the ford, she boldly rode in, her horse swam across the turbulent stream, and she continued her excursion to Cincinnati, arriving there without further peril in flood or field." In 1863 she removed to Dayton, where she lived till she was over fourscore.

Judge Spining has several descendants living here. Among them may be mentioned Mrs. Louisa King, Mrs. Jennie S. Mulford, Mrs. Mary C. Wade, Miss Elizabeth G. Spining, Mrs. Sarah Stewart, and Mrs. Mary McG. Stewart.

William King, dissatisfied with Kentucky on account of slavery, emigrated from that State to this vicinity in 1801. He was a remarkable man, distinguished for his strong convictions and his conscientious determination to carry them out at whatever cost. He was for many years an elder in the First Presbyterian Church, and had something of the Puritan and the Covenanter in his composition. He lived to a great old age, lacking at his death but three months of being one hundred years old. His two elder sons, John and Victor, removed to Madison, Indiana. His son Samuel married Mary C., daughter of John H. Williams. His daughter Jane married David Osborn. The Osborn family are descendants of Cyrus Osborn, who was here as early as 1797. Numerous grandchildren of David Osborn are living here; for instance, David L. Osborn, Cyrus V. Osborn, James Steele Osborn, Miss Harriet E. Osborn, Miss Harriet McGuffy Osborn. The older grandchildren of William King are Miss Nancy King, William B. King, John King, Mrs. Harriet Scott, and Mrs. Eliza Brenneman.

John H. Williams was an honored and highly esteemed citizen. His descendants are numerous and prominent. We can only mention Mrs. Hiram Lewis, Mrs. David Rench, Miss Susan Williams, Miss Nannie B. Williams, Mrs. Lucinda H. Campbell, John W. and Henry Stoddard, and Mrs. General S. B. Smith.

In December, 1803, Benjamin Van Cleve was appointed first postmaster of Dayton, and served till his death, in 1821. He opened the postoffice in his cabin, on the southeast corner of First and St. Clair streets. Previous to Mr. Van Cleve's appointment the only postoffice in the Miami Valley, and as far north as Lake Erie, was at Cincinnati. From 1804 to 1806 the people north of Dayton as far as Fort Wayne were obliged to come here for their mail. In 1804 Dayton was on the mail-route from Cincinnati to Detroit, and the mail was carried by a post-rider, who arrived and left here once in two weeks. Soon after, a weekly mail, the only one, was established. A letter from Dayton to Franklin, or any other town on the route, was sent first to Cincinnati and then back again around the circuit to its destination. A second route was soon opened from Zanesville, Franklinton, and Urbana to Dayton. The next improvement was a mail from the East by way of Chillicothe, arriving and leaving Sunday evenings.

In 1808 a committee of citizens—Judge Joseph H. Crane, George Smith, William T. Tennery, William McClure, and Joseph Peirce—employed William George to superintend the carrying of the mail to Urbana. It was necessary at that date that those interested in a proposed new mail-route should raise a fund to defray the expense of it, but the Postmaster-General agreed to allow toward the expense all that was paid in for postage, etc., at the new offices. The following interesting agreement between the committee and the Urbana mail-carrier was found a few years ago among the papers of William McClure, editor of the *Repertory*, which his brother-in-law, Judge James Steele, had preserved:

"WITNESSETH, That the said George, on his part, binds himself, his heirs, etc., to carry the mail from Dayton to Urbana once a week and back to Dayton for the term that has been contracted for between Daniel C. Cooper and the Postmaster-General, to commence Friday, the 9th inst., to wit: Leave Dayton every Friday morning at six o'clock; leave Urbana Saturday morning, and arrive at Dayton Saturday evening, the undertakers reserving the right of altering the time of the starting and returning with the mail, allowing the said George two days to perform the trip, the post-rider to be employed by the said George to be approved by the undertakers. They also reserve to themselves the right of sending way letters and papers on said route, and the said George binds himself to pay for every failure in the requisitions of this agreement on his part the sum equal to that required by the Postmaster-General in like failures. The said committee, on their part, agree to furnish the said George with a suitable horse, furnish the person carrying the mail and the horse with sufficient victuals, lodging, and feed, and one dollar for each and every trip, to be paid every three months."

Previous to this arrangement a public meeting had been called, where the committee on the new mail-route had been appointed.

Postage, usually not prepaid, but collected on delivery, was high, and money scarce. Few ever had a dollar in their possession. The Government would not accept payment in corn or pelts. Stamps were not used, but the amount due—usually twenty-five cents—was written on the outside of the letter, which was not enclosed in an envelope. It was a trial, especially in years when people had little in their own town to interest or amuse them, and were separated by a journey of many weeks from friends in the old home from whence they had emigrated to Dayton, to return the letter handed them at the office, because they had no money to pay postage. Mr. Van Cleve was a man of the period, and had a fellow-feeling for his penniless, but not necessarily poverty-stricken neighbors, and for a time he allowed them to take their unpaid-for mail. Soon, however, such notices as the following were of frequent occurrence in the newspapers: "The postmaster, having been in the habit of giving unlimited credit heretofore, finds it his duty to adhere strictly to the instructions of the Postmaster-General. He hopes, therefore, that his friends will not take it amiss when he assures them that no distinction will be made. No letters delivered in the future without pay, nor papers without the postage being paid quarterly in advance."

Mr. Van Cleve's successor as postmaster was George S. Houston, who came here from New Jersey in 1810, and entered into partnership with his brother-in-law, H. G. Phillips. Like Mr. Van Cleve, he was an unusually public-spirited citizen, as reports of societies and meetings in the old newspapers show, and a man of many avocations. From 1821 till his death, in 1831, he was editor-in-chief of the *Watchman*, cashier of the Dayton Bank, and postmaster. The postoffice was at his residence, a brick dwelling, still standing on the north side of Second Street, near Ludlow.

Joseph Peirce and Judge Joseph H. Crane, who signed the agreement with the Urbana mail-carrier, were very prominent citizens. They married sisters—the daughters of Dr. John Elliott. Joseph Peirce was born in Rhode Island in 1786, and was brought to Marietta in 1788 by his father, who served in 1779 as an aid-de-camp on the staff of General Horatio Gates, was a shareholder in the Ohio Company, and in 1789 one of the founders of Belpre, Ohio. Joseph Peirce spent his childhood in the stockades, Farmers' Castle, and Goodale's Garrison, in which the people of Belpre took refuge during the Indian war. About 1805 he came to Dayton, and in 1807 entered into a partnership with James Steele, which continued all his life. They retailed, as the manuscript advertisement which they circulated states, "all sorts of goods, wares, and commodities belonging to the trade of merchandising." He was a member of the Legislature in 1812. A letter written by him to a friend at this time refers in an interesting manner to the war then in progress. "Great unanimity prevails among the members [of the Legislature] so far. You no doubt have seen Governor Meigs's message. You will, in a few days, see the patriotic resolutions, approbating the general Government, that have been passed. I doubt we have promised more than most of us would be willing to perform, should we be put to the test. To-day I think we shall pass a law furnishing our militia on duty with about $5,000 worth of blankets." Dayton was the rendezvous of the Western troops in this war, and our merchants sold largely to the army, waiting, however, many a long month before they received their pay from the Government. Mr. Peirce was president of the Dayton Bank from 1814 till his death in 1821 of the fever which swept away a number of valuable citizens. The obituary notice published in the *Watchman* says that he received from his fellow-citizens many and various marks of their respect and confidence, and faithfully discharged the duties of all the public positions to which he was called. Fully appreciating the importance of a canal from the Ohio to Lake Erie, he was endeavoring to secure its construction when he died. He was an ardent supporter of Mr. Cooper in the latter's plans for the benefit of the town, and was held in the highest regard by his fellow-citizens in all public, business, and social relations. He was the father of J. C. and the late J. H. Peirce, and the grandfather of J. Elliott, Sarah H., Elizabeth F., and Howard F. Peirce, Mrs. H. E. Parrott, S. W. and J. P. Davies, Mrs. R. C. Schenck, and Mrs. Joseph Dart.

Judge Joseph H. Crane, the grandfather of J. F. S. and J. H. Crane, was noted for profound learning in his profession. He was a man of "wide and varied reading, and prodigious memory, especially familiar with English history and the English classics and poets." He aided in selecting the first books bought for the Public Library, and would buy only works of the highest character. The Dayton library and schools and other institutions received an impetus in right directions from cultivated and far-sighted men who came here in the first ten or twelve years of the history of the town, which is felt at the present day, and will never cease. Judge Crane came to Dayton when twenty-one, at the invitation of Mr. Cooper, from New Jersey, where he had studied law in the office of Aaron Ogden, a noted lawyer and statesman. He became invaluable as attorney and counselor to Daniel C. Cooper and the early settlers. He was elected to the Legislature in 1809. His colleague, David Purviance, in a letter to William McClure, editor of the *Repertory*, in the possession of one of the authors, says under date of December 29, 1809: "Mr. Crane is the *only lawyer* who is a member of the House of Representatives. He conducts with prudence, and is in good repute as a member." Crane was a young man and had his reputation to win at this period. He served in the War of 1812, enlisting with the other gentlemen of the town as a private, but at St. Mary's was promoted to sergeant-major of the post. From 1813 to 1816 he was prosecuting attorney, and was made judge in 1817. In 1828 he was elected to Congress, and served eight years. From 1836 till his death, in 1851, he practiced law in Dayton, venerated by all for his high character and great ability.

In 1804 Colonel Robert Patterson, whose name often occurs in the history of Kentucky and Ohio during the last years of the eighteenth century, came here from Kentucky. He settled on the farm now the site of the Cash Register Works, which have given his grandsons an international reputation in the business world. Colonel Patterson's early life was full of adventure and hairbreadth escapes from Indians and other perils of the Western wilderness. He was born in 1753 in Bedford County, Pennsylvania, and began his military career as a member of a company of rangers raised to protect the frontier of his native State from Indians. When twenty-one, he and several other young men started in boats from Fort Pitt for Kentucky, with nine horses and fourteen head of cattle, and supplies, implements, and ammunition. At Limestone Creek, in Kentucky, they met, "guarding a little corn-patch with their tomahawks," Simon Kenton and Thomas Williams, the only white men in what is now that State. In 1777 Patterson and his party cleared land and planted corn near a big spring, naming their camp "Lexington," in honor of the Revolutionary battle. Later, he entered land and laid out the city at this point. In 1787 he was one of the founders of Cincinnati. He accompanied General George Rogers Clark in the Illinois campaign in 1778, and Colonel Bowman in the expedition against the Shawnee towns at old Chillicothe in 1779; served as captain in 1780 in General Clark's raid on old Chillicothe and old Miami; was in command of a company of Logan's regiment in Clark's campaign, in 1782, against Indians at Piqua, on the Miami, and at Laramie. Colonel Logan's command camped three days at the mouth of Mad River; that is to say, at Dayton. In 1786 Patrick Henry, Governor of Virginia, commissioned Robert Patterson a colonel in the "State Line." In 1786 his regiment of Colonel Logan's division marched to destroy the Macacheek towns on Mad River. But for these battles and victories over the Indians, in which Colonel Patterson was for many years engaged, the Dayton settlement would have been an impossibility. His part in the history of our city is of the greatest importance, for he helped win its site from the Indians, and secured a peaceful and prosperous home for the pioneers. He was present with his regiment at "St. Clair's defeat" in 1791. In the War of 1812 he had charge of transportation of supplies from Camp Meigs, near Dayton, north to the army. All his later years he was a sufferer from wounds received in his campaigns.

Colonel Patterson's wife died in 1833. They had nine children, all deceased. Their son Jefferson (like his father, always called Colonel) was born in Dayton May 27, 1801, and was a man of high character and an influential citizen. He was a member of the Legislature at the time of his sudden death in 1863. Colonel Jefferson Patterson married, in 1833, Julia, daughter of Colonel John Johnston, who survives him. Colonel Johnston was a very noted man in Indian affairs, being in the employ of the United States Government. He succeeded in both doing justice to the Indians and securing the safety of the white inhabitants even during the War of 1812. Colonel Jefferson Patterson's children, Robert, S. J., J. H., and F. J. Patterson, and Mrs. J. H. Crane, are well known. Colonel Robert Patterson's daughter Catharine married, first, Henry Brown; second, Andrew Irwin; third, H. G. Phillips. Her children, the late Judge R. P. and Henry L. Brown, Mrs. Charles Anderson, and A. Barr Irwin, were long prominent in Dayton. Mr. Irwin and Mrs. Anderson now live in Kentucky.

After Benjamin Van Cleve closed his blockhouse school, children were dependent upon their parents for instruction till 1804, when Cornelius Westfall opened a school, probably on Main Street, next the High School lot. He was a Kentuckian, and, after he ceased to teach, was for many years clerk of the Miami Court of Common Pleas. His successor as teacher, in 1805, was Swansey Whiting, an educated man from Pennsylvania, who became a physician.

The town of Dayton was incorporated by the Legislature February 12, 1805. The act of incorporation provided for the election, by freeholders who had lived in Dayton six months, of seven trustees, a collector, supervisor, and marshal. The trustees were empowered to elect a treasurer, who need not be a member of their board, and to choose a president (in effect, mayor) and a recorder from their own number. The board of trustees was known as "the Select Council of the city of Dayton." Till 1814 annual public meetings were held, where estimates and expenditures for town improvement and government purposes were discussed and authorized by popular vote. Meetings of the Select Council were, for ten years, held at residences of members. Councilmen were fined twenty-five cents if thirty minutes late. In 1805 Council proposed raising the expenses of the town, which were seventy-two dollars, by taxation. But the proposition was defeated at a meeting of voters called to discuss it. Seventeen voted against taxation, and thirteen for it.

The first brick house erected in Dayton was McCullum's Tavern, two stories high and built in 1805 on the southwest corner of Main and Second streets. It was used as a hotel till 1870, when it was converted into a business house. In 1880 it was torn down. A bell in a belfry on the Second Street side of the roof called guests to breakfast, always served before daylight, and to the other meals, also ready at early hours. In 1812 a picture of the capture of the British frigate *Guerrière* by the American frigate *Constitution*, was painted on McCullum's sign, a large one fastened to a tall post on the pavement in front of the house. A highly colored engraving of this naval battle was a favorite ornament of Dayton parlors at that period. From 1805 to 1807 the county court was held at McCullum's, the commissioners agreeing to pay him twenty-five dollars a year for the use of as much of his house as would be needed.

The Dayton Social Library Society was incorporated by the Legislature in 1805, Mr. Cooper, who was a member of the Legislature at that date, no doubt attending to the matter. This was the first library incorporated in Ohio. The incorporators were Rev. William Robertson, Dr. John Elliott, William Miller, Benjamin Van Cleve, and John Folkerth. John Folkerth was treasurer; Robertson, Miller, and Elliott, directors. It is creditable to our pioneers that a library and an academy were established as early as 1805 and 1807. Benjamin Van Cleve was appointed librarian, and the books were kept at the postoffice, at St. Clair and First streets. When he died, Squire Folkerth took charge of them at his office, in the one-story extension of the building on the northeast corner of First and Main streets. Borrowers were assessed three cents for a drop of tallow, or for folding down a leaf, and in proportion for any other damage, and were fined one quarter of the cost of a book lent to a person not

From a portrait in possession of J. H. Patterson.

COLONEL ROBERT PATTERSON.

belonging to the society or allowed to be taken into a school. It was determined by lottery who should have the first choice, and so on, for each proprietor. The constitution provided for a monthly business-meeting of proprietors in the log-cabin meeting-house. In 1822 the *Gridiron* advertises a farce to be given by the Thespian Society for the benefit of the library. John W. Van Cleve said of this library: "The number of books is small, but they are well selected, being principally useful standard books, which should be found in all institutions of the kind. Among them are the *North American* and *American Quarterly Reviews* for the last few years." September 8, 1835, Henry Stoddard, William Bomberger, and J. W. Van Cleve, committee, advertised the library for sale at auction at the clerk's office at 2 P. M., Saturday, the 12th inst.

CHAPTER V

1805–1809

FIRST Disastrous Flood—Emigrants from New Jersey—Charles Russell Greene—Ferries—First Court-House—First Newspaper—First Brick Stores—James Steele—Robert W. Steele—Dayton Academy—James Hanna—John Folkerth—First Teachers in the Academy—William M. Smith—James H. Mitchell—E. E. Barney—Trustees of Academy in 1833—Collins Wight—Milo G. Williams—Transfer of Academy to Board of Education—Henry Bacon—Luther Bruen—Antislavery Excitement—Arrest and Suicide of a Fugitive Slave—Colored People Leave Dayton for Hayti—A Colonization Society Formed—Antislavery Society—Union Meeting-House, Principally Built by Luther Bruen—Dr. Birney and Mr. Rankin Mobbed—Dr. H. Jewett—Dr. John Steele—Advertisement of a Runaway Slave—Jonathan Harshman—First Brick Residence—The Cannon "Mad Anthony"—Rev. James Welsh, M.D.—Dr. John Elliott—Town Prospering—No Care Taken of Streets or Walks—Grimes's Tavern—Alexander Grimes—Reid's Inn—Colonel Reid—Second Newspaper, the *Repertory*—Advertisements in the *Repertory*—Matthew Patton—Abram Darst—Pioneer Women.

IN March, 1805, a disastrous flood—the first of any importance that had occurred since the settlement of Dayton—swept over the town plat. No levees had been built at this date, and when the town began to raise them they were repeatedly washed away. It took long and painful experience to teach the lesson that levees must be high and strong. John W. Van Cleve describes this flood in an address on the "Settlement and Progress of Dayton," delivered in 1833 before the Dayton Lyceum, a literary society, having a public library connected with it. The address was printed in a morning paper.

"In the spring of 1805," Mr. Van Cleve says, "Dayton was inundated by an extraordinary rise of the river. In all ordinary freshets the water used to pass through the prairie at the east side of the town, where the basin now is; but the flood of 1805 covered a great portion of the town itself. There were only two spots of dry land within the whole place. The water came out of the river at the head of Jefferson Street, and ran down to the common at the east end of old Market Street, in a stream which a horse could not cross without swimming, leaving an island between it and the mill. A canoe could be floated at the intersection of First Street with St. Clair, and the first dry land was west of that point. The western extremity of that island was near the crossing of Main and First streets, from whence it bore down in a southern direction towards where the sawmill now stands, leaving a dry strip from a point on the south side of Main Cross Street [now Third], between Jefferson Street and the prairie, to the river bank at the head of Main Street. Almost the whole of the land was under water, with the exception of those two islands, from the river to the hill which circles round south and east of town from Mad River to the Miami. The water was probably eight feet deep in Main Street, at the Court-house, where the ground has since been raised several feet.

"In consequence of the flood, a considerable portion of the inhabitants became strongly disposed to abandon the present site of the town, and the proposition was made and urged very strenuously that lots should be laid off upon the plain upon the second rise on the southeast of the town, through which the Waynesville road passes; and that the inhabitants should take lots there in exchange for those which they owned upon the present plat, and thus remove the town to a higher and more secure situation. The project, however, was defeated by the unyielding opposition of some of the citizens, and it was no doubt for the advantage and prosperity of the place that it was."

Some of us can remember how certain aged pioneers used to upbraid the founders of the town for putting it down in a hollow, instead of on the hills to the southeast, and expatiate on the folly which the people were guilty of in voting against the removal, after the terrible freshet of 1805, to high ground. "Some day there will be a flood which will sweep Dayton out of existence," those ancient men and women used to prophesy to their grandchildren.

In no way did Daniel C. Cooper confer a greater benefit upon his town than by inducing a number of men of superior education, character, and business capacity to come here from his native New Jersey and other States, between 1804 and 1808. About 1804 or 1805 arrived Charles Russell Greene, whose sister Mr. Cooper married. He was born in Rhode Island, but as, like his cousin Joseph Peirce, he was the son of a shareholder in the Ohio Company, his youth was spent at Marietta. The boys who came to Ohio in 1788 received a good education, for the company employed excellent teachers; and if these had been wanting, men, of whom there were many, of the ability and knowledge of Isaac Peirce and Charles Greene, fathers of Joseph Peirce and Charles R. Greene, were capable of instructing their sons themselves. When Charles R. Greene first came to Dayton, he was in business with Mr. Cooper. Afterwards he had a store of his own. He succeeded Benjamin Van Cleve in 1821 as clerk of the court, a position for which he was eminently fitted. He was remarkably elegant and fine-looking. An old gentleman who was a child when Mr. Greene died was fond of relating how admiringly the boys used to watch this handsome, graceful man, mounted on a beautiful, spirited white horse, taking his daily ride down Main Street out into the country. Mr. Greene married a daughter of Henry Disbrow, a prominent Dayton business man. They had six children: Luciana Zeigler, married J. D. Phillips; Sophia, married E. T. Schenck; Eliza, married David Z. Peirce; Cooper, died unmarried; Harriet, married David Junkin; Charles H., married Adeline D. Piper. All are deceased except Mrs. Schenck. Mrs. C. R. Greene died November 3, 1873.

Mr. Greene was a highly esteemed citizen, and his death in 1831 threw a gloom over the whole community. Even the man who, while under the influence of liquor, caused his death admitted that he had killed his best friend. The indignation against the murderer was intense. At a fire, which occurred here on the night of September 10, 1833, Mr. Greene, one of the fire-wardens, ordered Matthew Thompson, who was looking idly on, to assist in passing water in the leather buckets to the little engine, which was now always used in addition to the buckets. Thompson refused, and offering some resistance when the order was repeated, Mr. Greene was obliged to use force to compel him to obey. The next day, on the complaint of Thompson, Mr. Greene was summoned to appear before the squire. While he was being questioned, Thompson struck him with a club, death resulting in a short time. Mr. Greene's sister, Mrs. Cooper, by her third marriage became the mother of Major Fielding Loury, the father of Charles G. and Sophie Loury, Mrs. Anna Dana, and Mrs. Elise L. Smith.

There were no bridges over the Miami or Mad River in 1805; but there were two ferries over the Miami—one at the foot of First Street, at the old ford on the road to Salem, and another at the foot of Fourth Street, on the road to Germantown. The First-Street ferry was used till a bridge was built in 1819. Ferry rates were fixed by the county commissioners, as follows: loaded wagon and team, seventy-five cents empty wagon and team, fifty cents; two-wheeled carriage, thirty-seven and one-half cents; man and horse, twelve and one-half cents; person on foot, six and one-quarter cents.

In 1806 the first Court-house, a brick structure, fifty-two by thirty-eight feet in size, two stories high, was built on the present Court-house lot. The court-room was on the first floor, and the jury-rooms in the second story. In 1815 a cupola was built, in which a bell was hung in 1816. The building was removed about 1847, and that perfect piece of architecture, the "old Court-house," built on its site.

In July of this year a Mr. Crane, from Lebanon, Ohio, endeavored to establish a newspaper here. After issuing a few numbers, he was attacked with fever and ague, and, in consequence of this illness, returned to Lebanon, and abandoned his project. No file of this paper has been preserved, and even its name has been forgotten.

In 1806 two brick stores, one story high, were erected on the northeast corner of First and Main by Mr. Cooper, and one, two stories high, on the northeast corner of Main and First by James Steele. The latter building stood till 1865; it gave place to Turner's Opera-house. Brown & Sutherland had a frame store on Main, near Monument Avenue, and H. G. Phillips a log store on the southwest corner of First and Jefferson streets. In 1812 he built a brick store, with a handsome residence adjoining, on the southeast corner of Main and Second streets. The brick business houses of 1806 were very small, plain, and insignificant affairs, as those who remember the Steele store are aware. But Cooper's and Steele's stores drew business toward the center of town.

James Steele was born in Rockbridge County, Virginia, in 1778, and brought to Kentucky by his father in 1788. He came to Dayton from Kentucky in 1805, and was in business till 1807 with his brother-in-law, William McClure. From December, 1807, till 1821 he was in partnership with his wife's brother, Joseph Peirce. Before he came to Dayton, his life was one of hardship and anxiety on a Kentucky farm, where he labored strenuously to support and educate his fatherless brothers and sisters. He earned the capital with which he began business here by making trips on a flatboat, laden with farm products, from Kentucky to New Orleans. Like his son, Robert W. Steele, he was interested in every effort to promote the prosperity of the town, and gave money, time, and labor to schools, libraries, churches, benevolent societies, and to all organizations formed to secure public improvements. He was for many years a trustee of the old Dayton Academy, and was instrumental in securing the employment of E. E. Barney as principal. He was deeply interested in the second building erected by the First Presbyterian Church in 1839 (considered a model church), and gave to it largely of his means and personal attention. He died in 1841, just as it was finished. A friend described him as noted for unyielding integrity, candor, moderation, kindness, and benignity.

For fourteen years Mr. Steele was associate judge of Montgomery County, elected by the Legislature, and for four years was a member of the Ohio Senate. "On the bench he was distinguished for good sense, integrity, and impartiality," wrote Judge Crane. "As a legislator, in a period of great public excitement, though firm and consistent in his political opinions, he won the esteem and respect of his opponents by his candor and moderation." In 1824 he was one of the electors for President and Vice-President of the United States for the State of Ohio. His old friend Henry Clay was his candidate. From 1815 to 1822 he was a director in the Dayton Bank, and from the latter date till his sudden death, in 1841, president. The stone bank built in 1815, converted into dwellings, still stands on Main Street, next to the High School. In June, 1837, the Muscatine *Gazette* said that the Dayton Bank was the only one in the United States that had refused to respect President Jackson's Treasury order, and it was one of the three banks that continued to pay specie during that time of financial panic. But people preferred to take, and even hoarded, the notes of the bank. Mr. Steele served in the War of 1812. After the disgraceful surrender of General Hull, information was sent to Dayton that the Indians assembled near Piqua in council, emboldened by the success of the British, were dangerous, and threatening to attack the inhabitants. The news came on Saturday, and on Sunday morning at seven o'clock a company of seventy men, commanded by Captain James Steele, were ready to march to the front. The alarm proved groundless, and after a few days the company returned home, but Captain

Steele was retained in the service for some time by order of General Harrison, to superintend the building of blockhouses at St. Mary's for the protection of the people of that region.

In November, 1812, James Steele married Phebe, daughter of Isaac Peirce, who served as an officer in the Revolutionary army, and was a member of the Ohio Company. Mr. Peirce came to Marietta, Ohio, from Rhode Island with his family in 1788, and was in 1789 one of the founders of Belpre. Mr. and Mrs. Steele had two sons—Robert Wilbur, born in 1819, died in 1891 and Joseph Peirce, born in 1821, who entered into rest several years before the death of his idolized brother.

Robert W. Steele married, first, Elizabeth Smith, and five children of this marriage survive—Mary D., Sarah S., and Agnes C. Steele, of Dayton; Egbert T., of Spokane, Washington, married Louise White; William C., of Rocky Ford, Colorado, married May Carter. R. W. Steele married, second, Clara P. Steele, who, with one daughter, Charlotte H. Steele, survives him, and lives in Dayton. He was for thirty-three years member of the Board of Education, and for twelve years president; was one of the founders of the Dayton Library Association, and served for many years as director and president. After it was united with the Public Library in 1860, he was, excepting one or two years, till his death in 1891 a member of the Library Board. In 1844 he was one of the incorporators of Cooper Seminary, and a trustee till the school passed into private hands. He was nine years a trustee of Miami University, appointed by the Governor of Ohio. From 1858 to 1891 he was president of Woodland Cemetery Association; was a member, appointed by the Governor, of the Ohio State Board of Charities for five years; was actively engaged all his life in promoting agricultural and horticultural societies; was trustee of the Montgomery County Children's Home for nine years; was an elder in the Third Street Presbyterian Church for thirty-seven years, and a member of that church for fifty years. In the early history of railroads he was much interested in promoting those improvements, and was a subscriber to the stock of all the railroads, excepting three, entering Dayton. During the Rebellion he was active in promoting enlistments, and in aiding in providing for the comfort of the soldiers and their families. He was appointed by the Governor of Ohio and served as a member of the Military Committee of Montgomery County; was a member of the Sanitary

Commission, and Chairman of the Citizens' Committee to assist in raising the Ninety-third Regiment of Ohio Volunteer Infantry. He loved his native town with a personal love almost as strong and warm as that which he felt for relatives and individual friends.

The Dayton Academy was incorporated in 1807 by James Welsh, Daniel C. Cooper, William McClure, David Reid, John Folkerth, George T. Tennery, Benjamin Van Cleve, and James Hanna. Mr. Hanna was an influential citizen in early days. The family left Dayton many years ago. John Folkerth, one of the incorporators of the academy, was also one of the incorporators, in 1805, of the Library Society. He was elected first Mayor of Dayton under the charter of 1829. He was a man of sterling integrity, and a great reader of good books. He served in the War of 1812 as first sergeant in Captain Steele's company. In the early history of the town the greater part of the deeds were drawn by him, and his legible but peculiar handwriting is familiar to many. His daughter, Mrs. William Atkin, and his granddaughter, Mrs. D. W. Iddings, are widely known in Dayton.

Besides donations in money, Mr. Cooper presented for the use of the academy two lots on St. Clair Street, opposite Cooper Park, just north of Park Presbyterian Church, on which, in 1808, a two-story brick building was erected by subscription. He also gave a bell. In 1807 and 1808 a debating-club met on winter evenings in the academy.

This was the only boys' school in Dayton for many years. The first teacher was William M. Smith. He and his sons were prominent citizens. In his contract with the trustees he agreed to teach reading, writing, arithmetic, the classics, and the sciences. Teaching in elocution was also given prominence. In 1815 Mr. Smith had for assistant Rev. James B. Findlay, who afterwards became a distinguished Methodist preacher. About 1820 Mr. Smith was succeeded by Gideon McMillan, a graduate of the University of Glasgow, who in his advertisements made claims to great scholarship. Succeeding teachers were Captain McMullin; James H. Mitchell, a graduate of Yale, who afterwards followed the profession of civil engineer, and was a leading citizen for many years; E. E. Barney, a graduate of Union College, New York, and a remarkable teacher and man. Mr. Barney, by the introduction of the analytical method, exercised an important influence on our public schools. Teachers educated by him

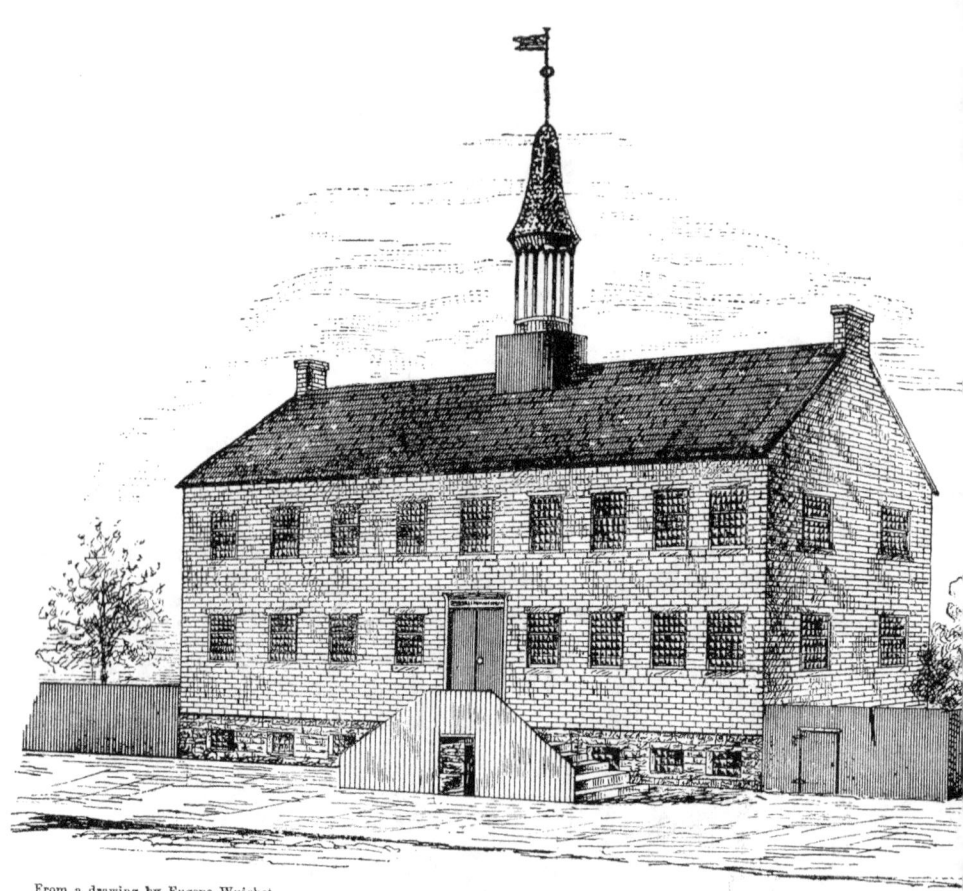

From a drawing by Eugene Wuichet.

THE OLD ACADEMY, 1833-1857.

carried these methods into the schools in advance of most places in the West, and gave them in their early history a high reputation. The year before Mr. Barney came, 1833, the old academy had been sold and a new one erected on the southwest corner of Fourth and Wilkinson streets. The trustees this year were Aaron Baker, Job Haines, Obadiah B. Conover, James Steele, and John W. Van Cleve. In 1840 Collins Wight, long known as a dealer in lumber, taught in the academy. He was succeeded in 1844 by Milo G. Williams, a teacher of large experience and reputation, who remained till 1850, when the academy was deeded to the Board of Education.

Among the early settlers of Dayton were Henry Bacon, Luther Bruen, and Jonathan Harshman—very unlike, but, nevertheless, all typical men. Mr. Bacon was a successful lawyer, and a man of unusual legal as well as literary acquirements. He served as prosecuting attorney, and ably discharged the duties of the office. He was endowed with much force and keenness of intellect, and "waked up sometimes, in addressing a jury, especially as a prosecutor of criminal cases, to flashes of eloquence." Two grandsons of Henry Bacon are prominent in Dayton—General Samuel B. and J. McLain Smith.

Luther Bruen was born in New Jersey in 1783, and came to Dayton in 1804. He was an influential and useful citizen, and noted for benevolence as well as for business talent. He has a number of descendants—Frank, Robert, and Mary Bruen, Mrs. Sella Wright, David B., Quincy, and Thomas Corwin, Mrs. Susie Zeller, Mrs. Dr. Pauley, Mrs. Charles D. Mead, Miss Mary and Miss Martha and William Brady.

Mr. Bruen was a practical abolitionist in times when to advocate antislavery principles required both moral and physical courage and enlightened views. A number of the founders of our city came to Ohio before 1808 because they did not want to bring up their children in a slave State. But there was little active opposition to what the father of one of them called "that great oppression" till 1832, when a respectable, industrious colored man, much liked by every one, a refugee from Kentucky who had lived here three years, was, in spite of protests and every effort for his legal protection on the part of the people, arrested by a party of slave catchers. The law delivered the negro over to his master. A great deal of sympathy and indignation were excited by this iniquitous proceeding, and citizens offered to buy his freedom and prevent his separation from his freeborn wife. The master declined to sell, when his agents wrote to him, so valuable a servant, and came himself to take "Black Ben" to Kentucky. Arrived at Cincinnati, the captive was confined for the night in a fourth-story room of a hotel. "All being safe, as they thought, about one o'clock, when they were in a sound sleep, poor Ben threw himself from the window, which is upwards of forty feet from the pavement." He was dreadfully injured, but lived two days. "A poor and humble being of an unfortunate and degraded race, the same feeling which animated the signers of the Declaration of Independence to pledge life, fortune, and honor for liberty determined him to be free or die. Mr. D. left this morning with the dead body of his slave, to which he told me he would give decent burial in his own churchyard. Please tell Ben's wife of these circumstances." Strange to say, the words first quoted are from a letter which Ben's master requested a friend to write to the Dayton *Journal*. Poor Ben's capture and suicide were not forgotten in Dayton.

Twenty-four people of color left Dayton on October 21, 1824, for Hayti. Their expenses were paid by the Haytian government, which was inviting negro emigrants from the United States, and sent an agent to New York to take charge of the large numbers who were willing to go; but citizens afforded aid, and felt much sympathy for those who went from Dayton. The departure was a scene of the greatest excitement—wild weeping, wailing, and shouting, and lamentations over the separation for life from friends and home; but nearly all who went from here soon found their way back again to Dayton. A colonization society was formed November 24, 1826, and the following gentlemen were appointed a committee to solicit subscriptions to the constitution: Aaron Baker, Henry Stoddard, Luther Bruen, O. B. Conover, and S. S. Cleveland.

In 1839 Luther Bruen was able to form an antislavery society, of which he was elected president. On South Main Street, west side, between Fourth and Fifth streets, a church known as the Union or Newlight Church, which was largely built with money subscribed by Mr. Bruen, was erected. Here lectures by famous antislavery leaders were frequently delivered. The meetings were frequently interrupted and the speakers treated with violence and indignity by angry proslavery crowds. In 1836 Dr. Birney and Rev. Mr. Rankin, who were invited to address an audience at the Union Church, barely escaped with their lives, and were hidden away for some hours, one at the residence of Dr. H. Jewett, a leading physician and active Abolitionist, and the other at the home of his relative, Dr. John Steele, who, though not an Abolitionist, believed in justice and free speech. The mob destroyed or injured the houses of Abolitionists and negroes, and tore to pieces the Bible, and broke the windows and stove at the church. Side by side in the *Journal* with the account of the organization of the antislavery society may be seen one of those coal-black little pictures representing a bareheaded colored man, carrying a bundle hung on a stick, and with negro quarters in the background, making all speed for the free States, which so often at this date appeared in the Dayton newspapers. The poor fellow is described as "likely and pleasant when spoken to, easily alarmed, and calling himself Washington, though that was not his name."

Jonathan Harshman came to Montgomery County from Maryland, at the age of twenty-four, in 1805, and purchased forty acres of land in what is now Madriver Township; but he and his family are so identified with Dayton that his life is part of the history of the town. The first three years after his arrival he spent in clearing his land, with the assistance of his neighbors, helping them in turn. In 1808 he married Susannah Rench, daughter of John Rench, an active and enterprising business man, who did much to promote the prosperity of the town. Among the latter's descendants are William H., Johanna, David C., and Charles Rench.

Mrs. Jonathan Harshman was, like many of the pioneer women, of whom their grandchildren are so proud, a strong character, energetic, industrious, and capable in many directions. In the period now reached there were not only housekeeping, cooking, and sewing to attend to, but cows to milk, butter to churn, poultry to care for, the smokehouse to fill with hams, sausage, and pickled pork; the vegetable garden to cultivate—in town as well as in the country. All these things were the duties of a housekeeper, and to these multifarious labors spinning and weaving were added. The spinning-wheel and loom were found in most houses. Many yards of linsey-woolsey were woven and made into summer clothes for children and grown people; while wool was woven into blankets, dress goods, cloth, and flannels for winter wear by the mistress of a family and her daughters. The "help," if any was employed, was some farmer's daughter, a friend or acquaintance, who was literally one of the family, though she received wages. Frequently the help was a bound girl, an orphan, whom the county was obliged to support, and whom the commissioners placed in a private family on condition that she should be free at eighteen and receive from her employers, on leaving them, a certain sum of money, clothes, and specified articles of furniture. No wages were paid her, but she received for her work food, clothing, and lodging.

In addition to his farming, Mr. Harshman engaged in milling and distilling, and opened with John Rench a store, trading for country produce, which they sent in flatboats for sale to Cincinnati or New Orleans. He accumulated a large fortune. In 1845 he was elected president of the Dayton Bank, and served until 1850. He was a member of the Twenty-fourth General Assembly of Ohio. In earlier years he was a stanch Federalist, and later an ardent Whig. In 1840 the famous Harrison convention was held in Dayton on the 10th of September. General Harrison, on his journey to Dayton, reached Jonathan Harshman's, five miles from town, on the evening of the 9th, and spent the night there. Early in the morning, his escort, which had been encamped at Fairview, marched to Mr. Harshman's residence, and halted till seven o'clock for breakfast, when it got in motion under command of Joseph Barnett, of Dayton, and other marshals from Clark County. Mr. Harshman died in 1850, and his wife in 1839. They had eight children. Elizabeth married Israel Huston, Catherine married Valentine Winters, Jonathan married Abigail Hiveling. These are all deceased, as are Mary, who became the wife of George Gorman, and Susannah, who married Daniel Beckel. Three sons—Joseph, George W., and Reuben—survive.

In the fall election of 1808 one hundred and ninety-six votes were cast at the Dayton Court-house. This year the first brick residence erected in town, a substantial, comfortable, two-story dwelling, was built by Henry Brown on the west side of Main Street on the alley between Second and Third streets. It was occupied till 1863 as a dwelling, and from then till it was torn down as a newspaper office. Mr. Brown kept in his stable a cannon, which, not so much because it was taken down to the river bank by an excited crowd and fired on the very rare occasions when there was anything to celebrate in Dayton, as on account of its imposing name, "Mad Anthony," was an object of awe and curiosity to all the boys and girls in town. Mr. Brown was engaged in trade with the Indians, and had obtained this cannon from them in exchange for his merchandise. It had been abandoned in the woods by one of the regiments of the Western army. As it was the only cannon in town for many years, it was quite an important possession. Finally it burst, killing the patriotic gunner who was firing it. At one time a company of mounted rangers was formed in Dayton, and called for the cannon the Mad Anthony Troop. When Mr. Brown first brought it here, it used to be fired on the vacant lots on Main Street, opposite his house.

Rev. James Welsh, M.D., and Dr. John Elliott, a retired army surgeon, both already mentioned, were interesting characters of this period. Dr. Welsh was pastor of the First Presbyterian Church from 1804 to 1817, and also practiced medicine and kept a drug-store. Notices to delinquent patients over his signature, like the following, frequently appeared in the newspapers: "I must pay my debts. To do this is impracticable unless those who are indebted to me pay me what they owe. All such are once more, for the last time, called on to come forward and make payment before the 25th of March next, or, disagreeable as it is, compulsory measures may be certainly expected." The death of Dr. Elliott, who died in 1809, was considered a great loss to the community, as he was socially and professionally popular. The *Repertory* contained a eulogistic obituary, and not only citizens, but large numbers from the country, attended his funeral. He was buried with martial honors, and Captain James Steele's troop of horse and Captain Paul Butler's company of infantry headed the procession to the Sixth-Street cemetery. These two military organizations were probably formed for defense against the Indians, at this date restive and threatening.

Between 1808 and 1810 Dayton began to grow and prosper. Two editors, a minister, a lawyer, a school-teacher, and three physicians were numbered among the inhabitants, and there were five stores and three taverns, all doing well. A square or two on First Street, and the west side of Main Street from Newcom's Tavern to the Court-house alley, except the corner on which stood McCullum's Tavern, and the site of Reid's Inn, were occupied by residences, separated from each other by several vacant lots. The east side of Main Street was not built up, and was covered with hazel bushes and wild fruit-trees, except the lots from the High School alley to the southeast corner of Main and First streets, which were occupied by Grimes's Tavern and Cooper & Compton's and Steele & Peirce's stores. The first-named store fronted on First Street. Dwellings were built close to the pavement, with no ground between, but there were large yards at the side and back of the houses. Streets were not graveled, no care was taken of walks, and fences were of the stake-and-rider or post-and-rail order.

Grimes's Tavern stood on the south corner of the first alley south of Monument Avenue. It was a one-story-and-a-half log house, and in the alley back of it were a log barn and feed-yard. A few years later, when it had ceased to be kept by its original owner, several frame additions and a large dining-room having been added, it became a popular place for parties and balls. Colonel John Grimes, the proprietor, was the father of Alexander Grimes, and the grandfather of Charles G. Grimes. Alexander Grimes was for many years (1831-1843) cashier of the Dayton Bank, and also in 1819 a director. No one was more thoroughly identified with this bank than he. On the 1st of January, 1843, he, as agent, closed up the affairs of the bank. At an early day he was in partnership with Steele and Peirce, under the name of Grimes & Company. In 1817 the firm was dissolved. Mr. Grimes married, first, Miss Gordon, and, second, Miss Maria Greene, a member of a leading Dayton family. In connection with Edward Davies, he was trustee of the estate of David Zeigler Cooper, heir of D. C. Cooper. The property rapidly increased in value, and was also a great benefit to Dayton as a result of their prudent and liberal management. Mr. Grimes served in the War of 1812.

Reid's Inn stood on the west side of Main Street, between First and Second streets, the present site of the First Baptist Church. The proprietor earned his title by service in the War of 1812. He was in command of the First Battalion of the First Regiment of Ohio Militia. The inn parlor was a favorite place for public meetings, in which Colonel Reid was a leading spirit, and in the large barnyard for years the menageries and museums which visited the town annually always gave their exhibitions. The "Inn or House of Entertainment"—as, to escape the tavern license of ten dollars, it was called in the advertisement inserted in the newspaper—kept by Colonel Reid was a frame building two stories high, with a belfry for the dinner-bell. On the large sign which, after the War of 1812, hung in a square frame from a tall post on the edge of the sidewalk, was painted a portrait of Commodore Lawrence, and a scroll bearing the words, "Don't give up the ship." The original small sign of the tavern, "Reid's Inn," hung below the larger one. Mr. Samuel Forrer, who staid at the inn in 1818, when he spent some time here, not then having become a permanent resident, "enjoying the hospitalities of the place, and the pleasures derived from the manly sports of those times," describes Colonel Reid as "a good man and excellent landlord." To Colonel Reid's very competent and energetic wife was, of course, due the bountiful, well-cooked meals and comfortable beds of Reid's Inn.

On the 18th of September, 1808, William McClure and George Smith began to edit and publish the second Dayton newspaper, the *Repertory*. It contained four pages of two columns each, was eight by twelve and one-half inches in size, and printed with old-fashioned type on a second-hand press. When five numbers had appeared, it was suspended till 1809, when Henry Disbrow and William McClure revived it as a twelve-by-twenty-inch sheet. It was published on Second Street, between Main and Jefferson streets, till 1810, when it ceased to exist. It was principally filled with foreign news several months old, but some local items can be gleaned from the file in the Public Library. Paul D. Butler advertises his "large and commodious house for sale; will answer for almost any business; good well and pump at the door, frame stable." Henry Disbrow offers a house and two lots, agreeing to take in payment "such produce as will suit the Orleans market," instead of cash, describing the property as "an elegant two-story frame house [not all the houses were log at this date], forty-five feet front and twenty-four feet back; a good kitchen adjoining; good well of water at the door; good nail factory and stable; situation good for either tavern or store; post-and-rail fence." Advertisements are inserted by John Compton, H. G. Phillips, and Steele & Peirce, merchants; John Dodson, carpenter; John Hanna, weaving establishment, south end of Main Street; John Strain & Co., nail factory; James Beck, blue-dying establishment; David Steele, cooper-shop, First Street, near St. Clair; Thomas Nutt, tailor; Matthew Patton, cabinet-maker. The advertisement of Mr. Patton is found in every number of the paper, showing that he had something of the modern enterprise in this respect. He served as first corporal in Captain Steele's company in 1812. He lived to an old age in Dayton and was highly respected and esteemed. He was the father of Captain William Patton, and has several grandchildren.

One of the earliest settlers and business men was Abram Darst, who came here from Virginia in 1805. "He was a man of sterling integrity, highly esteemed by the community, and occupied many positions of trust and usefulness. Mr. Darst died in 1865, aged eighty-three. His wife lived to be ninety-five, dying in 1882. She was a remarkable character, a typical pioneer woman, full of energy, and gifted with the faculty of taking excellent care of a large household, and at the same time assisting her husband in his business, as was the almost universal custom in that day." Life here was very much what it is at the present day among educated people in many a far Western settlement, who have gone west to make their fortunes. American women, when there is need of special effort, always prove that their sex in America has not degenerated during the past one hundred years. Many a lesson of cheerfulness, patience, industry, and thrift might be learned from the laborious, but contented, and, in the end, prosperous lives of the wives of the founders of Dayton. One of our wealthiest old merchants attributed his success largely to the assistance of his wife, brought up in a fashionable circle in an Eastern city. What was true of her was true of many others. When Robert Edgar was absent in the army during the War of 1812, his wife remained alone with her family in her lonely cabin, on the site of the Water Works, not only doing all the work of her household herself, but taking charge of the farm, so that when her husband returned things were not much less prosperous with them than when he left. But think of the burden of responsibility, labor, and anxiety that Mrs. Edgar and other wives of soldiers of 1812 bore in that dark era. Mr. and Mrs. Darst had ten children, of whom Miss Phebe and Mr. John W. Darst alone survive. Julia married James Perrine; Christina, W. B. Dix; Mary, Jacob Wilt; Sarah, W. C. Davis; Martha, George M. Dixon; and Napoleon B., Susannah, daughter of Valentine Winters, so that Abram Darst has many descendants in Dayton. We can only mention A. D. Wilt, Charles W., Fred T., Johnson P., Samuel B., and Rolla Darst, Mrs. Edward Fuller, Mrs. Joseph E. Bimm, Miss Fanny and Miss Mary Dixon, Mrs. George W. Shaw, Mrs. E. E. Barney, Miss Martha Perrine, who are grandchildren.

FIRST PRESBYTERIAN CHURCH, 1839–1867.

MAIN STREET IN 1846, LOOKING NORTH FROM BELOW THIRD.

Drawn by Henry Howe in 1846.

CHAPTER VI

1809-1812

WILLIAM EAKER—George W. Smith—Roads—Journeys to the East—Goods Brought by Conestoga Wagons and Broadhorns to Ohio—Packhorses Moving Up Main Street—Groceries from New Orleans by Keel-Boats—A Voyage from New Orleans Described—Country Stores—Drinking Customs—Flatboating South—Excitement When the Fleets of Boats Left Dayton—Arrival of a Large Keel-Boat—Fourth of July from 1809 to 1840—The First Drug-Store—Indians and Wild Animals Both Troublesome—Rewards for Wolf-Scalps—New Sidewalks and Ditches or Gutters—*Ohio Centinel*—Earthquakes—William Huffman—Ohio Militia Encamped at Dayton—Business Beginning of 1812—Horatio G. Phillips—J. D. Phillips—Obadiah B. Conover.

NO TWO Daytonians were ever more useful and prominent than William Eaker and George W. Smith. For a time they were in partnership. Mr. Eaker came here from Carlisle, Pennsylvania, at a very early day. He opened a store on Main Street in 1811, removing later to old Market or Second Street, where he continued in business till his death in 1848, making a large fortune. He was a stockholder and director in the first Dayton bank, founded in 1813, and remained a director till the bank ceased business in 1843. His store was very popular with customers, and he was indeed a general favorite in business and social circles, and noted for kind deeds. Probity, integrity, and goodness of heart were traits of character continually manifested by him during the course of his long residence here, and gained him the esteem and confidence of all. He was a stanch friend to all young men just entering business, as at the time of his death many prominent merchants and manufacturers were ready to testify. He was always a generous supporter of efforts to improve the town. He gave liberally to churches and charitable institutions. "At the outbreak of the Mexican War, he was one of the committee of citizens who pledged themselves to look after the families of volunteers, and to care for them in case the soldiers did not return. In every case these pledges were sacredly kept." In 1817 he married Letitia Lowry, who survived him thirty-four years. She was born in what is now a part of Springfield, Ohio, in 1799. Her father, Archibald Lowry, was the son of David Lowry, of Donnel's Creek, who came to the site of Dayton with the surveying party in 1795. He is mentioned in an earlier chapter as the first to send a flatboat south from Dayton, in 1799. Mr. and Mrs. Eaker are represented in Dayton by their only daughter, Miss Belle Eaker. The three sons—Frank, Charles, and William Eaker—are deceased.

George W. Smith, a native of England, came to Dayton from Virginia in 1804, and lived here till his death in 1841, at the age of fifty-seven. After dissolving partnership with Mr. Eaker, he was in business with Robert A. Edgar, and later with his son George. As he was a merchant, he was of course engaged in flatboating to the south. He built, near what is now known as Harries Station, extensive flouring-mills, a distillery, and houses for his workmen, calling the place Smithville. He was a man of wealth, and left a large estate. His first wife was a Miss Todd. Their two children died young. He married, second, Eliza Manning, and they had five children: James Manning,—lately deceased, leaving one daughter, Miss Lida Smith,—married Miss Caroline Shoup; George W.; Sophia, married Isaac H. Kiersteid; Louisa, married Captain Fletcher, U. S. A.; Ann, deceased, married W. G. Sheeley.

Roads, narrow, muddy, or cut up into deep ruts, were now opened to Piqua, New Lexington, Salem, Greenville, Xenia, Germantown, Lebanon, Franklin, and Miamisburg. Two years later a bridle-path was cut to Vincennes, two hundred miles distant. The State Road, known as the "Old Corduroy Road," which ran east and west through town, was built the same year. This was a road only in name, being almost impassable in wet weather. Mud-holes and low places were filled with poles, which floated, and through which the horses' feet would sink. Travelers were delayed for hours by such mishaps. In 1812 three roads used by the army were kept in tolerable condition. With this exception, till 1839 roads were either so muddy or so rough that it was difficult to drive or ride over them. Roads were poor even in more thickly settled regions. The journeys of our Dayton merchants to Philadelphia to buy goods, and of their wives to the old homes in the East, were made on horseback, with clothes packed in saddlebags, and babies carried in a net swung around the father's neck, and resting on the pommel of his saddle. The bridgeless streams had to be forded. "Is he a good swimmer?" was a common question, when a man was trying to sell a horse to a customer. It was necessary to carry arms, as the road for miles passed through unsettled forests, along an unbroken track, marked only by blazed trees and where Indians and wild beasts lurked. Travelers usually camped for the night, and ate and slept on the ground. The journey east could be made from Cincinnati to Pittsburg in a flatboat, but public conveyances of any kind were unknown.

Goods for Dayton merchants were brought as far as Pittsburg from Philadelphia, then the center of trade, in Conestoga wagons, and from Pittsburg to Cincinnati by river in "broadhorns"; thence they were either poled up the Miami, or brought here on packhorses. It was a common sight to see long line-teams, —often a dozen horses tied together,—in single file, the leader wearing a bell, and each horse carrying two hundred pounds, moving up Main Street. A train of this length was accompanied by three or four men, equipped with rifle, ammunition, ax, and blankets. Game in the woods supplied them with food. Men were stationed at each end, to take care of the leader and hind horse, keep the train in motion, and watch over the goods. Sometimes the train was composed of loose horses, taught to follow each other without being fastened together. Bells were attached at night to all the horses, and then they were turned out to graze.

Occasionally Dayton merchants purchased groceries brought up from New Orleans to Cincinnati in keel-boats or barges, and hauled here, about 1812,—when the army kept the road in tolerable condition,—in wagons.

The difficulties of an up-stream voyage are described in the following letter, written from Cincinnati, December 29, 1812, by Baum & Perry to Steele & Peirce, and found among the papers of the latter firm nearly eighty years after they received it: "We have just had the arrival of our barge from New Orleans. She was delayed at the falls for nearly two weeks before she could get over, detained five or six days waiting for the loading to be hauled from the lower landing to the upper, and finally had to come away with part of her cargo only, there being no wagons to be had, and ever since she left that place has been obliged to force her way for two weeks past through the ice. These are the circumstances which prevented her coming sooner. Knowing that sugar is much wanting at your place, have thought it advisable to load Mr. Enoch's wagon, and let it proceed to your town with that article, to wit, with six boxes, weighing as follows: 438 pounds for Mr. Henry Brown; 448 pounds, Cooper & Burnet; 432 pounds, Isaac Spining; 480 pounds, Robert Wilson; 510 pounds, Steele & Peirce; 430 pounds, Major Churchill." Freightage by wagon was one dollar per hundredweight. If a single box of sugar were taken, the price was twenty cents a pound, and eighteen and three-quarter cents per pound was charged if three boxes were bought.

Dayton merchants kept genuine country stores, and sold a very miscellaneous variety of articles. In front, close to the street, hitching-posts and feed-boxes were provided. Bottles of various kinds of liquor, principally whisky,—regarded in those days, according to Curwen, as "the elixir and solace of life," even by ministers and their most conscientious parishioners,—were displayed, flanked by glasses, on the counter, customers being expected to help themselves. Purchases were usually paid for in wheat, rye, corn, beeswax, tallow, corn-fed pork, and similar products that would sell at New Orleans; but cash was demanded if the grain, pork, etc., could not be delivered in time for the annual spring trip south by flatboat.

Flatboating south was a necessity, for there was no sale in Ohio for the articles received in exchange for goods by our merchants. The Great Miami was down on the map as a navigable stream, and towards the close of the flatboating era, and later, there were many attempts to introduce steamboats. Until 1828 our merchants depended principally upon keel-boats, built somewhat like canal-boats, and on flatboats for their connection with New Orleans, the only market for Western produce. Flatboatmen sold their boats—only used in descending streams, and kept in the channel by long, sweeping oars, fastened at both ends of the boat—when they arrived at New Orleans, purchased a horse, and rode home. The boats were inclosed and roofed with boards. On account of changes or obstructions in the channel or low water, it sometimes took a Dayton boat three weeks to reach Cincinnati.

May 24, 1809, the *Repertory* contains the first notice of a Dayton flatboat published here. It says: "A flat-bottomed boat, owned by Mr. Compton, of this place, descended the Great Miami yesterday. She was loaded with pork, flour, bacon, and whisky, and destined for Fort Adams." Later it is stated that "Mr. Compton's boat got safely through to the Ohio. Notwithstanding the representations made of the dangers of navigating the Great Miami, we are well convinced that nothing is wanting but care and attention to take our boats with safety from this place." Among the dangers encountered were dams and fish-baskets, or traps, which often wrecked the boats. Sometimes boatmen destroyed, or tried to destroy, these obstructions, the owners defending their property, and serious or fatal injuries resulting on both sides.

Between 1809 and 1810 Paul Butler and Henry Disbrow established a freight line of keel-boats between Dayton, Laramie, and St. Mary's, connecting our town with Lake Erie by way of the Miami, Auglaize, and Maumee rivers. They built the two keel-boats used for this line in the middle of Main Street, in front of the Court-house. When finished, they were moved on rollers up Main Street to the river and launched. Nine flatboats left on the 13th or 14th of May, 1811, for New Orleans. A private letter dated Dayton, March 28, 1812, says: "We had a snowstorm on Sunday last, eight inches deep, but, as it went off immediately, it did not swell the river sufficiently to let Phillips and Smith's boat out." It was customary for boats to wait for a freshet before starting. At the head of Wilkinson Street stood for many years Broadwell's old red warehouse, where shipments were made, and which was the scene in the spring of much hurry, bustle, and business. It was swept down stream itself in the flood of 1828. Boats built up the river used to come here, tie up, and wait for a freshet, when all the boats bound for New Orleans would set off together in a fleet. The departure of the fleet was an exciting event to farmers, distillers, millers, merchants, teamsters, boatmen, and the people generally, as the following description from the Dayton *Watchman* of May 26, 1825, indicates: "Rain had fallen on Wednesday, and continued till Friday, when the river rose. The people flocked to the banks, returning with cheerful countenances, saying, 'The boats will get off.' On Saturday all was the busy hum of a seaport; wagons were conveying flour, pork, whisky, etc., to the different boats strung along the river. Several arrived during the day from the north. On Sunday morning others came down, the water began to fall, and the boats, carrying about forty thousand dollars' worth of the produce of the country, got under way." In May, 1819, the *Watchman* announces, as a matter of public rejoicing, the arrival of a keel-boat from Cincinnati belonging to H. G. Phillips and Messrs. Smith & Eaker.

It was the first keel-boat that had for a number of years, on account of obstructions, ascended the Miami. The boat was over seventy feet long, and carried twelve tons of merchandise.

The Fourth of July was a grand occasion in Dayton in the first quarter of the nineteenth century. A public meeting was held beforehand, at which a committee of arrangements was appointed. Benjamin Van Cleve, Owen Davis, and William M. Smith served in 1809. The militia and the people from town and country, forming on the river bank at the head of Main Street, marched in procession to the Court-house. Here they heard an oration and patriotic songs; after which, reforming, they marched to the house of Henry Disbrow, where an elegant dinner was served, tickets costing fifty cents. Toasts were drunk and salutes were fired by the military companies, commanded by Captain Butler and Captain Steele. The afternoon was spent in sports and games, and there was a dance in the evening. In 1810 there was also a procession from the river to the Court-house, where the following exercises were listened to: Singing of an ode, prayer by Dr. Welsh, reading of the Declaration of Independence by Benjamin Van Cleve, and an oration by Joseph H. Crane. "The oration was eloquent and well adapted to the occasion." At noon there was a public dinner served under a bower, where seventeen toasts were drunk, a salute being fired as each toast was given.

In 1811 Dr. N. Edwards, Joseph H. Crane, and Joseph Peirce were the committee of arrangements. The procession was preceded by a sermon from Dr. Welsh, and followed at the Court-house by the usual exercises, Joseph H. Crane reading the Declaration, and Benjamin Van Cleve delivering the oration. This year political animosity, hitherto unknown in Dayton, had become so bitter that members of the two parties declined to dine together, as had been the custom on the Fourth of July, and unite in drinking toasts prepared by the committee of arrangements. There were two dinners, each under a bower prepared for the occasion; one at Mr. Strain's and the other at Mr. Graham's, formerly Newcom's. Each company drank seventeen patriotic toasts, and then an eighteenth toast, expressing their political opinions. Mr. Graham's guests drank to the accompaniment of a discharge of small arms the "Health of Thomas Jefferson, Late President of the United States." At Mr. Strain's the final toast was, "May our young Americans have firmness enough to defend their rights without joining any Tammany club or society." And it was drunk "under a discharge of cannon and loud and repeated cheerings." There was the usual military parade in the afternoon and a dance in the evening. Military companies were popular and militia trainings gala occasions. Business was suspended and crowds flocked into town to witness the drill and parade, when, as on September 17, 1810, Colonel Jerome Holt assembled the Fifth Regiment for training purposes.

In 1815 the young ladies of Dayton were invited to join the Fourth-of-July procession, assembling at Colonel Grimes's tavern. After the speeches, etc., at the Court-house, the procession marched to Republican Spring, where ladies and gentlemen dined together, as had not been the custom before on the national holiday. In 1816 the public meeting to make preparations for the Fourth of July was held at Reid's Inn. Dr. John Steele acted as chairman, and Benjamin Van Cleve as secretary, and Captain James Steele, Dr. Charles Este, George W. Smith, Fielding Gosney, James Lodge, Colonel John Anderson, and David Griffin were appointed a committee of arrangements. After the procession on the Fourth, Dr. Charles Este read the Declaration of Independence, and Benjamin Van Cleve Washington's farewell address. One hundred persons dined together at the house of Captain J. Rhea. Isaac Spining presided, and William George and Dr. Este were chosen vice-presidents of the occasion. Nineteen patriotic toasts were drunk with great hilarity. At four o'clock in the afternoon the ladies and gentlemen of the town and country "partook of a magnificent repast, furnished by the ladies, in the shade of the adjacent woods." In the evening there was a concert of vocal music at Mr. Bomberger's residence and a ball at Colonel Reid's inn.

In 1822 new features were introduced. Church bells were rung and cannons fired at daybreak and a flag run up on the town flagstaff. The exercises were held at the First Presbyterian Church. The procession was headed by the newly raised light infantry companies and riflemen. Captain Grimes's company wore a yellow roundabout coat, green collar and cuffs, white pantaloons, and red leggings. Captain Dodds's company were dressed in white roundabout, trimmed with black cord, pantaloons the same, and a citizen's hat with red feather. Captain Dixon's riflemen wore blue cloth roundabouts, trimmed with white cord, and white pantaloons. Captain Windbrenner's men were dressed in gray cloth coatees, trimmed with black cord, and pantaloons to correspond. After the militia came four Revolutionary veterans — Colonel Robert Patterson, Simeon Broadwell, Richard Bacon, and Isaac Spining, guarding the American flag and liberty cap. Judge Crane read the Declaration, and Stephen Fales "delivered a highly interesting and animating oration." The music "would have done honor to any place, and reflected great credit on the singers." The gentlemen dined at Mr. Squier's tavern, Judge Crane being elected president of the day, and Judge Steele and H. G. Phillips vice-presidents. After the regular toasts, the following volunteer toasts were given: By Judge Crane, "De Witt Clinton, the Able and Persevering Supporter of Internal Improvements"; by Judge Steele, "The Contemplated Canal from the Waters of Mad River to Those of the Ohio"; by Stephen Fales, "The Memory of General Wayne, the Deliverer of Ohio"; by Colonel Stebbins, officer of the day, "The President of the Day — a Descendant of a Revolutionary Officer, one of the first settlers in this place, and who has borne the heat and burden of the day with us: as distinguished for his modesty as his worth, his is the popularity that follows, not that which is pursued"; by Judge Spining, "May the cause that first inspired the heroes of '76 to shake off the chains of slavery be very dear, and supported by all true Americans"; by the four Revolutionary veterans, "The Heroes of the Revolution, that fell to secure the blessings of this day to us: may their children so maintain them that America may be a republic of Christians on the last day of time."

The first "jubilee of the United States," commemorating the fiftieth anniversary of the Declaration of Independence, was celebrated July 4, 1826, by a procession from the Court-house, services at the brick church, — First Presbyterian, — a dinner at Mr. Rollman's tavern, — formerly Newcom's, — and a picnic at the medical spring near the present buildings of St. Mary's Institute on Brown Street. The Declaration was read by J W. Van Cleve, and an oration was delivered by Peter P. Lowe. In 1832 Edward W. Davies read the Declaration, and Robert A. Thruston delivered an oration. Adam Houk was marshal of the procession, and G. C. Davis, Robert C. Schenck, Jefferson Patterson, Peter P. Lowe, and George Engle assistant marshals. The following gentlemen were the committee of arrangements: Thomas Clegg,

Drawn by Henry Howe in 1846.

A VIEW IN DAYTON IN 1846, FROM NEAR THE CORNER OF FIRST AND LUDLOW STREETS, LOOKING SOUTH.

From a water-color painting by John W. Van Cleve, in possession of Miss Martha Holt. Copyright, 1895, by Miss Martha Holt.

Charles G. Swain, David C. Baker, Charles R. Greene, George Grove, William Eaker, Peter Baer, Johnson V. Perrine, William Roth, John Engel, David Davis, Thomas Morrison, F. F. Carrell, Samuel Foley, and Thomas Brown. In 1840 the Declaration, "prefaced by some happy remarks," was read by John G. Lowe, and Peter Odlin was the orator of the day. The exercises were held at the Third Street Presbyterian Church. The Dayton Grays and the Washington Artillery, a new military company, paraded.

In April, 1809, Dr. Wood opened, in Reid's Inn, the first drug-store established here, advertising in the *Repertory* "medicines in the small" for sale. The first political convention held in Montgomery County convened September 6 of this year at the Court-house, David Reid, moderator; Benjamin Van Cleve, clerk. Six hundred votes were cast at the election, and the following ticket was elected: State Legislature, Joseph H. Crane, Montgomery County, David Purviance, Preble County; sheriff, Jerome Holt; coroner, David Squier; commissioner, John Folkerth.

Both Indians and wild animals were still troublesome in 1810. The Montgomery County commissioners paid thirty dollars in reward for wolf-scalps this year, and twenty-two dollars in 1811. There were two thousand four hundred Indians in Ohio in 1810; five hundred and fifty-nine lived at Wapakoneta, and many were now encamped at Greenville. Dayton people were very anxious, for Tecumseh and his brother, "the Prophet," were uniting the Indians in the West and South in a league against the whites, which two years later was useful to the British.

The town was slowly improving. The population in 1810 was three hundred and eighty-three. This year the Select Council provided for new sidewalks along Monument Avenue, then Water Street, from Main to Mill Street; on First, from Ludlow to St. Clair, except the south side of First, between Jefferson and St. Clair, and on Main, from Monument Avenue to Third Street. The ordinance directed the walks to be "laid with stones or brick, or to be completely graveled, and a ditch dug along the outer edge." People were forbidden, "except when it was absolutely necessary," to drive over the walks, and fines collected for infringing this law were to be appropriated for paving street-crossings. This ordinance caused general rejoicing, both among townspeople and visitors from the country, as is stated in the *Ohio Centinel*, a weekly newspaper eleven by nine inches in size,—a four-column folio,—which, on the 26th of July, succeeded the *Repertory*. Isaac G. Burnett, a man of talent and education, was the editor and publisher till 1813, when it was discontinued from want of patronage, most of the men being away with the army, and the women too busy with farm and domestic work to have time for reading. It was a very good paper, and the editorials are still interesting reading to any one who cares for our early history. It contained the official and legal announcements for the whole Northwest Territory, and had a large circulation as far as Detroit and Chicago. It was "Republican" in principle, but was far from being exclusively political. Its motto was, "With slight shades of difference, we have the same religion, manners, habits, and political principles."

In 1811 a comet was visible, and there were severe shocks of earthquakes throughout the Ohio Valley from 1811 to 1812. It was at this date that New Madrid, on the Mississippi, was entirely destroyed by earthquake. The superstitious were terrified by these "signs and portents" in sky and earth, regarding them as ominous of public or private misfortune. The *Ohio Centinel* gives graphic accounts of the shocks felt here on December 16 and 17, 1811; January 23 and 27, and February 13, 1812. While the alarming shocks were occurring at Dayton, the newspapers were filled with frightful descriptions of the catastrophe at New Madrid and startling earthquake news from other quarters, and it is no wonder that citizens read these reports with awe and dread, feeling that it was not improbable that a similar fate was in store for them. This year of disaster made a deep and never-forgotten impression. In illustration of the force of the earthquake on the 16th and 17th of December, when the earth was in a continual tremor, a pioneer grandmother used to relate an anecdote of a flighty little woman, who, partly for the purpose of asserting her own courage, of which, in fact, she had not a particle, and partly from a spirit of mischief and desire to shock her awestruck friends, threw herself laughingly on the ground, exclaiming: "How delightfully the world rocks! I like the motion." The poor, frightened lady probably thought it better philosophy to laugh than to cry; but the village gossips considered such conduct very unbecoming, and proof positive that she was an atheist.

The revenue of Montgomery County for 1811-12 was $1,748.87; the expenditures, $968.60.

In 1812 William Huffman came to Dayton from New Jersey.

He was for many years successfully engaged in business as a merchant and speculator in real estate. His stone house, the first stone residence built in Dayton, and which, according to pioneer habits, was both dwelling and store, stood on Jefferson and Third streets, on the site of the Beckel House. He and his wife lived to be very aged. Their son, William P. Huffman, deceased, was an enterprising citizen, doing much to build up the town. There were four daughters: Mary Ann, married Rev. David Winters; Catharine, Morris Seely; Eliza J., Alexander Simms; Lydia A., first, William H. Merriam, second, John Harries. Grandchildren: William H. Simms, Mrs. Ziba Crawford, William, Frank, George, Torrence, and Annie Huffman, Mrs. E. J. Barney, Mrs. J. R. Hedges, Mrs. C. F. Drury.

In January, 1812, the Government began to raise troops for the war with Great Britain. While the Ohio militia were encamped in Dayton, the rendezvous for the troops, D. C. Cooper employed them to dig a mill-race. The army also brought work and business of other kinds to town. Early in 1812 Joseph Peirce wrote to his brother-in-law, James Steele, who had gone east to buy goods: "Business quite as good as could be expected. Groceries, especially coffee, are scarce in town. I think eight or ten barrels would not be too much for us, if they can be purchased cheap. A good assortment of muslins to sell at twenty-five cents would be desirable, and if L. Pascson can furnish you with them as cheap for four months as for cash, I would purchase pretty largely." Soon after, he wrote to another relative that he had been so overwhelmed with business since the arrival of the troops that he had not had time to attend to his private correspondence.

Horatio G. Phillips was one of the several merchants who laid the foundations of large fortunes in 1812. He was a native of New Jersey, and the son of Captain Jonathan and Mary Forman Phillips. He was born in 1783. His father was an officer in the Revolutionary army. In 1803 H. G. Phillips and a party of friends came west to seek a new home. At Cincinnati, on his return from a visit to Natchez, Mississippi, where he had had some thought of settling, he met D. C. Cooper, a New Jersey acquaintance, and at his invitation came to Dayton in the winter of 1804-05. At the close of the year 1805 he made the long, lonely journey on horseback, without a companion, to Philadelphia. Having purchased goods in that city, he went to Lawrenceville, New Jersey, where, on April 10, 1806, he was married to Miss Eliza Smith Houston. The journey to Ohio was made on horseback to Pittsburg, thence by flatboat to Cincinnati, and from the latter place to Dayton in a wagon. Their home till 1812 was a two-story log house on the southwest corner of First and Jefferson streets. His store was in his dwelling. In 1809 he took his wife and their infant daughter back to New Jersey on a visit to the old home. They traveled on horseback, a lead-horse carrying their baggage. J. N. C. Schenck, of Franklin, Charles Russell Greene, and other merchants, going east for goods, traveled with them, all the men of the party being armed with rifles, as roaming bands of Indians made the journey through the woods dangerous. There were now occasional taverns, where a night could be spent in primitive style.

In 1812 Mr. Phillips built a two-story brick store and a residence on the southeast corner of Main and Second streets. Dayton was at this period the thoroughfare of all regiments and wagons bound for the seat of war, and the army brought a great deal of trade to Mr. Phillips and other business men. Troops were always stationed here, and their purchases added largely to the profits of our merchants. In 1812-13 Mr. Houston, whom Mr. Phillips sent to Philadelphia to purchase goods, bought more largely than the latter intended, and fearing the stock could not all be disposed of here, he opened a store at Troy, with Mr. Houston in charge. Fortunately, the war created a demand for pork, whisky, flour, and grain, taken in exchange for merchandise, and he accumulated a large amount of these articles at Troy and Dayton, which he sold at good prices at those towns, or at the forts between New Lexington and Urbana. In 1815 he opened a third store in Greenville, under the control of Easton Morris. He was actively engaged in business for many years, and retired in his old age. He was one of the founders of the first Dayton bank, and was interested in woolen mills at Hole's Creek. In 1830, in partnership with Alexander Grimes and Moses Smith, he laid out the town of Alexandersville. In 1843 or 1844 he, with others, purchased from John Kneisley the water-power afterwards owned by the Dayton Hydraulic Company. His partners were Daniel Beckel, J. D. Phillips, and S. D. Edgar. He was an ardent advocate of the building of turnpikes. The Phillips House, built in 1850, was named in his honor. In 1831 Mrs. Phillips died. "By her death society lost one of its most hospitable and gifted members and the church a liberal giver and an earnest, unselfish worker." In 1836 Mr. Phillips married Mrs. C. P. Irwin, who survived him many years. By his first marriage he had three children who lived to grow up: Elizabeth, deceased, who married John G. Worthington, and with her son and daughter lived in Washington; Jonathan Dickinson, born December 31, 1812, married Luciana Z. Greene, and died in 1871, his wife dying in 1881; Mariana Louisa, born March 30, 1814, married, first, Robert A. Thruston, and, second, John G. Lowe.

J. D. Phillips was a man of culture and taste, and very generous and public-spirited. When he gave anything to his native city,—and his gifts were large and frequent,—it was, if possible, beautiful as well as appropriate and useful. He was one of the founders of, and a very liberal contributor to, the Public Library, and the extent of his gifts in that and other directions was known only to a few intimate friends. He was a warm friend of the Public Library, and (about 1849) proposed to construct a room on the second floor of his new building especially adapted to the use of the library, and lease it to the association on very favorable terms. The proposition was accepted, and a room forty by sixty feet, with lofty ceiling, supported through the center by Corinthian columns, was prepared. This room was elegantly furnished by special subscription, at a cost of over two thousand dollars. It is safe to say that at that day there was no library-room in Ohio outside of Cincinnati that could compare with it in beauty and convenience. The room was finished in white and gold. A pair of handsome, large, revolving globes, in tall stands, and other ornamental and useful articles were, in addition to his contribution to the general fund, given by Mr. Phillips. He was very hospitable, and loved, for his own enjoyment as well as for the honor of the town, to entertain at his residence distinguished guests during their stay in Dayton. His elegant, large ball-room was the scene of many a brilliant reception.

Mrs. John G. Lowe has, through a long life, been noted for generosity and active interest in benevolent and religious work, following the example of her mother, who was a leader in every undertaking for the benefit of the community. During the War of 1812 Mrs. Phillips took sick and wounded soldiers, who were brought here from the battlefield, into her own home, and nursed them till they were well, and was one of the band of ladies who constantly forwarded provisions and clothes to soldiers at the front. Her daughter, Mrs. Lowe, was one of the founders and

8

hardest workers in the Dayton Sanitary Association, which met daily to cut out and make garments and pack boxes of food and comforts for our men serving in the army during the Civil War. Mrs. Lowe has seven children living: General Gates P. Thruston, Mrs. G. W. Houk, Mrs. Charles Newbold, Henry C. Lowe, Houston Lowe, Mrs. Fowler Stoddard, Mrs. Thomas Gaddis. A son and daughter, Dickinson P. and Jeannette J. Thruston, died in early manhood and womanhood.

J. D. Phillips had one son, Horace,—who married Miss Nannie Pease, and lives in Seattle,—and four daughters, Mrs. A. McD. McCook, deceased, Mrs. J. P. Davies, Mrs. J. Harrison Hall, and Miss Sophia Phillips.

In 1812 Obadiah B. Conover settled in Dayton. Mr. Conover, who came from New Jersey, was for some years engaged in blacksmithing and the manufacture of wagons, plows, and other farming implements. About 1820 he opened a store on the southeast corner of Main and Third streets, the property still belonging to his descendants, though the pioneer building has given way to a modern business house. He was much interested and very useful in city and educational affairs, and in church and in Sunday-school work. He married a daughter of John Miller, who came to Dayton in 1799. Some of the characteristics of the grandfather have been inherited by sons and grandsons, from whom schools, libraries, and other public matters have received intelligent and constant attention. Mr. and Mrs. Conover had five children, all, as well as their descendants, influential citizens. The sons, Harvey, Wilbur, and Obadiah, were men of superior talent and liberal education, who made themselves felt, the first two in Dayton, and the third in Madison, Wisconsin. The sons, and one of the daughters, Martha, who married Collins Wight, a prominent business man, are deceased. The second daughter, Hannah, married Colonel Hiram Strong, who was a gallant officer, and died in 1863 from wounds received in the battle of Chickamauga. Obadiah B. Conover has many grandchildren: Charles, Harvey, Lawrence, and Wilbur Conover, Mrs. W. A. Phelps, and Mrs. Emma Brown, children of Harvey Conover; Frank Conover, Hugh D. Conover, deceased, and Mrs. Mary C. Grundy, deceased, children of Wilbur Conover; Harry C. Wight, deceased, and Mrs. R. A. Rogers, children of Mrs. Wight; Mrs. Hannah Frank and Mrs. W. B. Gebhart, daughters of Mrs. Strong.

CHAPTER VII

1812-1816

DR. JOHN STEELE—1812 and 1813 Years of Excitement—Dread of Indians—Colonel Johnston's Control of the Indians—Madison Orders Out Ohio Militia—Battalion Muster at Dayton—Militia Bivouac Without Tents at Cooper Park—Governor Meigs Arrives—Issues a Call to Citizens for Blankets—General Gano and General Cass Arrive—Three Regiments of Infantry Formed—Captain William Van Cleve—General Hull Arrives—Governor Meigs Surrenders Command to General Hull—The Governor and General Review the Troops—The Three Regiments March Across Mad River to Camp Meigs—Leave Camp Meigs for Detroit—Munger's Brigade Ordered Here to Garrison the Town—Hull's Surrender—Consternation of the People—Handbills Issued at Dayton Calling for Volunteers—Captain Steele's Company—Kentucky Troops Arrive Here—Harrison Calls for Volunteers and Horses—Dayton Ladies Make One Thousand Eight Hundred Shirts for Soldiers—Expedition Against Indians Near Muncietown—Defeated Soldiers Bring Wounded to Dayton—Hospital on Court-House Corner—War—Jerome Holt—War Ended—Dayton Companies Welcomed Home—First Dayton Bank—*Ohio Centinel*—Stone Jail—Mr. Forrer's Reminiscences of Dayton in 1814—First Methodist Church—William Hamer—Aaron Baker—*Ohio Republican*—*Ohio Watchman*—Medical Societies—Dr. Job Haines—Female Charitable and Bible Society—First Market-House—Moral Society—Associated Bachelors—First Theater.

IN 1812 Dr. John Steele settled in Dayton. He was born near Lexington, Kentucky, and was graduated from the famous Lexington college, Transylvania University, of which his father, Robert Steele, was one of the founders. From college he went to the University of Pennsylvania, at Philadelphia, in which the celebrated Dr. Benjamin Rusk was professor, to attend medical lectures. Having received his diploma as a physician, he decided to make his home at Dayton, where his brother James had lived for several years. Soon after his arrival a military hospital, a frame building, was erected on the northwest corner of Main and Third streets,—the Court-house lot,—for the use of sick and wounded soldiers of the War of 1812, Dayton, as already stated, being a depot of supplies and a rendezvous for troops. Dr. Steele was placed in charge as physician and surgeon. During his residence in Dayton, while always ready to serve the public, he confined himself principally to the duties of his profession, in which he was very successful, and won a high reputation. Even to the present day many families remember his knowledge and skill as doctor and surgeon with gratitude, and speak of him with love and respect. He was remarkable for dry humor and wit, and his old patients recall and repeat his witty sayings with a relish heightened by the memory of the relief they brought amid the despondency and pain of the sick-room. Like his brother James, and like their grandfather and father before them, he was a very religious man, and long an elder in the Presbyterian Church. He was identified from its organization with the Third Street Presbyterian Church, and "only members of that church can know the respect and love in which he was held." He served as member and president of the City Council, was member and president of the Montgomery County Medical Society, a founder of and large contributor to the Library Association, an original stockholder in Woodland Cemetery Association, and prominently connected with all the benevolent and religious societies of his day. "With his name," writes a friend, "is associated all that is honorable, noble, and elevated in human nature." He was married twice, his first wife dying young. In 1823 he married Miss Cornelia King, of Morristown, New Jersey, who survived him twenty-five years. They had ten children: Augusta; Caroline, married W. F. Comly; Dr. Henry K., beloved in Dayton and Denver for the professional skill and delightful social qualities characteristic of his father, married Mary Frances Dunlevy; Clara, married R. W. Steele; James, married Sally Curd; Charlotte, married W. H. Harrison; Samuel, married Annie Mills; Cornelia, John, and William. Mrs. R. W. Steele, Mrs. W. H. Harrison, and Miss Cornelia Steele alone survive. Grandchildren: R. W. Steele, Miss Harriet D. Steele, Mrs. William Spalding, children of Dr. Henry K. Steele; Charlotte H. Steele, daughter of Mrs. R. W. Steele; Cornelia H. Steele, daughter of James Steele. Dr. John Steele died in 1854, aged sixty-three.

The years 1812 and 1813 were full of excitement and dread in Dayton. Fear of the Indians, large numbers of whom were friendly to Great Britain, rendered the war with that country especially menacing to the people of Ohio. There were two thousand Indians—Shawnees, Ottawas, Wyandots, Senecas, Delawares, and Muncies—in the State. Blockhouses were built

CENTRAL HIGH SCHOOL, 1857-1893.

in Montgomery County as a refuge for settlers of Preble, Darke. and Miami counties, who were considered in great danger. A hundred of them fled from their homes, and their flight increased the alarm of people in less exposed regions. Scouting parties of Miami County militia were constantly on duty north and west of Piqua. These companies were usually ordered to kill every Indian, and squaws and children were made prisoners. News was continually coming during the spring that men had been killed and scalped and found murdered in the woods; that white inhabitants were flying before the savages in every direction. On the 10th of May it was reported here that an Indian trader by the name of Conner, who resided at Fort Defiance, had been advised by friendly Indians to move in from the frontier, and also that the Prophet was rebuilding his town, and was as strong as ever; that he was seventy miles from Greenville, and would reach that place in about six weeks. On the 14th of May six Indians and a squaw were captured near Troy, and on the 15th five or six whites, while planting corn near Greenville, were attacked by Indians and one of them wounded. Our people knew that if the Prophet took any of the neighboring towns it would not be many hours before he arrived at Dayton. Colonel Johnston, by order of Governor Meigs, was holding a council of Shawnee chiefs from Wapakoneta at Piqua, and great anxiety as to the result of this conference was felt. The Indians decided for peace, but though Colonel Johnston, who, from long employment among them as a Government agent, understood them as few white men did, and had wonderful influence over them, believed their professions of friendship, the citizens of Ohio generally had no faith in their promises.

All through the war Colonel Johnston acted as mediator and peacemaker between the tribes and the whites, especially endeavoring to keep faith with the friendly Shawnees, and at the same time to defend Indians and citizens from each other. He pursued this noble course successfully, in spite of much opposition from his own people, by means of appeals through the newspapers, and various proclamations and stringent regulations. Soon after one of Colonel Johnston's appeals for a just and humane treatment of the Indians was printed, an article filled with abuse of him and the Shawnees was published in the *Ohio Centinel*. It was claimed that while he was assuring the people that the Indians would not be troublesome in any way, he directed them to bring him the ears of all the swine they had killed. The settlers insisted that the order would not have been issued if there had been no ground for complaints against the savages. Colonel Johnston's only object in publishing this order was to prove the innocence of his wards, if possible, or, if he failed in this, to provide some means of deciding what would be a full compensation for hogs that had been lost by their owners. The frontiersman could not, as a rule, believe an Indian less cruel and treacherous or more worthy of consideration than the wild beasts which he shot whenever he had an opportunity. Even the more intelligent and humane inhabitants of Ohio largely shared this distrust and contempt of Indians; and Indians professedly friendly did many things which confirmed the evil opinion the whites had of them.

President Madison ordered out one thousand two hundred Ohio militia in April, 1812, for one year's service, and Governor Meigs directed the major-generals of the Western and Middle divisions to report with their commands at Dayton on the 29th of the month. Major David Reid ordered the officers of the First Battalion, of which he was in command, to assemble for a battalion muster on the second Tuesday in April, at the usual parade-ground in Dayton, armed and equipped as the law required. At this muster orders were read, and also the bill for enrolling volunteers, passed by Congress on the 20th of February. On such occasions crowds of people gathered to enjoy the parade, and it was supposed that the patriotism and enthusiasm of spectators would be roused on the 14th of April, and that many recruits would be obtained. "It was expected," the editor of the *Ohio Centinel* writes, "that a sufficient number would volunteer to obviate the necessity of a draft, but only twenty stepped forward at the call of their country." The editor expresses his disappointment at this result in strong terms. Citizens had hardly had time as yet to realize that hostilities had really begun. The war excitement soon rose to fever-heat, and the *Centinel* never again reproved Daytonians for lack of patriotism. A company of Rangers was raised by General Munger at this date in this neighborhood, to be marched to Detroit. Governor Meigs came to Dayton on the 20th of April to inspect them. The company was partly composed of drafted men.

The uniform of the soldiers of 1812 was a blue coat, with scarlet collar and cuffs, and a cocked hat, with a cockade and white feather. The Governor appointed the 30th of April as a day of fasting and prayer, and appropriate religious services were held at the Dayton Court-house.

When, on May 1, the first companies of militia reached Dayton, though the Governor's order making this the rendezvous of troops had been published a month before, no arrangements had been made for their comfort. Till the middle of May they had neither tents nor camp equipage, and very few blankets. A number bivouacked without shelter on the commons now Cooper Park. Twelve companies, containing eight hundred men, were here by May 7, and eight or ten more arrived in a few days. As the town could not afford room for all these men, some camped a little south of Dayton.

Governor Meigs arrived on the 6th of May to give orders and inspect troops. The event was announced by the citizens by a salute of eighteen guns. He reviewed the militia in the afternoon, and the next day sent out an appeal from headquarters, McCullum's Tavern, southwest corner of Main and Second streets, to the citizens of Ohio, to men, mothers, sisters, and wives, for blankets for the soldiers. Each family was requested to "furnish one or more blankets," the appeal read, "and the requisite number will be completed. It is not requested as a boon; the moment your blankets are delivered, you shall receive their full value in money; they are not to be had at the stores. The season of the year is approaching when each family may, without inconvenience, part with one."

Soon after the Governor's arrival, he ordered General Munger and a small number of Dayton troops to make "a tour to Greenville, to inquire into the situation of the frontier settlements." On May 14 there were about one thousand four hundred troops here, the majority of whom were volunteers. Six or seven hundred of them were under the command of General Gano and General Cass. Six other companies arrived in a few days. Three regiments of infantry,—the First, Second, and Third,—numbering one thousand five hundred men, were formed on the 21st. These were the first regiments organized by the State of Ohio. After the companies were assigned to these regiments, and officers were elected, better military discipline was maintained than had been hitherto possible. The First Regiment encamped south of town, and the other two at Cooper Park.

Ohio's quota of troops having now been raised, Captain William Van Cleve's newly formed company of riflemen of this county was employed in guarding supply-trains on the road to St. Mary's. Captain William Van Cleve, brother of Benjamin, was born near Monmouth, New Jersey, in 1777. He was one of the original settlers of Dayton. Instead of coming on the keel-boat or pirogue with his family, he accompanied the Newcom party through the woods for the purpose of driving the cow of his stepfather, Mr. Thompson. He was married twice, and by his first wife, Effie Westfall, had several children. From the close of the war till his death in 1828, he kept a tavern at the junction of Warren and Jefferson streets.

In the latter part of May General Hull arrived at McCullum's Tavern, which he made his headquarters. The usually quiet village of Dayton was now all animation and noise, as officers, quartermasters, and commissaries were preparing for the departure of the regiments for Detroit. The broad and generally deserted streets, ungraveled, often knee-deep in mud, were alive with bustling citizens and country people, gazing with curiosity at the brilliant uniforms and equipments of the passing soldiers, and the stores were full of customers; companies were drilling; mounted officers and couriers galloping in different directions; lines of wagons and packhorses, laden with provisions and ammunition and camp equipage, coming in from Cincinnati or the neighboring places, and Montgomery County farmers and business men, even when they were enrolled among the volunteers, were many of them reaping a golden harvest. On the morning of the 25th General Meigs and General Hull, to whom the Governor had surrendered the command, reviewed and made addresses to the soldiers camped south of town. After dinner at noon at McCullum's, they reviewed and addressed the regiments at Cooper Park. Early the next morning the three regiments, with Hull and his staff at their head, crossing Mad River at a ford opposite the head of Webster Street, marched to a new camp,—which they called for Governor Meigs,—situated on a prairie three miles from town, on the west bank of Mad River. They raised the American flag, and, forming a hollow square around it, greeted it with cheers, and expressed their determination not to surrender it except with their lives.

On the 1st of June the First, Second, and Third regiments of Ohio militia and a body of cavalry, followed by a wagon-train and a brigade of pack-mules, left Dayton for Detroit. The Governor and his staff and strangers from Cincinnati and Kentucky, besides a crowd of people from the town and neighboring country, were collected to see the troops begin their march. They marched out the old Troy pike. A large number of men followed them for a day or two, some of them sleeping in camp one night. General Munger's command of militia was ordered here to garrison the town, protect stores and public property, and keep open a line of communication with the army at the front. This was service of importance, as quartermaster's ordnance and commissary's supplies were forwarded by way of Dayton.

The news of the surrender of Hull's army reached Dayton at noon on Saturday, August 22, and this terrible disaster occasioned much alarm. A handbill was at once sent out into the country from the *Centinel* office, containing the startling information just received, and urging every able-bodied man who could furnish a firelock to come to Dayton Sunday prepared to march immediately for the defense of the frontier, guard the public stores at Piqua, and watch the Indians in that region. So many poured into town, and so immediate was the response to the appeal, that the *Centinel* headed an editorial relating the occurrences of the next day or two, "Prompt Patriotism," and challenged "the annals of our country to produce an example of greater promptitude or patriotism." Though the news came Saturday noon, a company of seventy men, commanded by Captain James Steele, was by seven o'clock Sunday morning raised, organized, and completely equipped, and marched a little later in the morning to Piqua. All the men and women in town devoted themselves to the work of getting the soldiers ready, and few went to bed Saturday night. Five companies of drafted men from Montgomery and Warren counties arrived on Sunday. Monday and Tuesday troops were constantly departing and arriving. Two companies were left here at Camp Meigs. The Governor of Ohio, as soon as the bad news came, ordered forty thousand dollars' worth of public stores to be removed from Piqua to Dayton, and General Munger and his brigade soon accomplished this work. Captain Steele's company, no longer needed at Piqua, was ordered to St. Mary's,—the most advanced frontier post,—and the Captain was placed in command of the post. Joseph H. Crane was made sergeant-major. The Dayton company built blockhouses for the defense of St. Mary's. The pay-roll of Captain Steele's company was preserved, and its publication in a Dayton paper many years later enabled widows and children of the men whose names appear on it to obtain land-warrants from the Government. This pay-roll contained but fifty-two names, though seventy were enrolled on August 23, so that part of the men were probably engaged at this time in scouting or other duty. Perhaps some did not go farther than Piqua.

General Harrison spent the 1st of September, 1812, in Dayton, and a salute of eighteen guns was fired in his honor. While the citizens were receiving General Harrison in front of the Court-house, Brigadier-General Payne arrived with three Kentucky regiments, comprising one thousand eight hundred men, and, marching past the Court-house, halted at Second Street. The soldiers were also honored with a salute. Early in September General Harrison sent out a call for volunteers, to be commanded by himself, ordering them to "rendezvous at the town of Dayton on the Big Miami." He also issued a call for eight hundred horses provided with saddles and bridles, agreeing to pay fifty cents a day for them. The horses were to be received at Reid's Inn in Dayton. It is easy to imagine what a stirring place Dayton had now become. Some of the regiments which stopped over night camped, we are told, "in the mud on Main Street."

The troops at the front were in great need of blankets and warm clothes. The following appeal was sent to the ladies of Dayton from headquarters, St. Mary's, September 20, 1812:

"General Harrison presents his compliments to the ladies of Dayton and its vicinity, and solicits their assistance in making shirts for their brave defenders who compose his army, many of whom are almost destitute of that article—so necessary to their health and comfort. The material will be furnished by the quartermaster, and the General confidently expects that this opportunity for the display of female patriotism and industry will be largely embraced by his fair country-women.

"P. S.—Captain James Steele will deliver the articles for making the shirts on application."

Captain Steele's company, which had volunteered for short service, was returning home when this letter was written. The material for the shirts was obtained from the Indian Department, and had been prepared for annuities to tribes supposed to be friendly, but now in arms against the Government, and withheld in consequence of their present hostile attitude. "With a zeal and promptitude honorable to them and the State," and, of course, without compensation, the ladies of Dayton immediately went to work, and by October 14 one thousand eight hundred shirts were ready to send to the army—a good deal of sewing to accomplish without the aid of a machine in less than four weeks by the women of a village of less than one hundred houses.

On the 11th of December seven hundred men of the Nineteenth United States Infantry, who had remained in Dayton for ten days to procure horses, left under command of Lieutenant-Colonel John B. Campbell on an expedition against the Miami villages near Muncietown. The Indians were routed, but eight of our men were killed and forty-eight wounded, and nearly half the horses were killed or lost. Late in the afternoon of the day of the battle the army began its return march, carrying forty of the wounded, who were unable to ride, on stretchers. The men suffered all sorts of hardships, and nearly perished from cold, fatigue, and lack of food. On the 22d and 24th of December Major Adams, stationed at Greenville, and Colonel Jerome Holt, engaged in building blockhouses and protecting the frontier, came to their assistance and enabled them to continue their march. They reached Dayton on Sunday, the 27th, after traveling ten days. The *Centinel* says that "their solemn procession into town, with the wounded extended on litters, excited emotions which the philanthropic bosom may easily conceive, but it is not in our power to describe them."

The small military hospital on the Court-house corner, in charge of Dr. John Steele and assistant physicians, has already been mentioned. Some of Colonel Campbell's men were no doubt received at the hospital, but the soldiers were also taken into private houses, scarcely a family receiving less than four or five. The usual Sunday services were omitted, and the ladies of Dayton spent the day nursing the wounded and ministering to the needs of their worn-out comrades. Colonel Campbell's force marched to Franklinton in a few days, but those unable to accompany them were left here, and tenderly cared for by citizens. The ladies of Dayton, though not formally organized into a soldiers' relief society, were continually engaged in making or collecting clothes and supplies for Montgomery County volunteers in the field or in the hospitals. Both private and public supplies, though mud rendered the roads almost impassable, were constantly forwarded by army agents from Dayton. Supplies purchased here were delivered to Colonel Robert Patterson, forage-master at the Government storehouse, on the west side of Main Street, between Monument Avenue and First Street.

Jerome Holt, mentioned above, was a brother-in-law of Benjamin Van Cleve, and came to Dayton in the summer of 1796. They had been partners in Cincinnati. After John Van Cleve had been killed by the Indians, he assisted Benjamin in his first efforts to provide for the family. His wife, Anne Van Cleve, was born in Monmouth County, New Jersey, in 1775, and died in 1858 in Van Buren Township, where the Holts settled in 1797. He was appointed constable of Dayton Township in 1800, and elected sheriff of Montgomery County in 1809. From 1810 to 1812 he was colonel of the Fifth Regiment of militia. Three great-granddaughters, named Gusten, live in Dayton, and a descendant—Mrs. Lindsay—lives on the old Holt farm four miles north of Dayton. Jerome Holt died in Wayne Township in 1841, and was buried in Dayton with military and Masonic honors.

A new company was formed here in January, 1813, by Captain A. Edwards, and marched immediately. Captain Edwards, who was a Dayton physician, had served as a surgeon in the army in 1812.

In the fall of 1813 Perry's victory on Lake Erie, Harrison's defeat of Proctor, and the repulse of the British at the battle of the Thames, brought the war in the West to a close. Returning Ohio and Kentucky soldiers were now constantly on the march from the north through Dayton, and the town was full of people from different parts of the country, who had come to meet relatives serving in the various companies. Sometimes the volunteers, camped in the mire on Main Street, became a little noisy and troublesome. The Dayton companies received an enthusiastic welcome home. Streets and houses were decorated, and a flag was kept flying from the pole erected on Main Street. A cannon was also placed there, which was fired whenever a company or regiment arrived. The people, at the signal, gathered to welcome the soldiers, whom they were expecting, and for whom a dinner, on tables set out-of-doors, was prepared, and the rest of the day was given up to feasting, speech-making, and general rejoicing. Our Montgomery County companies had all returned by the 1st of December; but as they had been in

From a photograph by Wolfe.

NEWCOM'S TAVERN IN 1894. (USED AS A GROCERY.)

constant and active duty since their departure for the front, a number of brave men had fallen on the battlefield, and others came home in enfeebled health, or suffering from wounds which shortened their lives, so that many in this neighborhood had as much cause for sorrow as for joy when the troops gaily marched into town.

It is impossible for the present generation to realize the horrors and sufferings occasioned by the War of 1812. King says, in his history of Ohio, that an eye-witness described the country as "depopulated of men, and the farmer women, weak and sickly as they often were, and surrounded by their helpless little children, were obliged, for want of bread, to till their fields, until frequently they fell exhausted and dying under the toil to which they were unequal." There is slight record of the trials and labors of the people of Dayton during this period, but they no doubt had their full share.

The treaty of peace was not signed till 1815. When the news reached Dayton in February, the following article, headed "Peace," appeared in the *Republican:* "With hearts full of gratitude to the great Arbiter of nations, we announce this joyous intelligence to our readers. Every heart that feels but a single patriotic emotion will hail the return of peace, on terms which are certainly not dishonorable, as one of the most auspicious events we were ever called upon to celebrate. The citizens of Dayton have agreed to illuminate this evening. The people from the country are invited to come in and partake of the general joy." March 31 was appointed by the Governor of Ohio as a day of thanksgiving for the declaration of peace.

The mechanics of Dayton met at four o'clock in the afternoon of Saturday, March 15, 1813, at McCullum's Tavern, to form a mechanics' society. This was the first workingmen's association organized in Dayton. Workingmen and mechanics, as well as merchants and manufacturers, were prospering at the close of the war, and able to buy themselves homes. There was much successful speculating in real estate, and business was on the top wave for the next six or seven years.

The 5th of May of this year was set apart by the Governor of Ohio for a day of thanksgiving. In Ohio in early times thanksgiving was not always observed, and when the Governor issued a proclamation for the festival he was as likely to select Christmas or May-day as the last Thursday in November. The first proclamation of this kind in Ohio was issued by Governor St. Clair, December 25, 1788.

The first Dayton bank, called the "Dayton Manufacturing Company," was chartered in 1813. The following gentlemen constituted the first board of directors: H. G. Phillips, Joseph Peirce, John Compton, David Reid, William Eaker, Charles R. Greene, Isaac G. Burnet, Joseph H. Crane, D. C. Lindsay, John Ewing, Maddox Fisher, David Griffin, John H. Williams, Benjamin Van Cleve, George Grove, Fielding Gosney, and J. N. C. Schenck. The amount of stock issued was $61,055. The first loan was one of $11,120 to the United States Government to assist in carrying on the war. Banking hours were from 10 A.M. to 1 P.M. The president received a salary of one hundred and fifty dollars per annum, and the cashier four hundred dollars. H. G. Phillips was elected president in 1814, but resigned in a few weeks, and was succeeded by Joseph Peirce. On the latter's death, in 1821, Benjamin Van Cleve was elected; but he died in two months, and was succeeded by George Newcom. In the following year James Steele, who served till his death in 1841, became president, and George S. Houston cashier. After 1831 the bank was known as the "Dayton Bank." The bank closed up its affairs in 1843.

On the 19th of May, 1813, the last number of the *Ohio Centinel* appeared, and for a year and five months no newspaper was published in Dayton. As a consequence there is little material during this period for the history of the town.

The contract for building a new jail was sold to James Thompson, July 27, 1811, at public auction at the Courthouse, for $2,147.91. The jail was eighteen by thirty-two feet, and built of rubble-stone. A rented house was used for a jail till the new building was finished. It was not completed till December, 1813. The jail stood on Third Street in the rear of the Court-house, close to the pavement. It was two stories high, with gable shingle roof, running parallel with the street; a hall ran through the center of the house from the Third Street entrance. The prison occupied the east half of the building and the sheriff's residence the west half. There were three cells in each story. Those in the second story were more comfortable than the others, and were used for women and for persons imprisoned for minor offenses. One of the cells was for debtors, imprisonment for debt being still legal at that period. Often men imprisoned for debt were released by the court on "prison bounds" or "limits," upon their giving bond for double the amount of the debt. They were then permitted to live at home, support their families, and endeavor to pay their indebtedness, but were not allowed to go beyond the corporation limits. This jail was not considered a safe place of confinement for criminals, as persons on the sidewalk could look through the barred windows, which were about two feet square, into the lower front cell, and pass small articles between the bars. Though the cells were double-lined with heavy oak plank, driven full of nails, one night four prisoners escaped by cutting a hole in the floor, and tunneling under the wall and up through the sidewalk. About 1834 or 1835 a one-story building of heavy cut stone was erected in the rear of the jail. It contained four cells with stone floors and arched brick ceilings. This was the county jail until the fall of 1845, when a stone jail was built at the corner of Main and Sixth streets, the present workhouse.

Mr. Samuel Forrer, who visited Dayton in the fall of 1814, gives us, in his reminiscences, a glimpse of the town at that date· "At that early day there was a house and a well in an oak clearing on Main Street, near Fifth, surrounded by a hazel thicket. It was a noted halting-place for strangers traveling northward and eastward, in order to procure a drink of water and inquire the distance to Dayton." He describes the embryo city as still confined principally "to the bank of the Miami River between Ludlow and Mill streets, and the business — store-keeping, blacksmithing, milling, distilling, etc.— was concentrated about the head of Main Street."

In 1814 the first Methodist church was completed and occupied. It was a one-story frame building thirty by forty feet in size, and stood on a lot contributed by D. C. Cooper, on the south side of Third Street and a little east of Main Street. Previous to the building of this "meeting-house" Methodist services had been held in the open air, the Presbyterian log cabin, or the Court-house. As early as 1797 a Methodist class had been formed by William Hamer, a local preacher, which met in his house three miles up Mad River. Rev. John Kobler, sent out by Bishop Asbury to organize the Miami Circuit, preached in Dayton, as already mentioned, in August, 1798, and January, 1799. In April of the latter year class-meetings began to be held in the village at the house of Aaron Baker. Bishop Asbury preached here on the 22d of September, 1811, in the Court-house, to a thousand persons. Soon after, Rev. John Collins, who had preached here a few Sundays, persuaded the people to erect a church, and in a short time $457.55 had been subscribed for a building fund. The frame church was succeeded by two brick buildings on its site—the first, built in 1828, forty by fifty feet in size and twenty-four feet in height, and the second, built in 1849, fifty-five by eighty-two feet in size, and with a tower in front. In 1870 the congregation removed to the stone structure—Grace Methodist Episcopal Church—on the southeast corner of Fourth and Ludlow streets.

William Hamer, the first Methodist local preacher to hold services in this neighborhood, was one of the pioneers of 1796. He settled on a farm three miles up Mad River, and his place was known as "Hamer's Hill." His wife died in 1825. He died in 1827, aged seventy-five. Their son Dayton, born at Hamer's Hill in 1796, was the first child born after the original settlers arrived at the mouth of Mad River.

The name of Aaron Baker, the first Methodist class-leader in Dayton, often occurs in the early history of the town. He was born in Essex County, New Jersey, in 1773, visited Dayton in 1804, 1805, and 1806, and settled here with his family in 1807. He built McCullum's Tavern and the old brick Court-house.

In December, 1814, Charles Zull began to work a ferry across the Miami at the head of Ludlow Street. Farmers, leaving their horses and wagons hitched on the north side of the river, brought their produce over in the boat to trade at the stores.

The *Ohio Republican* appeared October 3, 1814, published by Isaac G. Burnet—who had published the *Centinel*, which it succeeded—and James Lodge. It was similar in appearance to the *Centinel*, and printed from the type used for that paper; price, two dollars per annum if paid in advance, two dollars and fifty cents if paid within the year, and three dollars if paid at the end of the year. Under the title was printed the motto: "Willing to praise, but not afraid to blame." It was devoted principally to literature and foreign events, little attention being given in newspapers of that era to home news. Mr. Burnet, who was elected to the Legislature a month after the paper first appeared, sold his interest to Mr. Lodge, who, as two-thirds of his subscribers did not pay for their paper, was obliged to cease publishing it October 9, 1816. In November of the same year Robert J. Skinner began to issue the *Ohio Watchman* at the former office of the *Ohio*

Republican, having purchased the material and good-will of the latter paper. Its first motto was, "Truth, equality, and literary knowledge are the grand pillars of republican liberty." For this was substituted in 1819, "A free press is the palladium of liberty." It was originally a four-column folio paper, enlarged in 1818 to five columns, pages twelve by twenty inches in size. The editor announced in 1816 that the paper should be genuinely Republican in principles, "that he was partial to the administration then in power [James Madison was President], but that he did not intend to permit party prejudice to blind his eyes or to make his ears deaf to the principles of truth. The price was the same as that charged for the *Republican*. In 1820 the name of the paper was changed, and it was henceforth known as the Dayton *Watchman and Farmers' and Mechanics' Journal*. It was now published by George S. Houston and R. J. Skinner, the latter retiring in 1822. The office was on the west side of Main Street, between First and Second, a few doors south of David Reid's inn. The publishers offered to receive in payment for their paper flour, whisky, good hay, wood, wheat, rye, corn, oats, sugar, tallow, beeswax, honey, butter, chickens, eggs, wool, flax, feathers, country linen, and cotton rags. In January, 1826, A. T. Hays and E. Lindsley purchased the paper, but it ceased to appear in November, 1826. From 1824 it bore the motto, "Democracy, literature, agriculture, manufactories, and internal improvements, the pillars of our independence." It was opposed to "mending" the Constitution, and in favor of the tariff of 1824. The three journals whose histories have just been given — really one paper under different names — were published once a week.

At an early date several medical societies were formed and met in Dayton, but in vain has an effort been made to trace their history. A call appeared in the *Ohio Centinel* for July 24, 1814, over the signature of A. Coleman, of Troy, for a meeting of the Seventh District Medical Society, to be held in Dayton at Major Reid's tavern, on the first Monday in September. On the 16th of October, 1815, Dr. John Steele, secretary of the Board of Censors of the Seventh Medical District of Ohio, announced in the *Republican* a meeting of the board at Dayton on the first Monday in November. All the physicians who had begun practice within the Seventh District since 1812, were requested to appear before the censors for examination. The penalty for neglect on the part of censors to attend this meeting was removal from office and election of others to fill their places. A number of physicians in the Seventh Medical District met at Dayton July 3, 1816, and formed the Dayton Medical Society, which was to meet here on the first Mondays of April, July, and November. Dr. John Steele was elected secretary. The Montgomery and Clark County Medical Society was organized May 25, 1824, at Reid's Inn. Dr. John Steele was president; Dr. Job Haines, secretary. Dr. William Blodgett is the only familiar Dayton name among the censors. At the annual meeting at Reid's Inn in 1828, Dr. William Blodgett was elected president, and Dr. Edwin Smith delegate to the medical convention. Among the members of the society were Doctors Job Haines, John Steele, and Hibberd Jewett.

Dr. Job Haines, mentioned above, was born and educated in New Jersey. Immediately after receiving his diploma as a physician, he came to Ohio, settling in Dayton in 1817. He was "remarkable for sound judgment and practical wisdom, as well as for modesty and humility." He stood high in his profession and in the estimation of the community in general; was Mayor of the city in 1833, and held other municipal offices. He was for forty years a member or elder in the First Presbyterian Church. The unobtrusive goodness, the quiet activity in benevolent work, of his daily life,—the fact that he was equally "a lover of truth, and a lover of peace, and a peacemaker," endeared him to all who knew him even slightly. Constant, year in and year out, were his gratuitous professional calls on the sick, poor, and afflicted. Never a day, probably, passed that he was not seen with a basket of nourishing food or dainties, wending his way to the bedside of one of these patients; and having made them comfortable physically, the visit closed, if the patient desired it, with a few words of prayer and a brief reading of the Bible. But he did not obtrude his religious views on others. He died July 23, 1860, aged sixty-nine.

The ladies of Dayton and the vicinity met at the house of Mrs. Henry Brown, on Main Street, next to the Court-house, at three o'clock on the afternoon of Wednesday, April 12, 1815, to organize the Dayton Female Charitable and Bible Society. Members were each required to contribute one dollar per annum for the purpose of purchasing Bibles, and to make a contribution of twenty-five cents every three months to the charitable fund. The society was organized for the purpose of gratuitously distributing the Bible and seeking the sick, the afflicted, and needy, particularly of their own sex, relieving their wants and administering to their comfort and giving consolation to them in their distress, as far as was in their power. The following ladies were elected officers of the society: President, Mrs. Robert Patterson; vice-president, Mrs. Thomas Cottom; corresponding secretary, Mrs. Dr. James Welsh; recording secretary, Mrs. Joseph H. Crane; treasurer, Mrs. Joseph Peirce; managers, Mrs. William King, Mrs. David Reid, Mrs. James Hanna, Mrs. James Steele, and Mrs. Isaac Spining. This was the first society of this kind organized in Dayton, though the ladies who formed it were previously and during the remainder of their lives noted for their benevolence and good works. A charity sermon for the benefit of the society was preached by Rev. Joshua L. Wilson, of Cincinnati, in the Methodist meeting-house on Sunday, June 25. A charity sermon was henceforth, as long as the Charitable Society existed, annually preached by Dayton ministers in turn.

Robert Strain opened in May, 1815, in his large brick building on the corner of Main and Fourth streets, the site of the United Brethren Publishing House, a travelers' inn, which was long a favorite tavern. A millinery shop was opened on June 26 by Ann Yamer on Main Street, south of Second. Besides attractive goods for ladies, she announced in the *Republican* a full stock of plumes and other decorations for military gentlemen, and that she was in need of a supply of goose-feathers. It will be seen that business was now advancing southward on Main Street.

The first market-house was opened July 4, 1815. The markets were held from four to ten o'clock in the morning on Wednesdays and Saturdays. The house was a frame building, and stood on Second Street, between Main and Jefferson. On either side of the interior were butchers' stalls, and there were stands for farmers and gardeners on the outside, under the wide-extending eaves. Two long horse-racks, or rails, extended from the building along Second or Market Street—as the part of Second Street on which it stood was then called—nearly to Main Street. On April 1, 1816, an ordinance took effect which forbade the sale, within the corporation, on any other than market day, of butter, eggs, cheese, poultry, vegetables, fresh fish, or meat, with some exceptions as to meat and fish, which could be purchased every day before eight o'clock in the morning. Prices were low in

1816; butter twelve and a half cents per pound; eggs eight cents a dozen. Flour, however, was five dollars per barrel, and the next year six dollars.

The *Watchman* says in July, 1822, when flour was two dollars and a half a barrel, butter five cents a pound, chickens fifty cents a dozen, beef one to three cents per pound, and ham two to three cents per pound, that the Dayton price-list, published weekly in the newspaper, had been noticed in the Eastern papers under the head of "Cheap Living," and the low prices of marketing here attributed to the scarcity of money in the West. The *Watchman* assured the people on the Atlantic Coast that the great abundance of country produce of all kinds was the true reason that living was cheap in Ohio, and that money "is quite as plenty with us as notions in the Eastern States!"

In spite of wretched roads and lack of forage, large numbers of cattle, horses, and hogs were driven, after the War of 1812, from this neighborhood to the Eastern market. The Rev. Timothy Flint says, in his "Letters on Recollections of the Last Ten Years in the Mississippi Valley," that on his journey west in November, 1815, he met a drove of one thousand cattle and hogs on the Alleghany Mountains, which were "of an unnatural shagginess and roughness, like wolves, and the drovers from Mad River were as untamed and wild in their looks as Crusoe's man Friday." These swine lived in the Mad River and Miami woods on beach-nuts and acorns, could successfully defend themselves and their young against wolves, and when desired for food were shot like other wild animals.

In 1815 there were about one hundred dwellings in Dayton, the majority of them log cabins. From 1814 to 1815 the revenue of the county was $3,280.51, an increase in one year of $1,431.64. The license for a store was fifteen dollars and the clerk's fee fifty cents in 1815.

Two clubs or societies of men were formed in July of this year—the Moral Society and the Society of Associated Bachelors. The object of the first organization, as its name would indicate, was to suppress vice and to promote order, morality, and religion, and more particularly to countenance, support, and assist magistrates in the faithful discharge of their important duties, and in enforcing the laws against Sabbath-breaking, profane swearing, and other unlawful practices. The society is careful to state in its constitution that it is not its intention to exercise a censorious

Jail. Old Court-House. New Court-House.

MONTGOMERY COUNTY BUILDINGS.

From a photograph by Appleton.

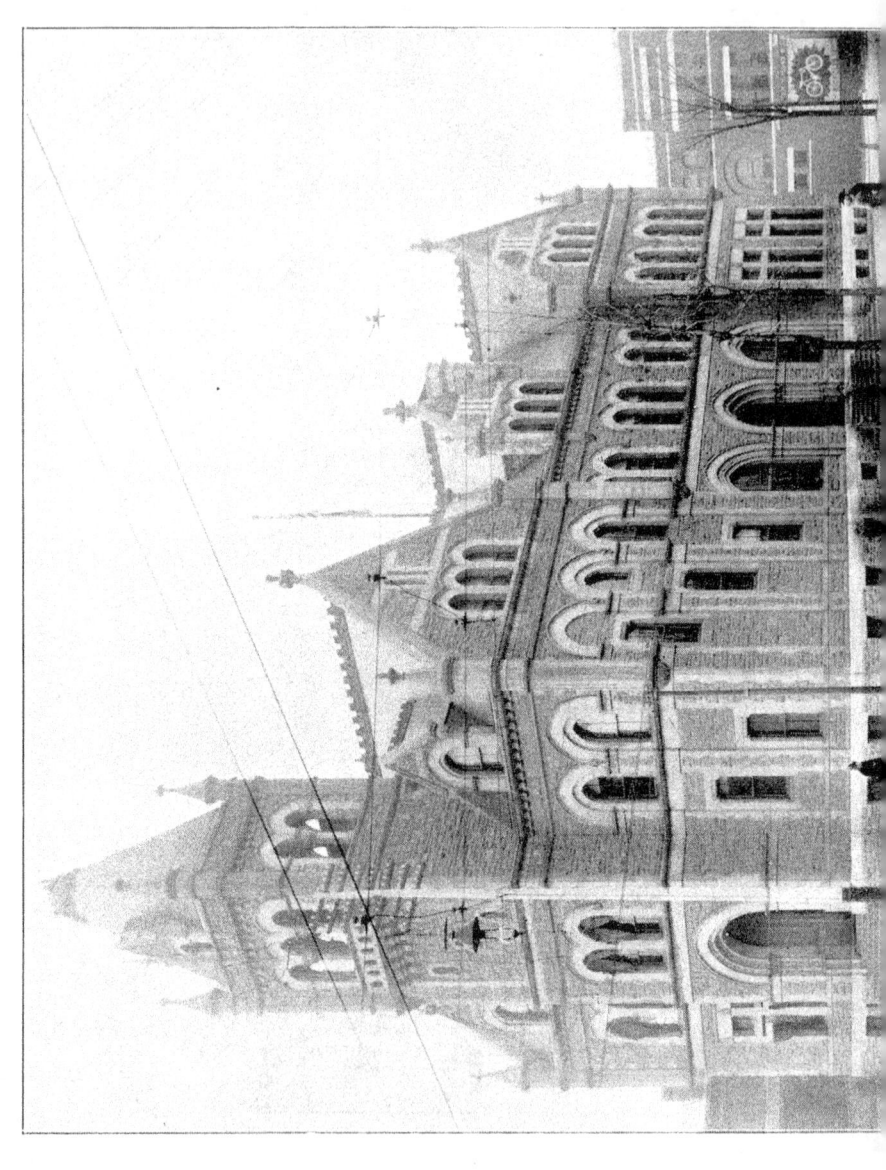

or inquisitorial authority over the private transactions or concerns of individuals. John Hanna was elected chairman; George S. Houston, secretary; managers, William King, Henry Robertson, Matthew Patton, John Patterson, and Aaron Baker. The meetings of the Moral Society were held on the first Saturday in October, January, April, and July. On the 12th of August, at two o'clock in the afternoon, the society assembled in the Methodist meeting-house to listen to a sermon from the Rev. Mr. Findlay. The Society of Associated Bachelors was intended for recreation, and usually met in Strain's bar-room. George S. Houston, secretary of the Moral Society, was at the same time president of the Associated Bachelors, so that the character of the two organizations could not have been as antagonistic as one might suppose. On the 24th of September, to the great satisfaction of the Moral Society, Mr. Houston was married to "the amiable Miss Mary Forman." Joseph John, secretary of the Associated Bachelors, was soon after married to Miss Jane Waugh, of Washington Township. The *Republican* made merry over the fact that both the president and secretary of the Society of the Associated Bachelors were married. Their successors were immediately elected—Dr. John Steele president, and Alexander Grimes secretary.

The grist-mill, and fulling-mill, and two carding-machines belonging to Colonel Robert Patterson, two miles from town, were destroyed by fire on the 7th of October. This was a calamity to many poor families, as well as to the proprietor, as there was a quantity of cloth and wool belonging to customers in the mills. They were soon rebuilt.

This year D. C. Cooper was president and J. H. Crane recorder of the Select Council of Dayton. D. C. Cooper was elected State Senator, and George Grove and George Newcom Representatives in the Legislature. Aaron Baker, who had no opponent, was elected coroner. In 1815 Mrs. Dionicile Sullivan opened a school for girls, in which were taught reading, writing, sewing, lettering with the needle, and painting,—the first school of the kind in Dayton.

Daniel C. Cooper was a member of the Legislature in 1816, and also president of the Town Council. Joseph Peirce was recorder; trustees, Aaron Baker, H. G. Phillips, Ralph Wilson, O. B. Conover, and George Grove. On the evening of April 22, 1816, the first theater was held in Dayton at the dwelling of William Huffman, on St. Clair Street. The much-admired, elegant comedy called "Matrimony, or The Prisoners," and the celebrated comic farce called "The Village Lawyer," were, the advertisement states, to be given, and between the play and the farce were to be presented two recitations, "Scolding Life Reclaimed" and "Monsieur Tonson," a fancy dance, and a comic song, "Bag of Nails." Tickets, fifty cents. Curtain to rise at half past seven precisely. Gentlemen were requested not to smoke cigars in the theater.

CHAPTER VIII

1816-1835

NEW Brick Court-House of 1817—Ferries—First Bridges—Sabbath-School Association—Sunday-School Society—Game Abundant—Flights of Wild Pigeons—Migrations of Squirrels—Fish—Stage-Coaches—St. Thomas Episcopal Church—Christ Episcopal Church—Shows—Volunteer Fire Department, 1820 to 1863—Leading Citizens Active Members—Feuds Between Rival Engine Companies—Financial Depression, 1820 to 1822—Fever——Lancasterian School—Francis Glass—*Gridiron* Newspaper—*Miami Republican and Dayton Advertiser*—George B. Holt—Consolidation of *Watchman* and *Republican*—Dayton *Journal*—Contribution to the Greek Cause—James Perrine, First Insurance Agent—First Baptist Church Built—Letter from Dayton in 1827—Canal Agitation—Dinner and Reception to De Witt Clinton—First Canal-Boat Arrives—Enthusiasm of the People—Extension of Canal by Cooper Estate—Law Providing for Election of Mayor—Town Divided into Wards—Temperance Society—New Market-House—Rivalry Between Dayton and Cabintown—Private Schools—Manual-Training School—Seely's Basin—Peasley's Garden—Miniature Locomotive and Car Exhibited in Methodist Church—Daytonians Take Their First Railroad Ride—Seneca Indians Camp at Dayton—First Public Schools—School-Directors—Steele's Dam—General R. C. Schenck—Political Excitement—Council Cuts Down a Jackson Pole—Cholera in 1832 and 1833—Silk Manufactory—The Dayton Lyceum—Mechanics' Institute—Six Libraries in Dayton—Eighth of January Barbecue—Town Watchmen—Lafayette Commemorative Services.

IT became necessary, on account of the increase of county business, to build a new Court-house in 1816. Finished in 1817, it was of brick, two stories high, forty-six feet front and twenty feet deep, and cost one thousand two hundred and forty-nine dollars. It stood on the corner of the Court-house lot. The *Watchman* rented the upper story in 1818, "at fifty dollars per year and free publication of the annual report of the treasurer and election notices." For same time the second-story rooms were rented for lawyers' offices.

In the spring of 1817 the advertisements of D. Stout, saddler, J. Stutsman, coppersmith, and Moses Hatfield, chairmaker, appeared for the first time in the *Watchman*. This year George

Newcom was elected State Senator, and William George and George Grove members of the lower house; D. C. Cooper, president of the Town Council; W. Munger, recorder; John Patterson, corporation treasurer.

Until 1817 Daytonians could only cross the rivers by fording or in a ferry. In December, 1817, a bridge at Taylor Street over Mad River, built by the county for one thousand four hundred dollars, was finished. It was a high, uncovered bridge, painted red. It fell into the river in 1828, but was rebuilt at once. In January, 1817, a stock company was incorporated to build the red toll-bridge across the Miami at Bridge Street. The following gentlemen were the incorporators: Robert Patterson, Joseph Peirce, David Reid, H. G. Phillips, James Steele, George S. Houston, William George, and William King. It was not finished till 1819. The people were very proud of this bridge, which the *Watchman* describes as "a useful and stately structure, . . . little inferior in strength and beauty to the best of the kind in the State, and renders the Miami no longer an obstruction to the free intercourse with our neighbors on the other side."

The Sabbath-School Association, the first organization of that kind in Dayton, was formed in March, 1817, through the influence of Rev. Backus Wilbur, pastor of the First Presbyterian Church—a very popular man, for whom a number of prominent citizens were named. He died in 1818. The inscription on his monument at Woodland Cemetery was written by the celebrated Rev. Dr. Archibald Alexander, of Princeton. A long obituary of Mr. Wilbur was published in the *Watchman* February 18, 1819. The Sabbath-School Association held its meetings in the new Presbyterian church. An annual fee of twenty-five cents entitled any one to membership. All denominations were represented, and most of the children of the town seem to have been enrolled. The list of names preserved in the history of the First Presbyterian Church is very interesting. Donors of five dollars or more became life-members. The society was managed by ladies, the officers consisting of a first and second directress, a secretary, treasurer, and five managers. The managers appointed the superintendent and the male and female teachers. The first board of managers consisted of the following ladies: Mrs. J. H. Crane, Mrs. Ayres, Mrs. Dr. Haines, Mrs. Hannah George, and Mrs. Joseph Peirce. Mrs. Sarah Bomberger was the first superintendent, and held the position for nearly twelve years.

Mrs. George, mother of Mrs. Bomberger, was for several years secretary, and was very efficient. Mrs. Bomberger was the daughter of Judge George, a leading citizen, who came to Dayton about 1805. In 1810 she married William Bomberger, who was county treasurer for fourteen years. Their children were George W., Ann, who married Peter P. Lowe, and William, who removed to Colorado and died there. In the spring of 1822 Mrs. J. H. Crane, first directress of the Dayton Sabbath-School Association, reported that they had distributed one hundred and sixty-five books during the previous year, had one hundred and twelve tracts and five miniature histories of the Bible on hand, and $19.75 in the treasury.

The Methodist Sunday-School Society was organized in July, 1818. Their meetings were held in the academy building. Adults and children were taught to read, and instructed in the Bible and catechism. There were, of course, no public schools here at that date.

D. C. Cooper and H. G. Phillips were the only persons in Dayton owning carriages in 1817.

The old Newcom Tavern was reopened in December by Blackall Stephens. The tavern was now called the "Sun Inn," and the swinging sign was decorated with a large picture of the sun. In an advertisement in the *Watchman*, with the sun flaming at its head, the house is described as "pleasantly situated on the bank of the Miami River," and the advantages of the inn, its comforts, sufficient supply of bed-linen, furniture, and other necessaries are set forth at length.

Game was nearly as abundant here at the date we have now reached as it was twenty years earlier. Mr. Samuel Forrer says in his reminiscences of Dayton in 1818 : "I remember that I killed three pheasants on the present site of Mr. Van Ausdal's house, in Dayton View. Quails, rabbits, etc., were found in plenty in 'Buck Pasture,' immediately east of the canal basin, between First and Second streets. Wild ducks came in large flocks to the ponds within the present city limits, but the ponds have since been mainly wiped out by drainage; and the fox-hunters had a great time on occasion by visiting the 'Brush Prairie,' within two miles of the Court-house. Deer, wild turkeys, and other game were killed in the neighborhood, and venison and wild meat were easily obtainable in Dayton." In 1821 Mr. H. G. Phillips frequently advertised a few coonskins for sale—used for caps.

The *Watchman* in April, 1822, notices a squirrel-hunt in Montgomery County lasting a day and a half, in which one thousand squirrels were killed, and their scalps produced in evidence.

Within the recollection of Robert W. Steele, as late as 1830 and 1840, game and fish were still abundant. An occasional deer could be found, and wild turkeys and pheasants were often shot by hunters. Squirrels and quails were thick in the woods and fields, and in the fall immense flights of wild pigeons alighted in the woods to feed on the mast. At irregular intervals one of those strange migrations of squirrels would occur, for which no satisfactory cause has been given by naturalists. Starting from the remote Northwest, they would come in countless numbers, and nothing could turn them from their course. Rivers were no impediment to them, and boys would stand on the shore of the Miami and kill them with clubs as they emerged from the water.

The rivers were still full of fish. No more delicious table-fish could be found anywhere than the bass, when taken from the pure, clear water of the Miami and Mad rivers of that day. On the mill-race, which has since been converted into the Dayton View Hydraulic, stood Steele's sawmill, which ran only in the daytime. At night the water was passed through a fish-basket, and each morning during the fish season it was found filled with bass of the largest size. In 1835 one Saturday afternoon a seine was drawn in the Miami, between the Main Street and Bridge Street bridges, and two large wagon-loads of fine fish were caught. Whatever hardships the pioneers of Dayton may have endured, they were in the enjoyment of luxuries that would have tickled the palate of an epicure. Fish-baskets, alluded to above, were usually made by building a dam on the riffles, so as to concentrate the water at the middle of the river, where an opening was made into a box constructed of slats, and placed at a lower level than the dam. Into this box the fish ran, but were unable to return. A basket of this kind remained on the riffle at the foot of First Street as late as 1830.

Previous to 1818 people wishing to visit Cincinnati were obliged to travel by private conveyance. But in the summer of this year a Mr. Lyon drove a passenger-coach from Dayton to Cincinnati once a week, beginning his trips in May. On June 2 D. C. Cooper, of Dayton, and John H. Piatt, of Cincinnati, began running a weekly mail-stage between the two towns, passing through Springdale, Hamilton, Middletown, and Franklin. Two days and a night were required for the trip, the night being spent in Hamilton. The fare was eight cents a mile, with an allowance of fourteen pounds of baggage. John Crowder, a colored barber of Dayton, and his partner, Jacob Musgrave, also colored, drove a coach and four that carried twelve passengers to Cincinnati and return in 1820. Timothy Squier ran a stage to Cincinnati in 1822. Five o'clock in the morning was the hour of starting by coach. Worden Huffman owned the stage-line to Columbus, which connected at that place with a coach to Chillicothe. In June, 1825, stages commenced running twice a week between Columbus, Dayton, and Cincinnati. When this line was first established, it was thought by many that all interested in it were throwing their money away. It was not long, however, before it became necessary to increase the number of trips to two a week, and finally a daily stage was established. In 1827 we were connected with Lake Erie by triweekly coaches, the trip taking four days. Daily coaches were started June 25, connecting at Sandusky with steamers for Detroit and Buffalo, and at Mt. Vernon with a stage for Cleveland. The fare to Cincinnati was three dollars, six dollars to Columbus, and twelve dollars to the lake. Four hundred and ninety-seven passengers by stage passed through Dayton in 1825. In 1828 there were stage-lines in every direction, twenty coaches arriving here every week.

In the era of ungraveled roads, when the coach went bumping over rough wagon-ruts, or splashing into deep mud-holes, or stuck fast in the mire, the journey to Cincinnati was a serious undertaking. It was ten or fifteen years later than 1825 before a short and pleasant trip could be made over an excellent turnpike in an "Indian bow-spring coach," which was superior to all sorts in use. A guard accompanied each coach, and the drivers were well behaved, and understood their business. In 1840 there were two daily lines of these coaches, owned by J. & P. Voorhees, one leaving at eight in the morning, and the other in the evening.

In 1818 George Grove and Judge George were elected members of the Legislature, and Warren Munger town recorder. George Newcom was elected State Senator in 1819, and Henry Stoddard and John Harries Representatives. The number of voters in Dayton in 1819 was seven hundred and sixty-five, and the number in Montgomery County two thousand seven hundred and eighty-five.

In 1819 St. Thomas Church—the first Episcopal church in Dayton—was organized by Bishop Chase with twenty-three members. In 1831 Christ Episcopal Church was organized by Rev. Ethan Allen, and in 1833 they built the first Episcopal house of worship erected in Dayton on South Jefferson, near Fifth Street.

Shows in Dayton were few and far between at that period. In 1819 an African lion was exhibited in the barnyard of Reid's Inn for four days, from nine in the morning till five in the afternoon. Patrons were assured that they would be in no danger, as the lion, "the largest in America, and the only one of his sort," was secured in a strong cage. Twenty-five cents admittance was charged; children, half price. In April, 1820, "Columbus," a large elephant, was on exhibition in the carriage-house of Reid's Inn—admittance, thirty-seven and a half cents; children, half price. In 1823 the advertisement of a menagerie, containing an African lion, African leopard, cougar from Brazil, Shetland pony with rider, ichneumon, and several other animals, appeared in the newspaper. A band, composed of ancient Jewish cymbals and numerous modern instruments, accompanied the show. The show at Reid's Inn in 1824 contained but one elephant. The first circus which appeared in Dayton exhibited in Reid's barnyard July 19, 20, and 25, 1825. No more circuses came till 1829, when two exhibited, both on July 5 and 6. In August, 1827, a traveling museum, consisting of birds, beasts, wax figures, paintings, etc., visited Dayton. One of the articles exhibited is advertised in a style worthy of Barnum, as "that great natural curiosity, the Indian mummy, which was discovered and taken from the interior of a cave in Warren County, Kentucky, where it was probably secreted in its present state of preservation for one thousand years." These museums, carried in cars or vans drawn by horses, traveled all over the Western country in early times. When they reached a town or village, the horses were unharnessed, and the cars were fastened together so as to make a continuous room for the display of the curiosities.

Cooper's Mills were burned on the 20th of June, 1820, and four thousand bushels of wheat and two thousand pounds of wool destroyed. They were soon after rebuilt by H. G. Phillips and James Steele, executors of the Cooper estate. This was the first fire of any importance that occurred in Dayton, and led to the organization of the first fire-company. Council provided ladders,

From a photograph by Wolfe.

CITY BUILDINGS.

From a photograph by S. C. McClure.

which were hung on the outside wall of the market-house on Second Street, and also passed an ordinance requiring each householder to provide two long, black, leather buckets, with his name painted thereon in white letters, and keep them in some place easily accessible in case of an alarm of fire. Before this no public provision for putting out fires had been made.

On the night of November 16, 1824, George Grove's hat-store and the shop of Hollis, the watchmaker, were destroyed, the loss being about one thousand dollars. This fire, which was the first of any size which had occurred since 1820, created a good deal of excitement, as the corporation ladders were not in their place at the market-house, and the whole dependence for extinguishing the fire was on the leather buckets of citizens. An ordinance was passed threatening persons removing the public ladders from the market-house, except in case of fire, with a fine of ten dollars, and providing that a merchant who was going to Philadelphia in the spring of 1825 should be furnished with two hundred and twenty-six dollars and directed to purchase a fire-engine.

On March 10, 1827, soon after the engine arrived, the first volunteer fire-company of Dayton was organized. George C. Davis was captain. At the same time a hook-and-ladder company, of which Joseph Hollingsworth was captain, was formed. John W. Van Cleve was appointed by Council chief engineer of the Fire Department. The following fire-wardens were appointed: James Steele, Abram Darst, Dr. Job Haines, and Matthew Patton. It was the duty of the wardens to periodically inspect the fire apparatus. A board of fire-guards was soon after appointed, whose duty it was to isolate and take charge of the neighborhood where the fire occurred while it was in progress and immediately afterward. The church bells sounded the fire-alarm, and fifty cents were paid to each sexton when the fire happened after nine in the evening. The one who rang his bell first received a dollar. The engine was a small affair, filled with the leather buckets, and the water was thrown by turning a crank in its side. Not much care was taken of it, for at a fire that occurred in 1831 it could not be used, as it was filled with ice, the water not having been taken out after a fire which had occurred several weeks before. A second engine was bought in 1833 and a third in 1834, by subscription.

In 1827 householders who had not themselves procured fire-buckets were provided with them by the town, the wardens distributing them at the engine-house, a frame building on the Court-house lot near the Main Street alley. Council expended $112.50 on buckets, half of which were kept at the engine-house and the rest at private dwellings. Buckets kept by citizens were for twenty years inspected every April by the wardens.

An alarm of fire brought out the whole population of the town, and the greatest excitement and confusion prevailed. Double lines were formed to the nearest pump, one line passing down the full buckets and the other returning the empty ones. Women were often efficient workers in these lines. The water in a well would soon be exhausted, and a move had to be made to one more remote. It was hopeless to contend with a fire of any magnitude, and efforts in such cases were only made to prevent the spreading of the flames.

In 1828 the following fire-wardens were appointed: James Steele, George W. Smith, Alexander Grimes, Matthew Patton, and Warren Munger; engineer, John W. Van Cleve. In 1833 a company, called the "Safety Fire-Engine and Hose Company, No. 1," was formed and offered its services to Council. To it was entrusted the new hand-engine, the "Safety," which had suction-hose and gallery-brakes, and five hundred feet of hose. The following were the first officers of the company: Foreman, James Perrine; assistant foreman, Valentine Winters; secretary, J. D. Loomis; treasurer, T. R. Black; leader of hose-company, Thomas Brown; assistant leader, Henry Diehl; directors, William P. Huffman, Jacob Wilt, Peter Baer, Henry Biechler, and Abraham Overlease. Fire-cisterns were built this year under the streets at First and Main, Third and Main, and Fifth and Main, and elsewhere. The cisterns were pumped full from neighboring wells, or filled by the engines, with hose, from the river or canal. In 1834 Alexander Grimes, I. T. Harker, John Rench, D. Stone, and others formed a company called the "Fire-Guards." They carried white wands, and it was their duty to protect property and keep order at fires. The following fire-wardens were appointed in 1836: First ward, Matthew Patton and Moses Simpson; second ward, James Steele and Abram Darst; third, Musto Chambers and Samuel Shoup; fourth, John Rench and David Osborn; fifth, A. Artz and William Hart.

A fire occurred here in 1839 which on account of bad management excited much indignation. According to the newspaper report, while the work of preservation was going on outside, an officious crowd, as was apt to be the case in those days, was playing havoc within doors. "In their eagerness to save the owners from loss by fire, they wrenched the doors from the hinges, pulled the mantels from their places, shattered the windows, and broke the sash." The next issue of the paper contained the following card from officers of fire-companies:

"Each company claims for itself the right to control its engine, hose, and pipe, and any interference by an individual not a member of the association is calculated to create useless altercation and to retard the effective operation of the firemen. The brakes of our engines are always free to those who desire to render effective aid. All we ask is that those who are not connected with the Fire Department would either remain at a distance or work at the engines, believing, as we do, that the confusion created at fires is occasioned by those who are not connected with the engines.

"E. W. DAVIES, President Second Engine Company.
"E. FAVORITE, Vice-President.
"V. WINTERS, Foreman Safety Engine and Hose Company.
"FREDERIC BOYER, Assistant.
"E. CARROLL ROE, President Enterprise Company."

It was difficult to maintain order in a volunteer fire department even when Dayton was a village, but as it grew into a city and the rougher elements of society were largely represented, fires became scenes of wildest excitement and disorder. There was a constant rivalry between the different companies as to who should reach the conflagration first, as to which engine threw the first water, as to which officer or private member deserved most honor for heroic or long-continued service. This led to bitter feuds: the hose of an engine was sometimes cut by members or adherents of another company; while striving for the most advantageous position or engaged in an altercation on other points, the men frequently came to blows and fought each other instead of the fire; stones were thrown, ladders, trumpets — anything that came handy was used as a weapon of assault or defense, and both firemen and spectators were often seriously injured. Going to a fire was like facing a mob, yet everybody went, whatever hour of night or day the flames broke out: such unusual excitement was not to be missed by the men and women of our then quiet little town. Every boy and nearly every man in town forty or fifty years ago was almost as ardent a partisan of the Independent Fire-Company, the Vigilance, the Deluge,

Oregon, etc., as of the political party to which by inheritance or conviction he belonged. But from 1856 there was, among the conservative class of citizens, a growing discontent with our unmanageable Fire Department. In 1863 the first steam-engine was purchased and our present splendidly equipped and perfectly ordered paid department inaugurated.

The flush times during the War of 1812 were followed by a serious and general depression in business throughout the United States, and the growth of Dayton till 1827 was slight. Gold and silver were withdrawn from circulation to the great injury of business in this region, where good paper currency was scarce. During 1820, 1821, and 1822, sales of all kinds were made by means of barter. Wolf-scalp certificates, called log-cabin currency, were taken instead of cash. There was some talk of returning to cut-money—dividing silver dollars into quarters, and Mexican quarters into three dimes. The Dayton Bank suspended specie payment several times during this period.

H. G. Phillips was president of the Town Council, and G. S. Houston recorder, in 1820; Aaron Baker, Luther Bruen, David Henderson, William Huffman, and Dr. John Steele, trustees. A fever prevailed during the summer and fall of 1821. There were seven hundred cases, and thirteen died. The population was one thousand. This year the three ponds southwest of town were drained—the "first two into the tail-race, and the other into the outlet from Patterson's pond to the river." Matthew Patton was president of Council, and G. S. Houston recorder, in 1821.

August 21, 1822, the Montgomery County Bible Society was organized at a meeting of which Joseph H. Crane was chairman, and G. S. Houston secretary. Dr. Job Haines was elected president; William King, Aaron Baker, and Rev. N. Worley, vice-presidents; Luther Bruen, treasurer; James Steele, corresponding secretary; George S. Houston, recording secretary; managers, John Miller, John H. Williams, John Patterson, David Reid, James Hanna, O. B. Conover, Daniel Pierson, Robert Patterson, James Slaght, John B. Ayers, Joseph Kennedy, Hezekiah Robinson, and Robert McConnel. This year was also formed the Dayton Foreign Missionary Society. James Steele was elected treasurer, and Job Haines secretary. The membership fee was fifty cents a year, which could be paid in money, clothes, kitchen furniture, or groceries, to be sent to the Indians, of whom a number still lived in Ohio.

In 1820 the Lancasterian or "mutual instruction" system of education was exciting great interest. Sharing in the general feeling in favor of the new method, the trustees of the Dayton Academy determined to introduce it in that institution. The trustees at that time were Joseph H. Crane, Aaron Baker, William M. Smith, George S. Houston, and David Lindsly. A house specially adapted to the purpose was built of brick on the north side of the academy, and consisted of a single room sixty-two feet long and thirty-two feet wide. The floor was of brick, and the house was heated by "convolving flues" underneath the floor. The walls were thickly hung with printed lesson-cards, before which the classes were marched to recite under monitors selected from their own number, as a reward for meritorious conduct and scholarship. For the youngest scholars a long, narrow desk, thickly covered with white sand, was provided, on which, with wooden pencils, they copied and learned the letters of the alphabet from cards hung up before them.

The following are some of the rules adopted for the government of the school:

"The moral and literary instruction of the pupils entered at the Dayton Lancasterian Academy will be studiously, diligently, and temperately attended to.

"They will be taught to spell, and read deliberately and distinctly, agreeably to the rules laid down in Walker's Dictionary; and in order to do that correctly they will be made conversant with the first rules of grammar. The senior class will be required to give a complete grammatical analysis of the words as they proceed.

"They will be required to write with freedom all the different hands now in use on the latest and most approved plan of proportion and distance.

"There will be no public examinations at particular seasons, in a Lancasterian school every day being an examination day, at which all who have leisure are invited to attend."

In 1821 the trustees adopted the following resolution, which would hardly accord with the present ideas of the jurisdiction of boards of education, or the authority of teachers:

"*Resolved*, That any scholar attending the Lancasterian School who may be found playing ball on the Sabbath, or resorting to the woods or commons on that day for sport, shall forfeit any badge of merit he may have obtained and twenty-five tickets;

and if the offense appears aggravated, shall be further degraded as the tutor shall think proper and necessary; and that this resolution be read in school every Friday previous to the dismissal of the scholars."

Gideon McMillan, who claimed to be an expert, having taught in a Lancasterian school in Europe, was appointed the first principal. In 1822 he was succeeded by Captain John McMullin, who came with high recommendations from Lexington, Virginia.

In 1823 there was a unique Fourth-of-July celebration under the direction of Captain John McMullin, of the Lancasterian School. A procession, composed of the clergy of the town, the trustees, and two hundred scholars, marched from the school on St. Clair Street to the First Presbyterian Church, where the Declaration of Independence was read by Henry Bacon, and a sermon delivered by Rev. N. M. Hinkle. It seems that Captain McMullin had served as a soldier, for the *Watchman*, in a notice of the celebration, says: "Captain John McMullin appeared as much in the service of his country when marching at the head of the Lancasterian School, as while formerly leading his company in battle."

In 1823 Francis Glass, an interesting man and remarkable scholar, taught a boys' school in Dayton.

The *Watchman*, on the 3d of September, 1822, contained the prospectus of the *Gridiron*, a weekly newspaper, edited and published by John Anderson, with the view of exposing and reforming people whose views of right and wrong differed from his own. The editor pledged his honor, liberty, and his life, if necessary, to the success of the *Gridiron*. The sheet was much dreaded by persons politically or otherwise obnoxious to the editor and contributors, and on it "evil-doers received a good roasting." Its motto was,

"....... Burn, roast meat, burn,
Boil with oily fat; ye spits, forget to turn."

The subscription price was one dollar per year, payable one-half yearly in advance, and it was printed on what was described as good medium paper, in octavo form. Thomas Buchanan Read, then living in Dayton, with his reputation all to win, was one of the contributors. A bitter political contest was being waged in Dayton at this period, and members of both parties, both in conversation and print, abused each other in a style that at the present day would have occasioned trial for slander. The *Grid-*

iron published the severest and most unjustifiable attacks on its opponents, or on unobtrusive citizens. Sometimes the broad burlesque or caricature of the articles excites a smile, but they are seldom even amusing. The writers are not restrained by truth, honor, or good taste, but indulge in wholesale abuse, which is unredeemed by genuine wit or humor. It is no wonder that such a scurrilous paper had a short career.

George B. Holt, better known now as Judge Holt, began to publish and edit, in 1823, a weekly Democratic paper, called the *Miami Republican and Dayton Advertiser*, which was continued till 1826. It was eleven by twenty-one inches in size. Judge Holt was a native of Connecticut, born in 1790, admitted to the bar of Litchfield in 1812, and came to Dayton in 1819. In 1828 he was elected judge of the Court of Common Pleas of Montgomery County by the Legislature, serving till 1836; elected again in 1842, serving till 1849. He was a member of the Ohio Legislature in 1824 and 1827, "and was conspicuously connected with some of the most important early legislation of the State." In 1825 the first act establishing free schools was passed by the Legislature. Judge Holt was an earnest and active advocate of the measure, and to him was greatly due the passage of the act. In 1850 Judge Holt, who "had a high reputation as a lawyer, and was popular among all classes of the people," was elected a member of the convention called to adopt a new constitution for the State of Ohio. He was prominent in the convention, which many of the most noted men in the State attended. From this period till his death, in 1871, he took little part in political or professional life, though he was an ardent supporter of the Union in the War of the Rebellion. He was learned in his profession, and was a man of keen, strong intellect and literary tastes. He was a member of the Presbyterian Church, and highly esteemed as a citizen. He has three daughters—Miss Eliza and Miss Martha Holt and Mrs. Belle H. Burrowes—and several grandchildren.

In 1826 William Campbell, of Westmoreland County, Pennsylvania, purchased and consolidated the *Dayton Watchman* and the *Miami Republican*. The new paper was published weekly, and was called the *Ohio National Journal and Montgomery County and Dayton Advertiser*. After a few weeks it was sold to Jephtha Regans, who, in 1827, sold one-half interest to Peter P. Lowe, and they carried it on together till 1828. It was Whig in politics, and its motto was, "Principles and not men, where principles demand the sacrifice." It was thirteen by twenty inches in size, with five columns to the page. The paper was now called the *Dayton Journal and Advertiser*. In 1828 J. W. Van Cleve purchased Mr. Lowe's interest. In 1830, Mr. Regans having died, Mr. Van Cleve entered into partnership with Richard N. Comly. In 1834 William F. Comly bought Mr. Van Cleve's share in the paper. Its size was increased to a seven-column folio, and it became the largest paper published in Ohio. Any one examining the files of the *Journal* of this date in the Public Library cannot but feel a pride in the fact that early Dayton had a newspaper of such excellence, whether as to print, or editorials and contributions. The owners' chief aim was to publish a paper of the highest character. R. N. Comly left Dayton many years ago, but William F. Comly is well known to the younger, as well as the older, generation of citizens. In his management of the *Journal* he exhibited a breadth of view, generosity, public spirit, and thorough disinterestedness of which only the noblest class of men are capable. The *Journal*, without regard to the popularity or financial success of the editor, advocated every city reform and improvement, and was a wonderful power for good. In so unobtrusive and matter-of-course a way was Mr. Comly's work for Dayton done that probably few are aware how greatly indebted the town is to him. In 1840 the *Journal* was changed to a daily, then to a triweekly. Since 1847 it has been published as both a weekly and daily.

February 9, 1824, a meeting was held at Colonel Reid's inn to raise money for the Greek cause. Simeon Broadwell was elected chairman, Dr. Job Haines secretary, and George S. Houston treasurer. One hundred and fifteen dollars were collected, and William M. Smith, George W. Smith, and Stephen Fales were appointed a committee to remit the money to the Greek Fund Committee of New York.

This year John Compton was president of the Town Council, and J. W. Van Cleve recorder.

The revenue of the town for 1825 was one hundred and seventy-two dollars.

In June, 1826, James Perrine was appointed agent for the Protection Insurance Company of Hartford, and was the first person engaged in that business in Dayton. Mr. Perrine was just beginning his long and honorable career as a merchant in Dayton.

From a photograph by Appleton.

STEELE HIGH SCHOOL.

There were eight hundred and forty-eight voters in Dayton Township in 1827. The population within the corporation was one thousand six hundred. Dr. John Steele was president of the Town Council, and R. J. Skinner recorder. George B. Holt was elected State Senator this year, and Alexander Grimes and Robert Skinner Representatives.

In 1827 the Baptist society, organized in 1824, built, on the alley on the west side of Main Street, between Monument Avenue and First Street, its first church, costing two thousand dollars.

The following is an extract from an interesting letter written December 11, 1827, by a person living in Dayton to a friend in New Jersey:

"I will now give you some account of our town. There are in it at present thirteen dry-goods stores, four public inns, seventeen groceries, one wholesale warehouse, two printing-offices, three wagon-maker shops, one carriage shop, four blacksmith shops, two sickle shops, one tinner shop, one coppersmith shop, three hatter shops, seven shoemaker shops, seven tailor shops, three tanyards, three saddler shops, three watchmaker shops, one brewery, one flour-mill with three run of stone, one sawmill with two saws, one fulling-mill, one set of carding-machines, and a cotton factory. There are six schools,—three with male, three with female, teachers,—one tallow-chandler, and two tobacconists. We have a market-house one hundred feet long, and it is well supplied. There have been brought to it during the last summer and fall twelve to sixteen beeves a week, and other meat, poultry, and vegetables accordingly. The productions of the country are much greater than can be consumed. The article of butter is very great. One merchant has taken in and sent to foreign markets thirty-two thousand six hundred pounds within one year. We have pork in the greatest of plenty. I was employed last year in taking in pork for Phillips & Perrine. We took in upwards of eighty thousand pounds at $1.50 per hundred. I started with it about the middle of February, and took it to New Orleans. This is the second trip I have made down the long and crooked streams of the Ohio and Mississippi. I shall commence taking in pork for Phillips & Perrine on Monday next, but I rather think I shall not take it to New Orleans for them this time, unless they give me higher wages. I went for them the other trips for fifty dollars the trip, the distance by water being over one thousand five hundred miles. I was gone each trip nearly ten weeks."

Thirty-six brick buildings and thirty-four of wood were erected in town during 1828. The population was one thousand six hundred and ninety-seven. Twenty stages arrived weekly. Dr.

John Steele was president of the Town Council, and John W. Van Cleve recorder.

A meeting was called at Colonel Reid's inn on the evening of June 29, 1821, to appoint a committee to coöperate with committees in other places to raise means to pay for a survey of the route for a canal from Mad River to the Ohio, and to ascertain the practicability and expense of such a canal. Judge Crane was chairman of this meeting, and G. S. Houston secretary. The following gentlemen were appointed to collect funds to pay for the survey: H. G. Phillips, G. W. Smith, Dr. John Steele, Alexander Grimes, and J. H. Crane. The law authorizing the making of a canal from Dayton to Cincinnati passed the Legislature in 1825.

On the 4th of July, 1825, Governor De Witt Clinton, of New York, assisted at the inauguration of the Ohio Canal at Newark. At a public meeting of the citizens of Dayton, James Steele and Henry Bacon were appointed a committee to wait on the Governor at Newark and invite him to partake of a public dinner in their town. Resolutions were also adopted and preparations made for his reception. Mr. Steele returned from Newark on the evening of Wednesday, the 6th, and reported that the Governor had accepted and would be here on Saturday. A number of gentlemen of Dayton and a detachment of the troop of horse commanded by Captain Squier met the Governor at Fairfield and escorted him to town. At 2:30 P.M. Governor Clinton and his suite, Messrs. Jones and Reed, Governor Morrow, Hon. Ethan A. Brown, Hon. Joseph Vance, Messrs. Tappan and Williams, canal commissioners, and Judge Bates, civil engineer, arrived at Compton's Tavern, on the corner of Main and Second streets, where they were received by the citizens. Judge Crane made an address of welcome, which was responded to by Governor Clinton. About four o'clock the guests and citizens sat down to an elegant dinner prepared for the occasion at Reid's Inn. Judge Crane presided, and Judge Steele and Colonel Patterson acted as vice-presidents. The dinner closed with appropriate toasts. In the evening Judge Steele gave a reception to Governor Clinton at his residence, on the site of Music Hall. The house, which stood far back from Main Street, as well as the yard, was brilliantly illuminated. Governor Clinton addressed the people from the porch which ran along the Main Street side of the house. On account of his advocacy of canals, Governor Clinton had long been popular in Ohio, and many boys were named for him. His Dayton namesakes were presented to him at the reception, and to each of them he gave a silver dollar. Some of the recipients of these gifts preserved them as souvenirs as long as they lived, though a silver dollar must have burned the pocket of a boy of that period, with whom a coin or money of any kind or amount was a rare possession.

It was suggested in October, 1825, that it would be a good plan to run the canal, which need not be wider than forty feet, down the middle of Main Street, reducing the sidewalks to twelve feet, leaving a roadway thirty-four feet wide on either side of the water, and rendering Main the handsomest street in Ohio. This proposed course of the canal was for a few days marked out by a line of red flags the length of the street. It was feared that the canal would be located a mile from the Court-house, which would seriously injure the town; and it was a great relief to citizens when the commissioners located it "on the common between the sawmill race and the seminary, on St. Clair Street." The construction of the canal was at first "violently opposed as a ruinous and useless expenditure"; but as soon as the law authorizing the expenditure was passed, and before the canal was located, the rapid improvement of Dayton and the increase in population proved the wisdom and foresight of those who, since 1818, had been agitating the subject of canal improvements in the Miami Valley. One of the objections against the canal urged by opponents of the project was that it could not be made to hold water. As the bed of the canal ran through loose gravel, there seemed to be force in the objection, and, indeed, some difficulty of this kind was experienced. The bottom of the canal, however, soon "puddled," and became water-tight.

The first canal-boat built in Dayton was launched near Fifth Street on Saturday, August 16, 1828, at 2 P.M. The citizens were invited to assemble at the firing of the cannon to witness the launch. The boat was called the *Alpha*, of Dayton, and was built for McMaken & Hilton by Solomon Eversull. The *Alpha* was pronounced by many superior to any boat on the line of the Miami Canal. As the water had not yet been let into the canal, a temporary dam was built across the canal at the bluffs, and water was turned in from the sawmill tail-race at Fifth Street. Trial trips were then made from the dam to Fifth Street and back. The Dayton Guards, a military company of boys organized a few weeks before, made the first trip on the *Alpha*. Friday evening, September 26, 1828, water was first let into the canal by the contractors from the mill-race at the corner of Fifth and Wyandotte streets. In January, 1829, citizens of Dayton were gratified with the sight so long desired of the arrival of canal-boats from Cincinnati. Four arrived during the day, each welcomed by the firing of a cannon and enthusiastic cheers from the crowd assembled on the margin of the basin.

The people made a festival of the completion of the canal, which, they congratulated themselves, had begun a new era of prosperity for the town, and took every opportunity to celebrate the event. There were several excursions, and on the evening of February 5, 1829, the canal being frozen over so that navigation was impossible, Captain Archibald, of the *Governor Brown*, which was embargoed by the ice at the basin, gave a handsome collation on board to a number of ladies and gentlemen. The next evening the captains of a number of boats lying in the basin partook of a canal supper at the National Hotel, and drank a number of toasts suitable to the occasion. On the 16th of April a steam canal-boat, called the *Enterprise*, arrived here. Two cords of wood were used in the passage from Cincinnati to Dayton. For many years it was believed that steam could be used in propelling boats on the canal, but after a fair trial it was found to be impracticable. Twenty hours from Cincinnati to Dayton by canal was considered a rapid trip. Merchandise was brought here from New York by water in twenty days.

The completion of the State canal, which ended at Second Street, was soon followed by the construction of a new basin, beginning at the terminus of the original one and extending to First Street. It was constructed by the Basin Extension Company, formed by H. G. Phillips and James Steele, executors of the Cooper estate, in 1830. Its object was to draw business to the part of town through which it passed. This new basin ran down the ravine, fifteen or twenty feet deep, which extended from the head of Mill Street to the corner of Platt and Harris, thence to the corner of Second and St. Clair, and down St. Clair to Fifth. "Through this ravine the waters of Mad River, breaking through the culvert in the levee near its mouth in spite of the exertions of men working night and day to prevent it, sought, at almost every flood, a channel through which to discharge themselves into the Miami below town.

Until the extension of the Miami Canal to the north in 1841, Dayton was at the head of navigation, and supplies of every kind for this region for a long distance around were forwarded from here. A brisk trade with Fort Wayne as a distributing point was kept up, and wagon-trains were constantly passing between the two points. Swaynie's Tavern, at the head of the basin, was the favorite resort of the wagoners, and his large stable-yard was nightly crowded with wagons, and his tavern with the drivers.

In January, 1829, there were one hundred and twenty-five brick buildings in Dayton, six of stone, and two hundred and thirty-nine of wood. There were two hundred and thirty-five dwelling-houses, and Presbyterian, Methodist, and Christian brick meeting-houses. This year Timothy Squier opened the National Hotel in the building on Third Street adjoining the Beckel House. The white population of Dayton in 1829 was two thousand two hundred and seventy-two; blacks, eighty-six. There had been an increase of six hundred and sixty-one in the population during the past fourteen months. The amount of merchants' capital returned by the assessor of Montgomery County for 1829 was one hundred and twenty-nine thousand eight hundred and eleven dollars. Under a new law passed by the Legislature, the free white male freeholders over the age of twenty-one who resided in the corporation one year voted for a mayor instead of a president of Council, and one recorder and five trustees. John Folkerth was elected Mayor, David Winters recorder, and Nathaniel Wilson, James Haight, John Rench, Luther Bruen, and William Atkins, trustees. An ordinance was passed by Council dividing the town into five wards. The improvements of the town were nearly all confined to the tract bounded by the river on the north and west, Mill and Canal streets on the east, and Sixth Street on the south.

At a meeting held in 1829 the first Dayton Temperance Society was formed. William King was moderator and Dr. Haines secretary of the meeting. The following persons were appointed to prepare a constitution and an address to the public: A. Baker, Daniel Ashton, D. Winters, D. L. Burnet, John Steele, Job Haines, H. Jewett, William M. Smith, and Henry Bacon. For some time the Dayton newspapers were full of arguments for and against temperance societies.

On July 27, 1829, it was decided that the new market-house,

which the city was about to build, should be located in the alley running from Jefferson Street to Main, between Third and Fourth streets. For the purpose of widening the market-space, property costing one thousand one hundred and ninety-six dollars was purchased by Council. A small building was put up on Main Street, which was extended to Jefferson Street in 1836. All the space east of the market-house of 1829 to Jefferson Street was given up to market-wagons. The old market-house on Second Street was abandoned April 24, 1830. A bitter rivalry existed between the parts of the town divided by Third Street. People living north of Third Street appropriated the name of "Dayton" to themselves, and in derision called that part of the town lying south of that street "Cabintown." When it was proposed to remove the market from Second Street to the present location, violent opposition was made, and every measure resorted to to defeat it. Two tickets were nominated for city officers, politics were forgotten, and this was made the sole issue. Cabintown proved numerically the stronger, and the fate of the market-house was sealed. When the market-house was moved, Thomas Morrison, who had it in charge, placed a large placard on it, "Bound for Cabintown," which was read with the deepest chagrin by the people on Market [now Second] Street. So bitter was the feeling that for a long time many persons refused to attend market at the new location.

Numerous advertisements of schools taught in Dayton appear in the newspapers between 1829 and 1834. In 1829 Edmund Harrison, a competent and successful teacher, taught what he called an "Inductive Academy" in a building which he erected for the purpose. He was followed by Ira Fenn. In 1832 an accomplished woman, Miss Maria Harrison, daughter of Edmund Harrison, taught a school for young ladies. In 1831 J. J. S. Smith, afterwards an eminent member of the Dayton bar,—father of S. B. and J. McLain Smith,—taught a school in the stone building on Main Street next to the High School. To illustrate how new ideas penetrated the West, it may be stated that Dr. and Mrs. Foster, in 1829, advertised a school to be conducted on the method of Pestalozzi.

Advertisements of singing-schools and writing-schools appear frequently. The flaming advertisement of D. Easton, teacher of penmanship, recalls the day before the invention of steel pens, when no small part of the time of the teacher was spent in making and mending quill pens. He offers to teach "the round running hand, the ornamental Italian hand, the waving hand, the swift, angular running hand without ruling, and various others, both plain and ornamental."

In 1833 David Pruden invited Milo G. Williams to come to Dayton to take charge of a manual-labor school to be established in a large brick building owned by him at the junction of Jefferson and Warren streets. Shops were erected for instruction in various mechanical trades. Mr. Williams was to conduct the academic, and Mr. Pruden the labor and boarding, department. A large number of boys from Cincinnati and other places were attracted to the school by Mr. Williams's reputation as a teacher, and the school for a time enjoyed great popularity. Both the principals were actuated by philanthropic motives in their attempt to combine intellectual culture with preparation for the practical duties of life; but they were at least fifty years ahead of their times, and the school was closed from lack of pecuniary success.

In 1830 a company was formed to construct a basin connecting the canal at its intersection with Wayne Street and a point at the southern extremity of the city. Morris Seely was the main mover in this project, and great expectations were entertained in regard to it. The Supreme Court had decided that the water-power within the city limits, and furnished by the canal, belonged to the State of Ohio, a decision which was afterwards reversed, and the water-power given to the Cooper estate. It was believed that this water-power could be leased and utilized along the proposed basin. Land was bought at what was then an extravagant price, and lots laid out. These lots were small in size, and arranged for factories, warehouses, and docks, such as would be required in a large city, but were unsuited to a place with the pretensions of Dayton. The scheme proved an utter failure, and left consequences that were an annoyance to the city for years afterwards. The lots were unsalable, and the method of platting a serious detriment to that part of the town. The canal, or ditch, as it was afterwards called, bred disease, and the city authorities were called upon to fill it up. Before the controversy was finally settled, the excitement ran so high that the sawmill of Mr. E. Thresher, located on the canal at Wayne Street, which used the ditch as a tail-race, was burned. A large part of the ditch is now filled up, and the lower end used as a city drain. In connection with the basin and on its bank a pleasure-garden was opened by A. M. Peasley on Warren Street. A small pleasure-boat was run from Third Street on summer afternoons to the garden, where refreshments were provided, and it was expected that large numbers of pleasure-seekers would resort there. Like the basin, the garden was ahead of the times, and after trial of two or three years was abandoned.

In 1830 Stevenson ran the first locomotive in England over the Manchester & Liverpool Railroad. The same year a miniature locomotive and cars were exhibited in Dayton in the Methodist church. The fact that the City Council by resolution exempted the exhibition from a license fee, and that the Methodist church was used for this purpose, illustrates the deep interest felt by the public in the new and almost untried scheme to transport freight and passengers by steam over roads constructed for the purpose. A track was run around the interior of the church, and for a small fee parties were carried in the car. A large part of the then citizens of Dayton took their first railroad ride in this way.

The population of Dayton in 1830 was two thousand nine hundred and fifty-four, a gain of one thousand two hundred and thirty-seven in little more than two years. This year eighty-one houses were built. In 1831 fifty brick and seventy-two frame buildings were erected. The population was three thousand two hundred and fifty-eight. Six thousand two hundred and nineteen passengers by coach passed through town this year.

In November about two hundred and fifty Seneca Indians, men, women, and children, on their way to the reservation west of the Mississippi River, encamped at the big spring on the north side of Mad River. They were here three days, and excited great curiosity by their singular, rude, and uncivilized habits and appearance. One of the gaping crowd, who was watching them at dinner, moved off in some confusion when an Indian, at whom he was staring, looked up and said, "Indian eats just like white man; he puts the victuals in his mouth." At this period no houses had been erected on the northwest corner of First and Jefferson streets, and the lots were used for shows. The Indians took great pleasure in riding on a merry-go-round, which was a feature of the show of 1831. One afternoon a crowd of them, all intoxicated, came whooping down First Street. Not satisfied with riding, they proceeded to break the merry-go-round and fight the owner and his customers. Nothing could be done with

Rike Building. Kuhns Building. City Buildings. United Brethren Publishing House.

From a photograph by Appleton. MAIN STREET, LOOKING NORTH FROM BELOW FOURTH.

them till the agent who had command of them arrived, armed with a club, which he used freely. Their submission was so sudden and entire as to be laughable. They feared the United States Government, which the agent represented, and fled before its representative like sheep to their camp across Mad River.

The first Dayton public school was opened December 5, 1831, by Sylvanus Hall, "approved teacher," in the school-room on Jefferson Street between Water and First streets. Public money was appropriated to support it, but the amount not being sufficient, each pupil paid a dollar per quarter for tuition. Three additional rooms were soon afterwards opened in different parts of the town for the convenience of scholars.

School-directors seem at first to have been appointed at public meetings of citizens. The following served during this period: Luther Bruen, Nathaniel Wilson, Henry Van Tuyl, Thomas Brown, William Hart, James Slaght, J. H. Mitchell, David Osborn, Ralph P. Lowe, Simon Snyder, and William H. Brown. The city charter of 1841 provided for the appointment by Council of a school-manager from each ward, and Council and this board worked together harmoniously for years. The tax levy for school purposes was so small that frequently the schools could only be kept open a few months. The teachers taught private schools in the houses the remainder of the year.

Just below the mouth of Stillwater the Miami makes a bend in the form of a horseshoe, inclosing in it that part of Dayton known as Riverdale. By cutting a race across the bend, a valuable water-power is obtained. About 1829 James Steele, who owned the land, completed a dam across the Miami and the race. In 1831 he erected a sawmill and afterward a grist-mill. This water-power is now known as the Dayton View Hydraulic. In digging the race an immense tooth of a mastodon was unearthed, which was deposited as a curiosity in the Cincinnati Museum. As no other part of the skeleton was found in the vicinity, it is supposed that the tooth was brought with the drift from some other region.

General Robert C. Schenck began the practice of law in Dayton in 1831. He was a public-spirited citizen, taking an active interest in all efforts for the improvement of the town, and impressing himself upon this community long before he attained a national reputation. He devoted much time and labor to the Dayton Lyceum, Mechanics' Institute, Public Library, Woodland

Cemetery, city park, the hydraulic, turnpikes, railroads, and public schools, and frequently gave gratuitous lectures at the invitation of his townsmen.

This year the rivers were very high at Dayton, and there was much destruction of property and great distress caused by the unprecedented height of the Ohio at Cincinnati. As soon as the news reached here that the homes of many poor people at Cincinnati had been washed away, a call for a meeting at the Court-house to raise funds for the flood-sufferers was published in the Dayton newspapers. At the meeting two hundred and two dollars were raised by subscription and sent by John W. Van Cleve, Mayor of Dayton, to the Mayor of Cincinnati, "to aid in relieving the distressed people of that city."

At no time in the history of Dayton, except during the Civil War, has there been as exciting a political campaign as that of 1832, preceding the second election of General Jackson as President of the United States. So bitter was the feeling on both sides in this contest that Whigs and Democrats, though neighbors and old friends, ceased speaking to each other on the streets. Previous to Madison's administration the people of Dayton seem to have been nearly all of one mind on the subject of politics, or at any rate not intense partisans; but for a number of years after that date an election rarely passed without several fights between the members of the two parties—usually on the corner of Main and Third streets, for the Court-house was the polling-place for the whole township, in which the territory now assigned to Harrison, Mad River, and Van Buren townships was then included. Late on the night before the Presidential election in 1832, a tall hickory pole was erected on the outer edge of the pavement in front of the Court-house, and from it floated the American flag. Great was the surprise and indignation of the Whigs when this pole greeted their eyes the next morning, and great the triumph of the party which had erected it. Crowds of Whigs gathered on the corners, muttering angry imprecations. It was evident that they would not permit the hickory tree to remain standing at the polls, and as certain that the Democrats would violently resist any effort which the other party might make to remove it, and that a pitched battle would ensue if the authorities did not interfere. A meeting of Council was held early in the morning, and presently those of the citizens who had not gone home to breakfast saw the Council, headed by the marshal, John Dodson, followed by John W. Van Cleve, the gigantic Mayor, ax in hand, and Dr. John Steele and F. F. Carrell, march to the hickory tree and form a circle around it. The Mayor notified the marshal of the order of Council just passed to "cut down the pole and drag it out as a nuisance." It was the duty of the marshal to perform this perilous act.

An account of this occurrence published in the *Journal* in 1889 called out two communications on the subject from eye-witnesses. One of them says: " In the face and in defiance of an outraged and infuriated collection (not mob) of red-hot Jackson Democrats — and what that meant could hardly be appreciated by one of this cold-blooded, law-abiding generation—the worthy marshal hesitated, as well he might. A man of lofty mien and determined purpose in every movement stepped to the front, seized the ax, and, wielding it as only a stalwart Kentuckian could wield it, with a few well-served strokes brought the offensive emblem to the ground. When it fell, there was a pause; not a cheer was heard from the Whigs, and only muttered curses from the Democrats. The audacity of this brave act of Dr. John Steele, a man universally known and respected, no doubt prevented a bloody riot." Another correspondent states that the pole was cut down by Herbert S. Williams. Probably both accounts were correct, as from the size of the pole it would require a good many strokes of the ax to fell it, and more than one hand may have been employed on it.

A canal-boat arrived in Dayton December 17, 1832, with twenty-five German emigrants on board, all of whom were ill with cholera, or something similar to it. One of them had died the day before the boat reached here. They all crowded into a small room together when they landed. Seven of the Germans and the two nurses employed by the town died. A board of health had been appointed by Council in the summer, so that all sanitary precautions were taken to prevent the spread of the disease, which was prevailing in other parts of the United States. The Board of Health consisted of a member of Council and two other citizens from each ward. The following persons were appointed: First Ward, Aaron Baker and George C. Davis; Second Ward, James Steele and William Bomberger; Third Ward, H. G. Phillips and Stephen Whicher; Fourth Ward, Dr. Haines and E. W. Davies; Fifth Ward, James Mitchell and William Patterson. There were thirty-three deaths here from cholera in 1833.

During 1832 fifty-one brick and sixty-two wooden houses were erected. A silk manufactory was established in town this year by Daniel Rowe. He made sewing-silk and the warp for coarse stuffs. Some handkerchiefs were also manufactured. He advertises in June that he has two thousand Italian mulberry trees ready to pluck, and will furnish leaves, silkworm eggs, and frames for those willing to raise cocoons for him on shares. He also offers to pay the highest price for cocoons delivered at the store of Swain & Demarest, and hopes by the next year to take all that the neighborhood could produce. A number of persons planted mulberry trees at this time, and expected to engage in raising silkworms. But the factory was not a success. A silk company, with a capital of one hundred thousand dollars, was formed in 1839, but also failed.

In 1832 the Dayton Lyceum was established, the object of which was "the diffusion of knowledge and the promotion of sociability." Meetings were to be held once a week " for lectures, communications, essays, and discussions of all subjects except theology and the politics of the day." It was also proposed to collect a cabinet of antiquities and minerals, and a library. A discourse was to be delivered " at the annual meeting of the society on the 27th of August, being the anniversary of the location of the town of Dayton." For several winters the Lyceum furnished courses of lectures and debates, which were of the highest interest and afforded great enjoyment to the people of Dayton. In 1833 the library of the Lyceum was kept at the house of Ira Fenn.

In 1833 the Mechanics' Institute was organized. The first secretary was Henry L. Brown, one of the best and most useful men who ever lived in Dayton. The object of the institute was "moral, literary, and scientific improvement." A library and reading-rooms were connected with it, and for many years a course of lectures was given each winter. A public address was delivered at the Court-house July 1, 1833, by Robert C. Schenck, in behalf of the Mechanics' Institute, and during its existence every citizen of Dayton who had any ability for lecturing was called upon for that service.

At this period there must have been unusual literary interest and activity in Dayton, for there were no less than six public libraries in existence, as we learn from notices in the newspapers. None of them were large, but in the aggregate they reached a wide circle of readers.

Charles Soule, afterwards a noted portrait painter, opened a store for the sale of engravings and for framing pictures in 1833. He also carried on "his old business of sign and ornamental painting" at his shop.

The second election of General Jackson to the Presidency was celebrated in Dayton on the 8th of January, 1833, by a barbecue on the common west of the basin, now Cooper Park. National salutes were fired during the day. Immediately on the arrival at noon of a canal-boat with from fifty to one hundred citizens of Miamisburg, "a hickory tree bearing the American flag, still larger and more majestic than that which on a previous occasion left a stump" (an evident allusion to the cutting down of the Jackson pole in 1832), was erected. A large number of people from this and adjacent counties were present on this occasion. After the erection of the pole a procession was formed, in front of which walked four Revolutionary soldiers bearing liberty-caps and two members of the Dayton Hickory Club carrying an appropriate banner, who were followed by another soldier bearing the American flag. After moving through the principal streets, the procession passed into the Court-house, where an address was made and resolutions were adopted. From the Court-house they proceeded to the common, where an ox was roasted whole, of which and other refreshments all were indiscriminately invited to partake. The barbecue was followed by some "spirited sentiments," after which the procession reformed and marched to the center of town, where it dispersed. A barbecue was usually an uninviting feast. The outer part of the ox was smoked and scorched, and the remainder uncooked, though the animal was always roasted for many hours. After the feast the almost untouched carcass was hauled off by horses, surrounded by a crowd of boys and dogs, to be disposed of by hogs and hounds.

There were one thousand and one buildings in Dayton in 1833. The population was four thousand. January 3, 1834, an ordinance was passed by Council for the appointment of one or more watchmen. They were to wear uniform badges and have the same power to call on persons to assist them in arresting offenders as the marshal had. The marshal and these watchmen constituted the police of Dayton.

Plans for a covered wooden bridge over the Miami River on Main Street were advertised for on the 28th of January, 1834.

The county commissioners, on June 4, 1835, appropriated six hundred dollars toward the building-fund, and the remainder of the money was raised by subscription. The bridge was opened for travel in 1836.

The news of the death of Lafayette was received in 1834, and commemorative services were held on the 31st of August. A procession, composed of the mechanics of the town, carrying handsome banners draped in black, and representing their different occupations, the Masonic Fraternity, and the Order of Independent Odd Fellows, formed about eleven o'clock, and marched to the Presbyterian church. The exercises were opened with an impressive prayer by Rev. E. Allen, after which a beautiful and feeling ode, written for the occasion by a young lady of Dayton, was sung by the choir. Robert A. Thruston delivered "an impassioned and eloquent delineation of the talents of the deceased patriot." Then an ode, written for a similar occasion in Cincinnati by James Hall, was sung by the choir. Solemn music by the Cincinnati band accompanied the exercises, which closed with a prayer and benediction by Rev. David Winters. The committee of arrangements on this occasion was composed of the following gentlemen: Thomas Clegg, George Owen, W. L. Helfenstein, E. W. Davies, Peter Odlin, John Steele, E. Browning, R. A. Thruston, E. Brabham, James Brown, Robert C. Schenck, John Anderson, Peter Baer, and C. G. Swain.

CHAPTER IX

1836-1840

MEASURES Proposed for Improving the Town in 1836—Proceedings of Council—Public Meeting to Sustain Council—Cooper Park—Dayton Business Men in 1836—Educational Convention in 1836—Shinplasters—Thomas Morrison—Zoölogical Museum—William Jennison—First Railroad—Turnpikes—First Public-School Buildings—Opposition to Public Schools—Processions of School Children and Other Efforts to Excite an Interest in Public Schools—Samuel Forrer Takes Charge of Turnpikes—His Biography—Midnight Markets—Cooper Hydraulic—Change of Channel of Mad River—First County Fair—*Morus Multicaulis* Excitement—Dayton Carpet Manufactory—Number of Buildings Erected in 1839—*Log Cabin* Newspaper—Harrison Convention—Numbers in Attendance—Hospitality of Dayton People—Banners Presented.

IN April, 1836, Council appointed a committee, consisting of Messrs. Stone, Smith, and Winters, to effect a loan in behalf of the corporation of from one to ten thousand dollars, at a rate of interest not exceeding six per cent., and for a period of not less than five years, the interest to be paid annually. The money so obtained was to be used in improving the streets and the appearance of the town. The following proceedings of the next meeting of Council describe the proposed improvements:

"The Common Council of the town of Dayton, at their meeting April 25, 1836, passed the following resolution: That they would appropriate and spend so much money (provided a loan can be obtained) as will make the following improvements, viz.: wharfing across the head of the State basin; improving the public commons as requested by D. Z. Cooper, in consideration of his releasing a part thereof for the benefit of the corporation, provided the balance be improved immediately; to extend the market-house on center market-space to Jefferson Street; to grade the streets and walks throughout the town, and so soon as the grade is correctly ascertained, to raise and lower the walks in the different wards to the said grade; to finish the cisterns already commenced with lime cement, and to purchase five hundred more feet of hose for the Fire Department."

As there was a difference of opinion in respect to the propriety of borrowing money and making the above improvements, it was resolved, on motion of the recorder, David Winters, "that all citizens interested in the above matter be requested to meet at the Court-house Wednesday evening next at early candle-lighting, and then and there express their approbation or disapprobation of the above measure." Peter Aughinbaugh was chairman of the town meeting called by Council, and Daniel Roe secretary. Addresses were made by Messrs. Robert C. Schenck, Ralph P. Lowe, Henry Bacon, and Daniel Roe. There was some opposition to the proposed improvements on the ground that they were more for ornament than use, and that they would increase the taxes, while the advantages would be unequally distributed. Council proposed to borrow ten thousand dollars, three thousand of which were to be expended on the park and the remainder on other improvements. After a full discussion a majority of the meeting passed resolutions commending the improvements contemplated by Council and the loan by means of which they were to be accomplished. They recommended that Council should apply one-tenth of any amount to be expended during the year in filling up the ditch commonly called "Seely's Basin."

An act of the Legislature, passed February 17, 1808, empowered Daniel C. Cooper to amend the original plat of Dayton as to lots 94, 95, 96, 97, 98, 99, 100, 141, 142, 143, and then set them apart as a common for the use of the citizens. To induce the citizens to convert the "commons" into a park that would be creditable, in December, 1836, David Zeigler Cooper, son of Daniel Cooper, executed a deed authorizing the city to lease lots 94, 95, and 96, and releasing any reversionary interest that might accrue to him. It was provided in the deed that the remaining ground should be enclosed, planted with trees, and forever kept as "a walk" for "the citizens of Dayton and its visitors." It was manifestly the intention that the proceeds from the leases should be used to keep the park in perfect order. In 1838 the "public square," as the park was then called, was prepared for and planted with fine forest trees, which the *Journal* of that day says was "a fair beginning for a work which promises to be a credit, as well as an ornament, to the town."

Major Daniel W. Wheelock, the efficient and public-spirited Mayor of Dayton during 1836, 1837, and 1838, suggested many of the new improvements, and energetically hastened the completion of those begun while he was in office. A number of new buildings were erected in 1836-37. Among the most impor-

From a photograph by Appleton.

FIFTH STREET, LOOKING EAST FROM MAIN.

tant was a handsome brick Catholic church. Thomas Morrison, builder, as stated in the Dayton *Journal*, reported the number of buildings put up this year as forty-five of brick and thirty-five of frame.

It may be interesting to mention the names of some of the business men whose advertisements appear in the *Journal* at this period. Numbers of them had been doing business in Dayton for many years. M. & G. A. Hatfield, chairmakers; T. & W. Parrott, merchants; John Bidleman, boot- and shoemaker; Swain & Demarest, produce dealers; Samuel Shoup, merchant; Simon Snyder and Samuel McPherson, tanners; Thomas Casad, hatmaker; Thomas Brown, builder; Richard Green, shoemaker; J. Burns, edge-tool manufacturer; H. Best, jeweler; James, Johnson V. & Henry V. Perrine, merchants; James McDaniel, merchant tailor; Aughinbaugh & Loomis, hardware; George W. Smith & Son, merchants; Samuel Dolly, coachmaker; E. Edmondson, tanner; Jacob Stutsman, coppersmith; Conover & Kincaid, merchants; T. Barrett and R. P. Brown, booksellers and bindery; E. Helfenstein & Co., hardware; Phillips, Green & Co., merchants; C. Koerner, druggist; Henry Herrman, merchant; Rench, Harshman & Co., produce dealers; D. Z. Peirce and W. B. Stone, grocers; C. & W. F. Spining, merchants; Brown & Hoglen, grocers; Daniel Roe & Sons, druggists; Daniel Keifer, cabinet-maker; Alexander Swaynie, produce dealer; J. Greer & Co., stoves; T. & J. H. Boyer, copper and tin shop; Brown & Peirce, merchants; Van Cleve & Newell, druggists; Estabrook & Phelps, grocers; Edwin Smith & Co., druggists; Morrison & Arnold, builders; Samuel Brady, merchant; R. A. Kerfoot, saddler; Abram Darst, grocer; J. O. Shoup, merchant.

This year a daily mail from Washington—through in fifty-six hours—was established.

A memorable convention was held in Dayton in August, 1836, in the interest of free schools. A committee of arrangements was appointed consisting of E. E. Barney, R. C. Carter, R. C. Schenck, George B. Holt, and Milo G. Williams. Delegates were present from Cincinnati and seven or eight other Ohio towns, and visitors from Belleville, New Jersey, and Detroit, Michigan. Rev. E. Allen was elected president, and Daniel A. Haynes secretary. The convention remained in session three days. Able addresses were made by Rev. W. H. McGuffey, D.D., a man of remarkable ability as a speaker, and afterwards the compiler of the famous readers that bore his name, and Dr. Harrison, an eloquent and distinguished professor in the Cincinnati Medical College. The discussions took a wide range, and were participated in by some of the most distinguished educators in the State. What advanced views were held may be learned from the resolutions adopted, which favored the establishment of normal schools, that teaching might become a profession; the introduction in the schools of the studies of geology and physiology; and the publication of a periodical to be called the *Teachers' Magazine*. The convention was fully reported in the Dayton *Journal*. The editors, R. N. and W. F. Comly, warmly and ably advocated the cause of public schools, and freely opened the columns of the *Journal* to the discussion of the subject.

The wild speculations which preceded and culminated in 1837 resulted in a complete prostration of business, from which the country did not recover for many years. The failure of many banks, and the suspension of specie payments by the others, made money, and especially silver change, excessively scarce. As a substitute for small coin, "shinplasters," or promises to pay fifty, twenty-five, or ten cents on demand, printed on ordinary paper, were issued by merchants, grocers, and others. Thomas Morrison, who was an extensive owner of real estate, which was a basis for credit, issued a large amount of these "shinplasters." It was so easy and tempting to issue money which was current to be redeemed in the future, that it is not surprising that an amount was put out much beyond the original intention. When the time came for redemption, the following advertisement in the *Journal* of June 26, 1838, shows the unpleasant position in which Mr. Morrison was placed:

"PUBLIC NOTICE—SHINPLASTERS IN DANGER.

"FELLOW-CITIZENS: I am compelled to leave town to fulfill a contract that I have undertaken—that is, to build a mill at the falls of Greenville Creek for G. W. Smith. I leave Dayton at this time with regret, because the law prohibiting the circulation of small notes or shinplasters is soon to take effect, and I wish to satisfy my fellow-citizens that I am not the man under any circumstances to take advantage of that law, by which the State allows me to act the rascal. No; it is vain to try to induce me to do so. I intend to redeem every note I have put in circulation, and that as soon as I return, and will do it with pleasure and satisfaction. I desire my fellow-citizens and all who have confidence in my word of honor — and I trust there are some who believe I will do as I say — not to refuse to take them till my return, when every cent shall be paid, with the addition of six per cent. interest for every day the notes are left unredeemed after the 1st of July. On my return I will give public notice, so that the holders of my notes may call. It has been an unprofitable business, but it shall end honestly."

In the end Mr. Morrison redeemed in full all the "shinplasters" he issued. Mr. Morrison came to Dayton at an early day, and was for many years the leading contractor and builder of the town. His son, David H. Morrison, a skillful civil engineer and founder of the Columbia Bridge Works, married Harriet, the daughter of Robert J. Skinner, the pioneer newspaper publisher and editor. Mary Morrison married Dr. M. Garst, and Maria, Daniel Garst.

A number of citizens assembled on the 16th of September at the Court-house for the purpose of establishing a zoölogical museum. A committee, consisting of John W. Van Cleve, Dr. John Steele, William Jennison, and Thomas Brown, was appointed to ascertain whether a suitable room could be obtained, and funds for paying for it secured. A room was procured at the head of the basin, but the place was unsuitable and not attractive. The idea of establishing a public museum would not have suggested itself to the citizens of Dayton at that early date but for the presence here of a very accomplished naturalist, William Jennison, who had been for a number of years engaged in such work in Germany, and being connected with foreign societies of naturalists, would be able to procure from abroad almost any specimens desired, merely by applying for them and paying the cost of transportation. He had a number of birds prepared by himself in the best manner, and handsomely arranged in glass cases; and also hundreds of insects classified and arranged in scientific order, and affording, by the variety of size and color, a most beautiful sight, though "the poor fellows were impaled with pins." All these he offered to place in a public museum, and to devote part of his time to the work of increasing the collection. But the project was soon abandoned, and he removed his birds and butterflies to his residence, — then a short distance out of town, but now on Linden Avenue, within the corporation, — where he had a garden and greenhouse, in which he raised fine flowers for sale. He was an object of curiosity to the people when he went out, net in hand, to collect butterflies for his cabinet and natural-history specimens to exchange with his friends across the Atlantic. Mr. Jennison was an elegant and accomplished man, with the courtly manner of a gentleman of the old *régime*. He spoke English perfectly, which was probably due to the fact that his mother was an Englishwoman of rank, whom his father, Count Jennison, of Heidelberg, had married while minister of the Kingdom of Würtemberg to the Court of St. James. Washington Irving, in a letter published in the second volume of his biography, gives an interesting account of a visit which he paid in 1822 to Count Jennison and his amiable and agreeable family. He describes the Count as an elegant and hospitable and highly cultivated man, who spoke English as perfectly as an Englishman.

A meeting was held on the evening of the 18th of November, 1837, at the Court-house for the purpose of exciting an interest in the Mad River & Lake Erie Railroad Company, incorporated in 1832 and organized in 1834. Since the election of officers of the company nothing further had been done. Jonathan Harshman, Robert C. Schenck, and Peter Odlin took a prominent part in the meeting, and resolutions were passed urging the raising of stock and the speedy commencement of the road. The law affording State aid to railroads had recently been passed by the Ohio Legislature.

An act was passed on the 24th of March, 1836, by the Legislature "to authorize a loan of credit by the State of Ohio to railroad companies, and to authorize subscriptions by the State to the capital stock of turnpike, canal, and slack-water navigation companies." Dayton was one of the first towns to take advantage of the provisions of the act guaranteeing the aid of the State to works of this description, and before the repeal of the law in 1840 it had been the means of putting in the course of construction five turnpikes, the aggregate length of the five roads being one hundred and forty miles, and other turnpikes were in contemplation. To the abundance of gravel, which made the construction of turnpikes cheap and easy, are due our excellent turnpikes leading in every direction to the neighboring towns. By 1850 Dayton had fourteen turnpikes.

The subscription books of the Dayton & Springfield Company were opened January 19, 1838, and the contract made on the 12th of May. This turnpike, to induce travel through Dayton, was built in the same style as the National Road, especially at its junction with the latter, and with similar bridges, stone culverts, toll-gates, and mile-stones. Comfortable brick taverns were erected a few miles apart along the pike. It was a great disappointment to the people of Dayton that the National Road did not pass through here. Strenuous efforts were made to induce Congress to locate the road through Dayton, and, having failed, equally strenuous efforts were made to have the route changed. Many familiar names occur in connection with the turnpikes —Peter Odlin, R. C. Schenck, Horace Pease, H. G. Phillips, Joseph Barnett, Thomas Brown, Thomas Dover, J. W. Van Cleve, J. H. Crane, Jonathan Harshman, John Kneisley, V. Winters, Abram Darst, and David Z. Peirce.

On May 7, 1838, a public meeting was called at the Court-house to discuss the erection of public school-houses, and how much money should be raised by taxation for the purpose. Strenuous opposition was made to the levy of the tax by a few wealthy citizens; but, after a heated discussion, the measure was carried by a large majority. The amount to be raised was six thousand dollars, and two school-houses—one in the eastern and one in the western part of the town—were to be built. The opposition did not end with the meeting. It was believed that it could not be proved that the law had been complied with in giving notice of the meeting. This had been anticipated by Mr. E. E. Barney, who had taken the precaution to post the notices in person, and, accompanied by a friend, had visited them from time to time to see that they were not removed. The houses—considered models in that day—were built. The majority of the children attended private schools, and all sorts of efforts were made by enlightened citizens to increase the popularity of the public schools.

On the Fourth of July, 1838, Mr. Elder's school paraded on Main Street, escorted by the Blues and Grays,—the militia companies of the town,—and then gave a concert at the Methodist church. At a public meeting in 1839 it was resolved that the Fourth of July should be celebrated by a procession of the public, private, and Sunday schools of the town, with exercises at Cooper Park and a picnic-dinner for the children. Children and teachers marched on one side of the street, and parents and citizens on the other. In 1856 the school year closed with a procession and picnic across the river. The City Council and School Board headed the procession. Each school carried a beautiful silk banner.

Two brass bands enlivened the procession. At the grove there were declamations and songs, an address by the president of the board, and delivery of diplomas to High School graduates. In 1859 there was a similar procession and picnic.

In 1839 Mr. Samuel Forrer, at the earnest solicitation of the directors, consented to take charge of the turnpikes as engineer and general superintendent. The roads placed under his supervision were the Dayton & Lebanon, Dayton & Springfield, and the Great Miami turnpikes. The Ohio Legislature, for partisan reasons, had just excluded Mr. Forrer from the Canal Board, thus depriving the State of a faithful and competent officer. But as Dayton could now secure the constant aid of his invaluable talents and experience in the various public improvements in which the citizens were interested, and which, although of a local character, deeply concerned a large proportion of the people, there were some among us, the *Journal* says, selfish enough not to regret the change. For some years the county commissioners have had the supervision of the turnpikes. The toll-gates, which used to be encountered every few miles along the road, have been abolished by a law permitting the purchase of the pikes by the county from the companies.

Samuel Forrer was reappointed in the spring of 1837, by the Board of Public Works, principal engineer on the lines of the Wabash and Erie and Miami canals. This appointment, as the proper administration of the canal involved the prosperity of Dayton, was a matter of rejoicing here. A number of Dayton young men went out with Mr. Forrer to learn civil engineering. Howe's "Historical Collections of Ohio" contains, in the chapter on "Pioneer Engineers of Ohio," by Colonel Charles Whittlesey, the following interesting biographical sketch of Mr. Forrer:

"No engineer in Ohio spent as many years in the service of the State as did Mr. Forrer. He came from Pennsylvania in 1818, and in 1819 was deputy surveyor of Hamilton County, Ohio. In 1820 Mr. William Steele, a very enterprising citizen of Cincinnati, Ohio, employed Mr. Forrer at his own expense to ascertain the elevation of the Sandusky and Scioto summit above Lake Erie. His report was sent to the Legislature by Governor Brown. This was the favorite route [for the Erie Canal], the shortest, lowest summit, and passed through a very rich country. The great question was a supply of water. It would have been located, and in fact was in part, when in the summer and fall of 1823 it was found by Judge D. S. Bates to be wholly inadequate. Of twenty-three engineers and assistants eight died of local diseases within six years. Mr. Forrer was the only one able to keep the field permanently and use the instruments in 1823. When Judge Bates needed their only level, Mr. Forrer invented and constructed one that would now be a curiosity among engineers. He named it the Pioneer. It was in form of a round bar of wrought iron, with a cross like a capital T. The top of the letter was a flat bar welded at right angles, to which a telescope was made fast by solder, on which was a spirit-level. There was a projection drawn out from the cross-bar at right angles to it, which rested upon a circular plate of the tripod. By means of thumb-screws and reversals, the round bar acting as a pendulum, a rude horizontal plane was obtained, which was of value at short range.

"Mr. Forrer was not quite medium height, but well formed and very active. He was a cheerful and pleasant companion. Judge Bates and the canal commissioners relied upon his skill under their instructions to test the water question in 1823. He ran a line for a feeder from the Sandusky summit westerly and north of the watershed, taking up the waters of the Auglaize and heads of the Miami. Even with the addition the supply was inadequate. Until his death in 1874 Mr. Forrer was nearly all the time in the employ of the State as engineer, canal commissioner, or member of the Board of Public Works. He was not only popular, but scrupulously honest and industrious. His life-long friends regarded his death as a personal loss greater than that of a faithful public officer. He was too unobtrusive to make personal enemies, not neglecting his duties, as a citizen zealous but just. He died at Dayton, Ohio, at 10 A.M., March 25, 1874, from the exhaustion of his physical powers, without pain. Like his life he passed away in peace at the age of eighty, his mind clear and conscious of the approaching end."

In the winter of 1838 the experiment was tried of having market on Monday, Wednesday, and Friday afternoons, and in the early morning on the other three days. But the people soon returned to what Curwen calls "our midnight markets," the bell ringing at four o'clock in the depth of winter, and the people hurrying at the first tap to the market-house, as a short delay would deprive them of their favorite cut of meat or first choice of vegetables and force them to fill their baskets with rejected articles. As in New York two hundred years ago, "such was the strife among the thrifty townsfolk to be on hand at the opening of the market, and thereby get the pick of the goods, that long before noon the bulk of the business was done." This custom of market before daybreak, in spite of its discomfort, continued for many years.

In spite of the hard times, Dayton was prosperous in 1838. The following improvements were made that year: Council expended about six thousand dollars in improving and beautifying the town; the streets and pavements were graveled, guttered, and macadamized for the first time, though the work had been begun three years before; eighty-nine buildings, fifty-six of brick and thirty-three of frame, were erected, and more would have been put up if it had been possible to obtain sufficient brick and timber. The principal buildings erected were two brick district school-houses, the first that were built in Dayton, and the Third Street Presbyterian Church. This was also of brick, seventy-two by fifty-two feet in size, "of approved architectural beauty," and cost fifteen thousand dollars. The dwellings in town were all occupied to their fullest capacity, and there were none for rent or for sale.

The most valuable improvement made this year was the Cooper Hydraulic, constructed by Edward W. Davies and Alexander Grimes, agents of the Cooper estate. "It is an enterprise," said the *Journal*, "for the projection and completion of which all who have the prosperity of Dayton at heart will cheerfully accord to the gentlemen above named due credit for their public spirit." The hydraulic was seven hundred feet long and fifty feet wide, with twelve feet head, and was built between Third and Fifth streets, west of Wyandotte Street. "A bend in Mad River at the northeast corner of the town extended south from the aqueduct to First Street, and along that street, crossing what is now Keowee and Meigs Street, thence in a northwest direction, crossing Taylor Street south of Monument Avenue, and on and across Monument Avenue to and uniting with the Miami River at a point about four hundred feet south of the present mouth of Mad River." In 1840 Mr. Davies and Mr. Grimes, as a further improvement to the Cooper estate, "caused a survey to be made for a new channel for Mad River from the

From a photograph by Bowersox.

YOUNG MEN'S CHRISTIAN ASSOCIATION BUILDING.

aqueduct straight to the Miami River." It was finished in the winter of 1842. Originally a bayou extended up Mad River from the Miami to Keowee Street.

Dayton Township was divided March 12, 1839, into two election precincts, the first precinct voting at the Court-house and the second at Houk's Tavern on Market Street.

The Montgomery County Agricultural Society had been organized September 11, 1838, with Colonel Henry Protzman president, and Charles Anderson secretary. The first Montgomery County Agricultural Fair was held in Dayton at Swaynie's Hotel, at the head of the basin, October 17 and 18, 1839. At eleven in the morning on the 17th a procession of about three hundred persons interested in the society marched, headed by a band of music, through the principal streets to the hotel, where the anniversary address was delivered by D. A. Haynes. The display of horses, cattle, and farm products was fine. The committee on silk, Daniel Roe, C. S. Bryant, John Edgar, Peter Aughinbaugh, Charles G. Swain, W. B. Stone, and R. N. Comly, awarded a premium, a silver cup worth ten dollars, for the greatest amount of silk produced from the smallest number of *multicaulis* leaves. Other valuable premiums were awarded by the society, but the cup was offered by members of the Silk Company.

The mention of the *Morus multicaulis* tree recalls to memory one of those strange manias that occasionally sweep over the country. The tree had recently been introduced from China, was of rapid growth, and furnished abundant food for silkworms. It was believed that the cultivation of this tree, and the use of its leaves to feed silkworms, would make the United States the great silk-producing country of the world. The most extravagant price was paid for young trees, and thousands of acres were planted. Wide-spread ruin was the result, and hundreds of persons lost their all in this wild speculation.

Swaynie's Hotel, where the first Montgomery County Agricultural Fair was held, was finished in April, 1839. It was considered a first-class house, and regarded with pride by the people of Dayton. All the carpets in the hotel were manufactured by the Dayton Carpet Company, and were of such superior texture, designs, and colors that guests of the house could with difficulty be convinced that they were made west of the Alleghany Mountains. The Dayton carpets were sold in the stores at Cincinnati and other Western towns as imported carpets, and purchasers did not discover the deception.

The number of buildings erected in Dayton in 1839, as counted by Thomas Morrison, was one hundred and sixty-four of brick, thirty-six of wood, and twenty-six intended for business houses. A new First Presbyterian Church took the place of the old one built in 1817. A Baptist church was also built on the corner of Fourth and Jefferson streets, forty by sixty feet in size and seventy-five feet in height. The front presented a very neat specimen of the Grecian Doric architecture. The cost of the whole, including the lot, was six thousand dollars. A number of improvements were made along the hydraulic. Mr. Thomas Brown, after particular inquiry made at the request of the *Journal*, reported that four million five hundred thousand bricks were made in Dayton during 1839. The number on hand he computed at five hundred thousand, which gave four millions as the number of bricks laid during the year.

In February, 1839, the prospectus of the *Log Cabin* newspaper, published in Dayton by R. N. and W. F. Comly, appeared. The *Log Cabin* was continued during the Harrison campaign, and after enough subscribers were obtained to pay expenses, was gratuitously distributed as a campaign document. A large picture of a log cabin, with a barrel of hard cider at the door, occupied the first page of the paper. The illustrations were drawn and engraved by John W. Van Cleve. The price of the paper was fifty cents for thirteen numbers. Two files of the *Log Cabin*, which attained a national reputation, are on the shelves of the Dayton Public Library.

The population of Dayton was now six thousand and sixty-four.

Never in the history of the Northwest has there been a more exciting Presidential campaign than that which preceded the election of General W. H. Harrison, and nowhere was the enthusiasm for the hero of Tippecanoe greater than in Dayton. A remarkable Harrison convention was held here on the date of Perry's victory on Lake Erie, and tradition has preserved such extravagant accounts of the number present, the beauty of the emblems and decorations displayed, and the hospitality of the citizens and neighboring farmers, that the following prophecy with which the *Journal* began its account of the celebration may almost be said to have been literally fulfilled: "Memorable and ever to be remembered as is the glorious triumph achieved by the immortal Perry on the 10th of September, 1813, scarcely less conspicuous on the page of history will stand the noble commemoration of the event which has just passed before us." Innumerable flags and Tippecanoe banners were stretched across the streets from roofs of stores and factories, or floated from private residences and from poles and trees. People began to arrive several days before the convention, and on the 9th crowds of carriages, wagons, and horsemen streamed into town. About six o'clock the Cincinnati delegation came in by the Centerville road. They were escorted from the edge of town by the Dayton Grays, Butler Guards, Dayton military band, and a number of citizens in carriages and on horseback. The procession of delegates was headed by eleven stage-coaches in line, with banners and music, followed by a long line of wagons and carriages. Each coach was enthusiastically cheered as it passed the crowds which thronged the streets, and the cheers were responded to by occupants of the coaches. Twelve canal-boats full of men arrived on the 10th, and every road which led to town poured in its thousands early in the morning.

General Harrison came as far as Jonathan Harshman's, five miles from town, on the 9th and passed the night there. Early in the morning his escort, which had been encamped at Fairview, marched to Mr. Harshman's and halted there till seven o'clock, when it got in motion under command of Joseph Barnett, of Dayton, and other marshals from Clark County. A procession from town, five miles long, under direction of Charles Anderson, chief marshal, met the General and his escort at the junction of the Troy and Springfield roads. The battalion of militia, commanded by Captain Bomberger, of the Dayton Grays, and consisting of the Grays and Washington Artillery, of Dayton; the Citizens' Guards, from Cincinnati; Butler Guards, of Hamilton, and Piqua Light Infantry, were formed in a hollow square, and General Harrison, mounted on a white horse, his staff, and Governor Metcalf and staff, of Kentucky, were placed in the center. "Every foot of the road between town and the place where General Harrison was to meet the Dayton escort was literally choked up with people."

The immense procession, carrying banners and flags, and accompanied by canoes, log cabins furnished in pioneer style, and trappers' lodges, all on wheels, and filled with men, girls, and boys, the latter dressed in hunting-shirts and blue caps, made a magnificent display. One of the wagons contained a live wolf enveloped in a sheepskin, representing the "hypocritical professions" of the opponents of the Whigs. All sorts of designs were carried by the delegations. One of the most striking was an immense ball, representing the Harrison States, which was rolled through the streets. The length of the procession was about two miles. Carriages were usually three abreast, and there were more than one thousand in line. The day was bright and beautiful, and the wildest enthusiasm swayed the mighty mass of people who formed the most imposing part of "this grandest spectacle of time," as Colonel Todd, an eye-witness, termed the procession. The following description of the scene, quoted by Curwen from a contemporary newspaper, partakes of the excitement and extravagance of the occasion:

"The huzzas from gray-headed patriots, as the banners borne in the procession passed their dwellings, or the balconies where they had stationed themselves; the smiles and blessings and waving kerchiefs of the thousands of fair women, who filled the front windows of every house; the loud and heartfelt acknowledgments of their marked courtesy and generous hospitality by the different delegations, sometimes rising the same instant from the whole line; the glimpses at every turn of the eye of the fluttering folds of some one or more of the six hundred and forty-four flags which displayed their glorious stars and stripes from the tops of the principal houses of every street, the soul-stirring music, the smiling heavens, the ever-gleaming banners, the emblems and mottoes, added to the intensity of the excitement. Every eminence, housetop, and window was thronged with eager spectators, whose acclamations seemed to rend the heavens. Second Street at that time led through a prairie, and the bystanders, by a metaphor, the sublimity of which few but Westerners can appreciate, likened the excitement around them to a mighty sea of fire sweeping over its surface, 'gathering, and heaving, and rolling upwards, and yet higher, till its flames licked the stars and fired the whole heavens.'"

After marching through the principal streets the procession was disbanded by General Harrison at the National Hotel on Third Street. At one o'clock the procession was reformed and moved to the stand erected for the speeches "upon a spacious plain" east of Front Street and north of Third. Mr. Samuel

Forrer, an experienced civil engineer, made an estimate of the space occupied by this meeting and of the number present at it. He says: "An exact measurement of the lines gave for one side of the square (oblong) one hundred and thirty yards and the other one hundred and fifty yards, including an area of nineteen thousand five hundred square yards, which, multiplied by four, would give seventy-eight thousand. Let no one who was present be startled at this result or reject this estimate till he compares the data assumed with the facts presented to his own view while on the ground. It is easy for any one to satisfy himself that six, or even a greater number of individuals, may stand on a square yard of ground. Four is the number assumed in the present instance; the area measured is less than four and one-half acres. Every farmer who noticed the ground could readily perceive that a much larger space was covered with people, though not so closely as that portion measured. All will admit that an oblong square of one hundred and thirty yards by one hundred and fifty did not at any time during the first hour include near all that were on the east side of the canal. The time of observation was the commencement of General Harrison's speech. Before making this particular estimate I had made one by comparing this assemblage with my recollection of the 25th of February convention at Columbus, and came to the conclusion that it was at least four times as great as that." Two other competent engineers measured the ground, and the lowest estimate of the number of people at the meeting was seventy-eight thousand, and as thousands were still in town it was estimated that as many as one hundred thousand were here on the 10th of September.

Places of entertainment were assigned delegates by the committee appointed for that purpose, but it was also announced in the *Journal* that no one need hesitate "to enter any house for dinner where he may see a flag flying. Every Whig's latchstring will be out, and the flag will signify as much to all who are a hungry or athirst." A public table, where dinner was furnished, as at the private houses, without charge, was also announced as follows by the *Journal:* "We wish to give our visitors log-cabin fare and plenty of it, and we want our friends in the country to help us." A committee was appointed to take charge of the baskets of the farmers, who responded liberally to this appeal.

In early times, when hotel and boarding-house accommodations in Dayton were very limited, it was the custom, whenever there was a political or religious convention, or any other large public meeting here, for the citizens to freely entertain the delegates at their homes. At night straw-beds were laid in rows, a narrow path between each row, on the floors of rooms and halls in both stories of dwellings, and in this way accommodation was furnished for many guests. The making of the ticks for these beds before the days of sewing-machines, required many days of labor, often principally done by the hostess. As late as 1853, when the first State fair was held in Dayton, public-spirited citizens who could afford the expense exercised this generous but somewhat primitive hospitality. When a meeting was of a religious character, the different denominations assisted in entertaining the guests. During the 1840 convention the hot dinner, which was served if possible on such occasions, was supplemented by large quantities of cold roast and boiled meats, poultry, cakes, pies, and bread that had been prepared beforehand. A few wealthy housekeepers employed men cooks and other additional assistance during the convention. But there were no caterers or confectioners in those days, and good domestic help was rare, so that a great part of the labor of preparing for their hungry crowd of guests was performed by Dayton ladies with their own hands.

All the houses in Dayton occupied by Whigs were crowded to their fullest capacity during the Harrison convention, and again at the Clay convention in 1842. One family, according to a letter from its mistress written at the time, entertained three hundred persons at dinner one day in 1842, and the same night lodged nearly one hundred guests. Thirty Kentuckians left that afternoon, or there would have been over one hundred lodgers. The writer states that the houses of all her friends and relatives were as crowded as her own, and says that this lavish hospitality was a repetition of what occurred in 1840. The letter contains an interesting description of a morning reception for ladies during the convention of 1842 at the residence of Mr. J. D. Phillips, where Mr. Clay was staying. A crowd of women of all ranks and conditions—some in silk and some in calico—were present. Mr. Clay shook hands with them all, afterwards making a complimentary little speech, saying, among other graceful things, that the soft touch of the ladies' hands had healed his fingers, bruised by the rough grasp of the men, whom he had received the day before.

Among other interesting occurrences during the Harrison convention was the presentation, on the 9th of September, of a beautiful banner to the Tippecanoe Club of the town by the married ladies of Dayton. The banner was accompanied by an eloquent address written for the occasion by Mrs. D. K. Este, and was presented in the name of the ladies to the club, who were drawn up in front of the residence of Mr. J. D. Phillips, by Judge J. H. Crane. It was decorated on one side with an embroidered wreath, with a view of General Harrison's house in the center, and on the other side with a painting of Perry's victory on Lake Erie, executed by Charles Soule "with the skill and taste for which he is so distinguished."

On the 11th of September the young ladies of Dayton presented a banner, wrought by their own hands, to General Harrison. Daniel A. Haynes made the presentation speech. The convention was addressed by many noted men. General Harrison was a forcible speaker, and his voice, while not sonorous, was clear and penetrating, and reached the utmost limits of the immense crowd. Governor Metcalfe, of Kentucky, was a favorite with the people. A stonemason in early life, he was called "Stone-Hammer" to indicate the crushing blows inflicted by his logic and his sarcasm. The inimitable Thomas Corwin held his audience spellbound with his eloquence and humor, and R. C. Schenck added greatly to his reputation by his incisive and witty speeches. Joseph H. Crane, R. S. Hart, and other Daytonians spoke.

PROTESTANT DEACONESS HOSPITAL.

From a photograph by Wolfe.

Dayton From 1840 to 1896

CHAPTER X

DAYTON FROM 1840 TO 1896

THE Beginning of "the Forties"—Distinguished Visitors—Schools—Oregon—West Dayton—Banks—Police Department—New Jail and Court-House—Cemeteries—Dayton Bar—General Robert C. Schenck—Clement L. Vallandigham—Thomas Brown—Prominent Physicians—Public Library—Churches—Floods—Cholera—The Mexican War—First Telegraph Message—Gas and Electric Light—Railroads—Street-Railroads—Fire Department—Water-Works—Dayton Orphan Asylum—Young Men's Christian Association—Woman's Christian Association—Young Women's League—St. Elizabeth Hospital—Protestant Deaconess Hospital—Musical Societies—Literary Clubs—Improvements—Manufacturing and Mercantile Interests—Natural Gas—Newspapers—Periodicals—David Stout—Ebenezer Thresher—Valentine Winters—Frederick Gebhart—Robert W. Steele.

By the beginning of "the forties" many of the toilers who had made the early history of Dayton slept in the little green graveyard on Fifth Street. There were a few left—old men and women who told the fireside tales, or watched with quiet wonder the enterprises of the new generation, treading with careful steps the newly made streets and pavements, or venturing out on the smooth roads, with bridges, toll-gates, and taverns, that were being built in all directions.

This bright, hospitable little town seems to have had some distinguished visitors. In 1842 it was enlivened by another convention and honored by the presence of the great Clay. Again all were made welcome. Receptions, banquets, banner presentations, and speeches were the order of the day. In the autumn of 1843 John Quincy Adams passed through Dayton on his way to Cincinnati.

The early settlers had ever been anxious to secure for their children the advantages of civilization which they had willingly abandoned for themselves, and now the public schools, under the care of a faithful board of directors, were getting a foothold in spite of hard times, for in 1842 four schools were opened,—two in houses built for them in 1837 and two in rented rooms,—but were thriftily closed before the end of the second quarter to avoid debt; and it was not until 1849 that the full school year was reached. But there was no lack of fine private schools. Milo G. Williams took charge of the Dayton Academy in 1844, and taught there until 1850; and in 1845 Cooper Female Seminary was opened, in charge of E. E. Barney, and at once became known throughout Ohio, by reason of the strong personality, magnetism, and culture of Mr. Barney, as an attractive and scholarly institution—qualities which also distinguished it under the management of Miss Cox, whose name is held in thankful remembrance by many of the brightest women of Dayton and other Ohio cities.

The Roman Catholic Church in 1847 added St. Joseph's to its parochial schools, and in 1849 St. Mary's Institute.

In the spring of 1850 the Central High School of Dayton was opened. In the fall it was located in the old academy building, where it remained until 1857, when a new building was put up for it on the same ground—on the southwest corner of Fourth and Wilkinson streets, where the Central District School now stands. James Campbell, who was afterwards superintendent of schools, and who was a dear lover of books, served as principal for eight years. Miss Mary G. Dickson, upon whom much practical work must have fallen; James Turpin, whose name stood for music in Dayton; and, later, dear old Jean Bartholomew, genial, easy, and far from a fiery Frenchman, completed the first short list of teachers, whose names, "like a waft from the gracious spring," take back to youth many staid and sober men and women of to-day. Since then the roll of teachers and pupils has lengthened and the curriculum broadened, but the same spirit of zeal, energy, and enthusiasm rules in the new High School building, occupied since 1892, and named in honor of one of the best friends of the schools—Robert W. Steele. The new building is situated on the southeast corner of Main Street and Monument Avenue, and is one of the finest in the country, having cost over a quarter of a million dollars.

A normal school was opened in the autumn of 1869 for the higher education and training of teachers. The free night schools were established in 1877. A manual-training school was opened January 2, 1896, in the Central District School building.

There are now nineteen district schools, with twenty-nine buildings conveniently located in the various parts of the city. Many of these buildings are large, handsome in appearance, and well equipped with modern improvements.

In 1845 Dayton began to spread itself. That part of the city called "Oregon" was platted; also, about the same time, the part lying west, between Wolf Creek and the Germantown pike, which was called "Miami City," now "West Dayton." The common from 1845 to 1855 was the unenclosed ground west of Ludlow Street to the river and south of the old graveyard.

The warfare of President Andrew Jackson upon the United States Bank and the refusal of the Ohio Legislature to renew its charter compelled the closing, on the 27th day of January, 1843, of one of the soundest banks in the country—the old Dayton Bank. Dayton remained without banking facilities for more than two years. In 1845 two strong, conservative banks were started—the Dayton Bank and the Bank of Dayton. Fifty years of fair business prosperity, with the advantages of the banking law of 1863, have since given us a number of reliable and successful banks.

In 1841 an ordinance was passed providing that for the protection of the city two constables should be elected each year in addition to the marshal and deputy. It would seem that Dayton was once a very good little city, but in 1850 sixty men were added to this body. That Dayton, as a certain small boy said of himself, "grew bigger and bigger and badder and badder," is indicated by the organization in 1873 of the metropolitan police force, with a chief, two lieutenants, twenty-six patrolmen, three roundsmen, and three turnkeys, the arrangement being similar to that now in force. The city had no prison before 1858, its few offenders being confined in the county jail. Then an old engine-house on Main Street, between Fifth and Sixth, was fitted with cells and so used. In 1872 the United Brethren church, near the corner of Sixth and Logan streets, was bought and remodeled for a city prison. In 1875 the county commissioners vacated the stone jail on Main Street, and it has since then been used as a work-house.

The old Court-house, on the northwest corner of Main and Third streets, was completed in 1850. "An exceptionally fine reproduction of Grecian architecture, it was at the time of its erection the finest building in the State, and is still regarded as one of the notable buildings of the city." The new Court-house on Main Street, north of the old one, was completed in 1884.

It was decided in the spring of 1869 that a new jail was needed for the county. It was placed west of the Court-house, on Third Street, and completed in February, 1874.

John W. Van Cleve, of whom a biographical sketch has been given in a previous chapter, had a very tender feeling for this corner of the earth, which his father had helped to hew out of the wilderness. He was one of those who "call every bush my cousin." Original in character, odd in appearance, the jolly band of children who followed his burly figure through many holiday excursions grew wiser, happier, and healthier. Men and women found in him an intelligent, cultivated, and agreeable companion, and a very true and loyal friend. As a citizen he was advanced, enterprising, and of unbending integrity. As previously stated, to him more than to any other we are indebted for our beautiful Woodland Cemetery. He made the suggestion of a rural cemetery, and from the organization of the Woodland Cemetery Association, in 1842, to the time of his death, in 1858, served as its president and gave to its affairs an amount of labor and watchful supervision which money could not have purchased. In June, 1843, the cemetery was opened, being the third rural cemetery of any importance established in the United States. Robert W. Steele became the president upon the death of Mr. Van Cleve, and served with the same unselfish sagacity until his death in 1891. Since the death of Mr. Steele, Jonathan H. Winters has been the president of the association.

The ground for St. Henry's Cemetery was purchased by Archbishop Purcell and used as a burial-place by the Roman Catholics until 1872, when land was purchased for Calvary Cemetery, two and a half miles south of the city, on a commanding bluff, with a wide outlook over the neighboring hills, valleys, and river.

The Hebrew Congregation purchased an acre on Brown Street in 1851, which is no longer in use, a new cemetery having been located near Calvary on the bluffs.

The first member of the Dayton bar, Judge Crane, with his well-trained mind, legal learning, courteous and commanding bearing, simple life, and kind and helpful friendliness, had unconsciously done much to mold the character and ambitions of the young lawyers who were his companions and successors, so that the spirit of integrity came to be a characteristic of the early Dayton bar. Of the members of this early bar, Charles Anderson became Governor of Ohio, four were judges, two members of Congress, and ten members of the Ohio Legislature. Among the later members Judge Haynes is perhaps the oldest and most respected. John A. McMahon, who represented the

Third Ohio District in Congress for three terms, and Lewis B. Gunckel, who served in Congress and other political capacities, and whose services in connection with the location of the Soldiers' Home in Dayton and its management are especially appreciated, stand at the head of the profession at present.

If "the baton of a marechal is hidden in every soldier's knapsack," there must have been much in the saddle-bags which young Robert C. Schenck brought to Dayton in 1831 of which even he had no knowledge, for his musings as he followed the narrow trail through the quiet wood were only of the fortune he must make and of how he would some day write his name beside those of Crane, Holt, Anderson, and Thruston. The youth was not ill equipped—with a nature which time showed to be strong and deep, unlimited energy, a brain full of wit, and a mind original and logical, stored and trained by six years at Oxford, Ohio, where he had graduated first in his class, and in the office of one of the most distinguished legal practitioners of Ohio—Thomas Corwin, of Lebanon. The saddle-bags contained one very tangible treasure in the sealed letter from Mr. Corwin to Judge Crane—the "open sesame" to needed opportunity, for when the Judge had read it and taken a keen, quiet look at the slim, pale-faced, pale-haired young man, he invited him to become his partner. So, instead of waiting and hoping for a client, he had for the next three years the care of one of the largest practices in Ohio, Judge Crane having been called to Washington soon after.

In politics Mr. Schenck was an ardent Whig. He was a captivating speaker, and did yeoman service in the Harrison campaign. In 1841 he was elected to the Ohio Legislature, from which he and other Whig members resigned in order to defeat the Democratic "gerrymander bill." The next year he was returned to the Legislature. In 1843 Mr. Schenck was elected to represent this district in Congress, where he spent eight active years and was ranked among the foremost men of his party. In 1851 he was appointed United States Minister to Brazil. Having performed some important diplomatic services, he returned to Dayton in 1856.

Robert C. Schenck was said by Lincoln to have been the first man who in a public address named him for the Presidency.

When "with a voice that shook the land, the guns of Sumter spoke," Mr. Schenck offered his services to the Government and was made a brigadier-general. He commanded a brigade at the battle of Bull Run, and did good service by his "gallantry in action and coolness and discretion in retreat." In the second battle of Bull Run he was shot in the wrist while urging his men on with uplifted sword. While suffering from this wound he received the commission of major-general. Still unfit for active service, he was given command of the Middle District, where he filled a difficult place with sagacity and skill. Being again elected to Congress in his old Third District, in 1863, he resigned his commission in the army. It has been said that "a history of the course of General Schenck in the Thirty-ninth and Fortieth Congresses would be a complete history of the military legislation of the country through the most eventful years of the War to its close."

Appointed by General Grant Minister to Great Britain in 1871, he represented the United States at the Court of St. James for five years. During this period he was also a member of the Joint High Commission providing for the Geneva Conference. And to the zeal and ability, tact and experience, of Robert C. Schenck America is very much indebted for that peaceful settlement. This was the crowning achievement in the life of the old statesman.

General Schenck was ever a fearless fighter, and while he was a man with many loyal friends, his extremely frank and caustic speech had made bitter enemies, who were able to darken somewhat, by annoying and unfounded charges, the last days of a man who had for more than forty years put the interests of his country before his own, and used in her service talents and energies which, applied to his chosen profession, would undoubtedly have brought him fortune, friends, and fame.

It seems well to tell the story of General Schenck's life at some length, not because it is full of interest, as it is,—not because he served his country well, as he did,—but because he belonged to Dayton—was her most distinguished citizen: his fame was hers; he loved the place, cast his first and last vote at her polls, and now sleeps on one of her sunny hillsides with the companions of his youth.

To the older men of Dayton there are few names that bring more stirring memories than that of Clement L. Vallandigham, who came to Dayton in 1847,—a lawyer by profession, by instinct a politician. He had the qualities of his ancestors,—Scotch-Irish and Huguenot,—ability, courage, ambition, and dogged determination, qualities which, after a series of defeats, gave him a

From a photograph by Appleton.

FIRST PRESBYTERIAN CHURCH.

From a photograph by Appleton.

THIRD STREET PRESBYTERIAN CHURCH.

seat in the Congress of 1856, and kept him there until 1862. Vallandigham's opposition to the War was so radical, his principles so boldly declared, his influence in his party so great, as to induce his arrest by the Government in May, 1863, his trial by a military commission, and banishment to the South. In June of the next year he ran the blockade from Wilmington to Bermuda, and from there to Canada, where he remained at Windsor until the following spring. While there he was nominated by acclamation Democratic candidate for Governor of Ohio, and defeated by John Brough, of which Senator Sherman has just said, "I have always regarded Brough's election in Ohio upon the issue distinctly made, not only as to the prosecution of the War, but in support of the most vigorous measures to conduct it, as having an important influence in favor of the Union cause equal to that of any battle of the War." In June, 1864, Mr. Vallandigham returned to his home in Dayton, where he was received by an immense crowd of sympathetic and enthusiastic friends. From this time he was again a familiar and striking figure at Democratic meetings and conventions. In May, 1871, he presented to the convention in Dayton his "New Departure" resolutions. Soon after, he delivered the last and probably most powerful speech of his life. Mr. Vallandigham formed a law-partnership in 1870 with Judge Haynes. In June of the following year he was leading attorney for the defense in an important murder trial at Lebanon. While demonstrating his theory in regard to the alleged murder, he accidentally shot himself, and died the next morning. Then once again the name of Vallandigham brought together a great concourse of people. This time they followed him quietly, and left him sadly in the peace which comes to all—under the sod.

Among the portraits in the large history of Dayton, Ohio, published in 1889, is one with the trembling, unsteady signature of an old man—"Thomas Brown." Life was still attractive and full of interest to this bright-eyed, active, helpful, genial old man when the angel of death led him gently over the threshold into the promised land one day in May, 1894. Mr. Brown had been one of Dayton's best citizens since 1828. "A man of public spirit, fully up with the times, and always at the front in all public enterprises," he was a Christian and a gentleman of the old school. Born in 1800, Mr. Brown had seen the century from the beginning almost to the end.

In 1840 the medical profession was represented in Dayton by such old-school gentlemen and positive characters as Dr. John Steele, Dr. Job Haines, and Drs. Hibberd and Adams Jewett. Later came many others, among them Dr. Clarke McDermont, who served the soldiers with heart and hand; Dr. Armor, and Dr. John Davis. Of the charter members of the Montgomery County Medical Society, organized in 1849, only two survive— Dr. Carey, lovingly remembered by many friends and patients here, now a citizen of Indianapolis, and Dr. J. C. Reeve, whose keen, sensitive, scholarly face is still a familiar one among us.

Perhaps, among the many who spend long summer hours under the trees in Cooper Park, idly watching the little crowd that passes along the sun-flecked walk, and in and out of the open door of the Library, there are a few who wonder what it is— this strange hunger for books, not knowing it was that which made the beautiful building possible, and stored it with treasures to which all are made welcome; for it is a very common instinct among those who love books to pass their blessings on. This feeling led to the establishment of libraries and lyceums, and to the organization in 1847 of the Dayton Library Association, which soon started on a pleasant and useful career, with an opening list of a thousand books. In a little town of scarcely twenty thousand people a library association was a luxury that must be paid for with work and self-denial. The cheerful givers were called upon again and again, while other friends labored earnestly with tongue and pen, that the good work might go on. The money which had been gathered by taxation for school library purposes was used in Dayton for a central library, which started in 1855 with one thousand two hundred and fifty carefully selected books free to all. In 1860 it was determined that the public interest would be best served by the union of the two libraries; so the Library Association transferred its valuable library and furniture to the Board of Education. The united books, the cheerful room, an ever-ready librarian, and the prosperity of an assured income, combined then to make the Dayton Public Library the object of pride, pleasure, and profit to the citizens of Dayton which it is now. In 1888 the library was removed to the stone, fireproof building in Cooper Park—one of the finest in the West— which it now occupies; and in its commodious quarters, with more than thirty-five thousand catalogued books, and a well-equipped museum, it is the center of attraction for a large number of citizens.

Dayton has never been lacking in churches. In 1842 Dr. Barnes was preaching in the First Presbyterian Church, the second that had been built on the corner of Second and Ludlow streets, where a handsome stone one now stands. The Third Street Presbyterians built a brick church on the corner of Third and Ludlow streets in 1842, which they occupied until it was torn down to make way for the present handsome stone structure. The town clock which many remember on the old Second Presbyterian steeple, was purchased and first placed on the tower of Wesley Chapel in 1851. The First Baptist Church had finished an edifice on the corner of Jefferson and Fourth streets, where they remained until the removal to their present quarters on Main Street. Christ Episcopal Church, on Jefferson Street, was then almost ten years old, and was not abandoned until 1874, when a new one was completed on First Street. The First United Brethren Church was organized in 1847 in a small room in the Oregon Engine-House. Their first church building was erected in 1852 on Sixth Street near Logan, and served the congregation until 1873, when the lot on Fifth Street between Main and Jefferson was bought, on which their church now stands. The Methodists, who were among the earliest settlers of Dayton, had already outgrown two churches when a new brick one was erected on Third Street in 1849. In 1866 more room was needed by the congregation, and a lot on the corner of Fourth and Ludlow streets was purchased and a new building dedicated in 1870. The First Reformed Church had finished their building on Ludlow between Second and Third streets in 1840. The First English Lutherans built their first house of worship on the southwest corner of Fourth and Jefferson streets in 1841. Their present church building was erected in 1860, and dedicated in January, 1861. The first Hebrew congregation was organized in 1850. They met in the old Dayton Bank building until 1863, when they purchased the old Baptist church. Since then a handsome synagogue has been built on Jefferson between First and Second streets. The first Roman Catholic family came to Dayton in 1831. By 1837 the Franklin Street church was built, and in 1873 a very large new one just east of the old site was dedicated. The first church for colored people was organized in 1842. From these various beginnings have sprung many churches and missions, until now, looking down from the surrounding hills, nothing is more striking than the number of slender spires in the once little town below that has come to be called the "City of Churches."

Dayton was much terrified and incommoded by the flood of 1847. Some money was lost, but no lives. The heavy rainstorms of September, 1866, again produced a flood, which cost, in losses to individuals and public property, no less than two hundred and fifty thousand dollars. After this disaster the waterway was broadened and the bridges lengthened. Another general flood occurred in February, 1883, and an extraordinarily heavy storm visited the city in 1886.

In the summer of 1849, by a cholera epidemic Dayton lost more than two hundred of her people.

For the first half century Dayton, like a happy young mother, kept her children close about her; but the modern restless feeling began to come. Some talked of the gold of California, and took the long and toilsome trip as if it were a journey to Fairyland. Some talked of politics and some of war. Blaine says, "There was not in the whole country a single citizen of intelligence who was indifferent to Clay or Jackson." A little later the men of Dayton were watching the battles of the political giants with the same eager interest. Some had been captivated by the "Fifty-four forty, or fight" campaign cry. Others would have left that question to time. Some were for the annexation of Texas and the acquisition of Mexican territory. Others felt that a war with Mexico would have no excuse of justice or necessity. Yet when the election of Mr. Polk gave an unquestionable verdict in favor of annexation, and when on May 13, 1846, war with Mexico was formally declared, the citizens of Dayton sprang forward to defend the country, and Dayton became a rallying-point for the enlistment of soldiers. The militia of the county, organized as the First Brigade, commanded by Brigadier-General Adam Speice, was attached to the Tenth Division of Ohio Militia. Public meetings were held and offices opened for recruiting.

On the 20th of May the First Brigade of the Tenth Division was ordered to assemble at Dayton with a view to immediate organization for service. As the numbers of the companies were not quite full, the National Guard, Captain Hormell, began recruiting on the 26th at their armory; the Dayton Dragoons, changed to Dayton Riflemen, Captain Giddings, at McCann's store. The Riflemen and National Guard were the first to start for Camp

From a photograph by Appleton.

GRACE METHODIST EPISCOPAL CHURCH.

From a photograph by Appleton.

CHURCH OF THE SACRED HEART.

Washington, the rendezvous for Ohio volunteers. They boarded the canal-boats, amid music and cheering, just at sunset on the 4th of June. It is safe to say that the most of Dayton watched the slow boats towed off and the bright new banners vanish in the distance. There were sad hearts, of course; but many also who were eager to follow. So by June 9 another company was ready to leave, but could not be accepted by the Government, too many men having already volunteered for the necessities of the service. By August the three Ohio regiments were beside the Rio Grande, and later took a brave part in the battle of Monterey. Eight Dayton men were lost in this battle.

In 1847 the Fifteenth Regiment of regulars was raised to serve during the war. In one of the companies there were twenty-two Dayton men. Edward A. King was appointed captain of this company, which left Dayton on the 24th of April, 1847, a great crowd watching its departure also. The time of the first two companies having expired, they were mustered out of service at New Orleans June 11 and 12. Company B reached Dayton on the 26th with a tattered flag and but forty men; Company C, a few days later. The people turned out from town and country — five thousand of them — and waited at the foot of Main Street with the militia, music, and guns until the slow little canal-boats brought them back. In response to the next call for troops the "Dayton German Grenadiers" were raised, Captain John Werner. These were with Scott at Contreras, Churubusco, Chapultepec, and the city of Mexico. In July, 1848, they returned with only thirty-six men. Peace was proclaimed by President Polk July 4, 1848. The military spirit seems to have lingered in Dayton long after the end of the war, and was kept up by reviews, sham-battles, and parades. The largest of these demonstrations was in 1858, when Governor Chase reviewed the Ohio troops at Dayton.

The first telegraph message was received in Dayton September 17, 1847. In the next few years other lines were built, which have since been consolidated, until now there are but two offices in the city.

The population of Dayton in 1848 was fourteen thousand.

Houses were first lighted by gas in 1849, but street lights came a little later. At present the city is well supplied with both gas and electric light.

Curwen says, in 1850: "Dayton is on the natural route of the great chain of railroads that are destined at an early date to connect the extreme West with the Atlantic cities. The completion of the several lines of railroads now in process of construction and contemplated will afford a continuous chain from St. Louis to all the great commercial cities of the East. What has been done may be briefly stated. The Lake Erie & Mad River Railroad [from Dayton to Sandusky] terminates here. Over this road there passed last year over one hundred and eight thousand people. The Dayton & Western Railroad [from Dayton to Richmond, Indiana] when completed will be one of the best roads in the country. The road from Dayton to Greenville will be in operation early in 1851." It is safe to say that Mr. Curwen's predictions have been amply fulfilled. Dayton now has eleven railroads, which form parts of four great systems. The period of which Curwen writes was also one of great prosperity for the canals, which showed little diminution for the next ten years.

The first street-railroad was chartered in 1869, as the "Dayton Street Railroad," though generally known as the "Third Street Railroad." Others followed rapidly until in 1896 there are few parts of the city not reached by street-cars. Electricity has taken the place of horse-power on all but one road.

After a discussion of several years the volunteer fire department in Dayton was succeeded by a paid force, and the first steam fire-engine was purchased in 1863. Dayton now has one of the most efficient and best-equipped fire departments in the country.

At the spring election of 1869 the question was put to the people whether water-works should be erected, and was answered in the affirmative. On April 1, 1870, the water-works committee made a report to Council to the effect that the machinery and fixtures placed in position were in successful operation, and up to and over the standard guaranteed by the company; from which time Dayton has been one of the most fortunate cities in her unfailing supply of pure, cold water.

The Dayton Female Orphans' Association was incorporated in 1844. The first home, a small brick building on Magnolia Street, was used until the erection of the new one across the Miami River. In 1867 the commissioners of Montgomery County determined to take charge of the Dayton Orphan Asylum. A new home was built in Harrison Township and opened in 1867. The number of children taken care of averages of late years about a hundred.

The Dayton Young Men's Christian Association had its origin in a great religious revival in 1869 and 1870, the object of the association being "the physical, intellectual, social, and spiritual improvement of young men." The first home of the association was on the second floor of the *Journal* building, north of the Court-house. In the spring of 1875 funds were raised, and the old Dunlevy residence, on Fourth Street, bought, remodeled, furnished, and occupied within a single month. A fine gymnasium was opened in 1885, which only demonstrated the need of greater facilities. In 1886 fifty-five thousand dollars were contributed towards a new building, which was at once begun, and dedicated in the following year. The property is now valued at over one hundred thousand dollars, and the value of the work done for young men is inestimable.

The Woman's Christian Association was organized in 1870. Encouraged by the success of the young men's association, and hoping to work in unison with them, their work has been crowned with even greater success than could have been hoped. The work is of varied character. A widows' home is sustained, and a woman's exchange operated. There are many committees for visiting the Soldiers' Home, the hospitals, the jail, and for missionary work. The day and night classes and lunches for working girls have been among the modern and successful experiments. The old Winters homestead on Third Street was bought in 1891, and now forms the attractive and convenient home of the society.

The Young Women's League, organized in 1895, has a large membership — principally of working women — and a comfortable club-house, on Jefferson Street, south of Fifth.

St. Elizabeth Hospital was started on Franklin Street, near Ludlow, in 1878, in a very modest way by two Sisters of the Poor of St. Francis. They soon found that there was a broad field for their work. More room was needed. The Sisters selected six acres of land in Browntown, which were purchased, and the corner-stone laid in 1881 for a large building. There, supported by voluntary contributions, they are quietly doing a noble work.

The Protestant Deaconess Society of Dayton was organized in August, 1890. At first two or three deaconesses from Cincinnati nursed in private families. In October, 1891, a temporary hospital was opened on Fourth Street near St. Clair, under the direction of the society. Its usefulness proved that such a hospital, home, and training-school for nurses was needed for the growing city. On Sunday, October 14, 1894, a new building was dedicated. It was built on the ground of the old Widows' Home, which had been bought and donated for the purpose by Mrs. J. H. Winters. Crowning an eminence overlooking the city, it stands "a stately and massive edifice, built for a noble cause and dedicated to it." "Behold," says Mr. Simonds, the president of the society, "how great a matter a little fire kindleth."

The Dayton Philharmonic Society was organized in 1874, and has achieved a decided success. The Mozart Musical and Literary Society was organized in 1888. There are also the Harmonia, the Young Men's Christian Association Orchestra, Maennerchor, and other musical societies.

The Woman's Literary Club of Dayton was organized in 1889. It has a limited membership, meets in the Woman's Christian Association parlors, and has been a pronounced success from the first day. A number of other woman's clubs have since been formed — the "H.H." Club, organized in 1891, the Friday Afternoon and Emerson clubs of more recent date.

The Present Day Club, formed in January, 1895, is an organization composed of about three hundred representative men, who spend an evening every two weeks during the greater part of the year in the discussion of important topics relating to social, literary, educational, religious, economic, and other problems.

In 1885 Professor J. A. Robert began the improvement of the land along the western levee, and, by filling and protecting it from the river by a fine wall, has added a beautiful street to the city from Monument Avenue to Fifth Street, finished in July, 1887.

On the 22d of October, 1892, the Columbian Centennial was appropriately celebrated in Dayton by an immense procession of military and civil societies, school-children, and industrial exhibits, followed by appropriate addresses and music in Cooper Park.

The manufacturing interests of Dayton have long been prominent. There has been a steady and substantial growth in the number and size of manufacturing establishments, until in 1894, according to the report of the State Labor Statistician, the city ranked as the third in the State in number of industries, capital invested, and wages paid, and fourth in the value of its manu-

From a photograph by Wolfe.

SYNAGOGUE OF THE JESHURUN CONGREGATION.

From a photograph by Wolfe.

Chapel. Office.

factured products. Many of its establishments are very large, some employing from one to two thousand persons, and a number of them are known in almost every part of the globe.

The stores, banks, building-associations, insurance companies, and other branches of trade conduct a large amount of business, and rank high in the commercial world.

Within the last few years a complete sewer system has been projected and largely finished, and the principal streets of the city have been handsomely paved with asphalt, brick, sandstone, and granite; and many of the residence streets have been parked by narrowing the roadway and making lawns along the borders of the sidewalks. These improvements, together with the large number of shade-trees which abound in the city, make the streets very attractive.

In 1889 natural gas was introduced in Dayton for fuel purposes. Although not sufficiently plenty to supply many factories, it has proved a great convenience to housekeepers.

Dayton, since the earliest days, has seldom been left for any length of time without a newspaper. The *Journal* was descended from a long line of plucky ventures. It was a Republican paper, ably conducted after 1835 by the Comlys. It had been a weekly and a triweekly, and in 1847 became a daily, and as such has continued to the present day, with a short interregnum after the burning of the office, presses, and materials by a mob in May, 1863. Soon after this Major William D. Bickham took charge of and made the *Journal* into a paper of national reputation. Mr. Bickham was a bold and brilliant writer, an astute and enthusiastic politician, a man whose death, in 1894, left a vacancy in political and newspaper circles difficult to fill. The *Journal* is now conducted by the sons of Mr. Bickham.

In 1842 the Democratic party in Dayton was represented by the *Western Empire*. Some years later the *Daily Empire* was published irregularly, finally becoming a regular evening paper. It was continued until 1863, when the editor was arrested and the paper suppressed because of an article which it published in regard to the arrest of Vallandigham. A new paper was soon started, and has continued to the present day under the titles of *Daily Ledger, Herald, Herald and Empire, Democrat,* and *Times.*

The *News* is an afternoon daily issued from the same office as the *Times.*

The *Volks-Zeitung*, started in 1866, has always been an independent paper.

The *Daily Herald* was started in 1879 as an independent journal.

The *Press*, first issued in 1891, is a Republican afternoon paper.

Including the above, there are published in the city seventeen secular and thirty-two religious periodicals, making a total of forty-nine periodical publications.

Among the men whose active business life made them well known in the years preceding and following the War were several who should be mentioned at length in the history of these periods. The eldest of these was David Stout, who came to Dayton in 1812. He was a native of Pennsylvania, and was seventeen years old when he became a citizen of the growing town. He soon engaged in business for himself, and for nearly half a century was actively interested in various lines of business, being the first man in the city to engage in the sale of stoves. He was at one time a member of the Town Council, for twenty years treasurer of the town and of the School Board, a director of the Cooper Cotton Factory and Dayton Carpet Company, one of the organizers of the first public light company, treasurer of the Dayton Gas Light and Coke Company, and a stockholder in the Woodland Cemetery Association. On the corner where the Atlas Hotel now stands he built one of the first brick residences in Dayton, which remained unaltered until 1892. In 1839 he moved into his new home on the northeast corner of Second and Perry streets, where he dispensed a liberal hospitality during the Harrison convention in 1840, and in 1842, at the Henry Clay convention, entertained one hundred and eight guests over night and many more at dinner. David Stout was remarkable for his kindness and benevolence to individuals. He had eight children and numerous descendants, many of whom now live in the city. Three of the children are now living and reside in Dayton — Elias R., Atlas L., and David Orion.

Another pioneer in prominent business enterprises of the city, when once it began to extend its operations, was Mr. Ebenezer Thresher, one of the first manufacturers of agricultural implements and of railroad cars. Mr. Thresher had been born and brought up in Connecticut, receiving an extended education and entering the ministry in New England. Failing health compelled him to relinquish other plans, and led him in 1845 to come west to engage in business. With Mr. E. E. Barney and Mr. Packard, he organized in 1849 the firm of Thresher, Packard & Company, manufacturers of agricultural machinery, and soon after of railroad cars. This was the beginning of the great "Car Works" which have helped to make Dayton known throughout the world. In 1854 Mr. Thresher retired, founding later his varnish business. During the remainder of his long life, which continued till 1886, he was prominent in religious and educational circles, especially in the enterprises of the Baptist Church, of which he had always been an influential member. Two sons and two daughters are still residents of the city.

Much of the history of banking in Dayton centers around the name of Mr. Valentine Winters. Mr. Winters came to Dayton from Germantown in 1825, and was employed in the dry-goods store of Andrew Irwin, and later with Harshman & Rench, in which firm he soon became a partner. He was prominent in the commercial circles of Dayton for a half-century, conducting at first a dry-goods and general merchandise store, and afterward engaging in banking. He was cashier of the Dayton Bank, organized in 1845, and afterward was one of the proprietors in the banks of Harshman, Winters & Company, V. Winters & Son, and the Winters National Bank. Mr. Winters was a member of the first board of directors of the Dayton & Western Railroad, and with his partners, Jonathan Harshman and E. F. Drake, constructed the first railroad in Minnesota, connecting St. Paul and Minneapolis. In 1839 he was foreman of the Safety Engine and Hose Company. In the War of the Rebellion he was a loyal supporter of the Government, and gave the assistance of his bank to the support of the finances of the State and Nation. Mr. Winters was a member of the Third Street Presbyterian Church, and gave liberally to the Young Men's Christian Association and Woman's Christian Association. In 1829 he married Catharine Harshman, a daughter of Jonathan Harshman, and had eleven children,—four sons and seven daughters, —a number of whom, with their descendants, still live in the city.

Another figure well known on our streets for nearly forty years was Mr. Frederick Gebhart. Mr. Gebhart came to Dayton from Pennsylvania in 1838, being then forty years of age. He was soon after followed by his brothers Herman and George, whose business interests were closely allied to their brother's. In 1839

Mr. Gebhart opened a dry-goods store, removing a little later to the building on Third Street so long occupied by his successors, D. L. Rike & Company. After a number of years he entered the linseed oil business, and until his death in 1878 was interested in enterprises which would add to the prestige of the city. The descendants of these three brothers form one of the large and influential families of the city.

No history of Dayton would be complete that had not much to say of Robert W. Steele. Quiet student though he was, he touched the life of the place on every side, for he was a lover of men and of books, of his country and home. He was born in 1819 to a life of ease and all honorable traditions. He was the son of an earnest, self-reliant pioneer, who had been a merchant, a soldier when needed, trustee of the Presbyterian Church, of Miami University, and of the Dayton Academy, one of the founders of Woodland Cemetery, president of the Dayton Bank for nearly forty years, a judge for fourteen years, one of those chosen to cast the electoral vote of Ohio for Clay, and who had died in the midst of a busy, active career. This was the example which the past gave to the young man who was met at the threshold of manhood by the knowledge that such a life could not be his. He was prohibited by his physician from continuing the study of law. If he could not practice his profession, could not do his own work as he had planned, "Very well," he said to himself quietly and bravely, "I shall help others to do theirs"; and this, I take it, was the key-note to his life—he was a helper.

"Whoever thou art whose need is great,
In the name of the all-compassionate and merciful One I wait."

Men and women went to the quiet study where he loved to sit, with books climbing the walls around him, and usually came away comforted. The teachers learned to come,—the pupils, too,—for he was a member of the Board of Education for thirty years, and its president for twelve of them. He was one of the founders of the Library Association, and for years director and president. When the association was united with the Public Library, he was chairman of the Library Committee until he resigned in 1875. Later he became a member of the reorganized Library Board, and served until his death. His love for books was the enthusiasm of his life. The feeling that other men put into business and professions he lavished upon these quiet friends. He knew a good book by instinct, was a fine critic, and a writer himself, having done considerable work for newspapers, and published numerous essays, and histories of the library, cemetery, public schools, and early Dayton.

He was member and treasurer or president of every horticultural society of Dayton, as well as the Ohio State Board of Agriculture. He was interested in the early railroads centering in Dayton, and a subscriber to the stock of all of them but one.

When the War of the Rebellion came, he felt deeply. Loving his country as he did, he served it well. If he could not fight himself, he could help the soldiers in a hundred ways; he could care for the wives and children at home, and uphold the Government through the darkest days. He served on the Military Committee of Montgomery County, was a member of the Sanitary Committee, and chairman of a Citizens' Committee.

No reform or change for the better in his native city ever lacked the hearty sympathy and cordial support of Robert Steele. He was an elder in the Third Street Presbyterian Church for forty years. He was secretary of the Woodland Cemetery Association, and its president when he died. He served five years as a member of the State Board of Charities.

When death laid its touch on that kindly heart to still it, and men sorrowed to know they should meet that quaint figure no more; when he lay asleep in the dear old home his father had built, and was carried over its threshold to the Woodland they had both tended and cared for,—who could say now which of the two men had done more for humanity?

CHAPTER XI

DAYTON IN THE CIVIL WAR

THE Opening of the War—Fall of Sumter—Recruiting—Dayton Light Guards—Light Artillery—Lafayette Guards—Departure of Troops—Anderson Guards—Dayton Riflemen—Zouave Rangers—Buckeye Guard—State Guard—Camp Corwin—Camp Dayton—Families of Soldiers Cared For—Advancing Kirby Smith—R. C. Schenck Elected to Congress—Union League Formed—Arrest of Vallandigham—*Journal* Office Burned—Morgan's Raid—Colonel King—*Empire* Office Mobbed—Procession of Wood-Wagons—Women's Work for the Soldiers—The Home-Guard—Return of Companies A and E—Another Call for Troops—Last Draft of the War—Lee's Surrender—Assassination of Lincoln—Admiral Schenck—Rear-Admiral Greer—Paymaster McDaniel—National Military Home—Soldiers' Monument.

THE War of the Rebellion did not come upon the country like a sudden summer shower. The great clouds gathered slowly, and hung dark and menacing long before the storm broke. There were enough men of both parties in Dayton who had accepted the decision of the people in the election of Mr. Lincoln to make it a city sternly loyal and practically helpful to the Government, yet there were also many firm in their devotion to States' rights and bitter in their opposition to the war; and the Third Ohio District was represented by a man who had proclaimed as his position that "if any one or more of the States of the Union should at any time secede, for reasons of the sufficiency and justice of which before God and the great tribunal of history they alone may judge, much as I should deplore it, I never would, as a Representative in Congress, vote one dollar of money whereby one drop of American blood should be shed in a civil war." So there was a season of suspense; the people waited with bated breath; men eyed one another with grave distrust. With Southern confidence at its height, and Northern courage at its lowest point, Mr. Lincoln began his journey to Washington. The people, waiting for a sign, watched the quiet progress, read the tender words to the South, the strong and temperate inaugural, and of the refusal to recognize the Southern commissioners. They also read events, and began to see the patience and self-control, the grand courage and wisdom, of their leader, who, as is now clear, "came as one appointed to a great duty, not with rashness, not with weakness, not with bravado, nor shrinking, but in the perfect confidence of a just cause, and with the stainless conscience of a good man."

When Sumter fell, the excitement in Dayton was painful in its intensity. The people were full of just wrath, and eager to avenge the insult to the flag. If there was a citizen who had not heard the news, he read it in the morning paper with the proclamation calling for seventy-five thousand men beside it. Recruiting was begun at once. Four days later three companies were starting for Columbus—the Dayton Light Guards, Captain Pease; Light Artillery, Captain Childs, and the Lafayette Guards, Captain Deister, marching to the train through great, cheering crowds, anxious to show that for once all were united to defend the country. The men who had been loyal by reason of intelligence, judgment, and expediency experienced a new feeling as the hot wave of enthusiasm swept over the land. On the 18th of April Colonel E. A. King was appointed to take charge of the camp at Columbus. On the same day the Anderson Guards opened recruiting lists. By the next night sixty-four men had enrolled and the company organized and left the next morning. The streets were crowded with people, singing "The Star-Spangled Banner," cheering and waving handkerchiefs and flags; and it must be confessed there were tears among the women as they took up their heavy task of watching and waiting and working. The men filed out of the armory through the shouting crowd, and soon another hundred had gone, making almost five hundred men (four hundred and eighty-five) in answer to the first call for three months' volunteers.

Upon their arrival at Columbus, the first three Dayton companies were assigned to the First Regiment Ohio Volunteer Infantry. This regiment was ordered and started to Washington April 19, had its first fight at Vienna, and covered itself with glory at Bull Run. The Dayton Riflemen and Anderson Guards were ordered to Camp Jackson, and later assigned to the Eleventh Ohio Volunteer Infantry and sent to help construct Camp Dennison, where they were kept drilling for six or seven weeks.

In June Company A (the Riflemen) reënlisted for three years. Part of Company G reënlisted and part returned to Dayton.

These were busy, unselfish days for those at home. The doctors offered their services free to families of volunteers, and the druggists offered to fill prescriptions without charge. The sum of five thousand dollars was quickly raised for immediate wants. The Board of County Commissioners and the City Council each appropriated ten thousand dollars for the soldiers' families. Other large sums of money were constantly coming in. All sorts of donations were made. The ladies' societies went to work with a will. No one was too old or too young to work in some way.

The Zouave Rangers tendered their services as a home-guard, were accepted, and served for three months. The Buckeye Guard was in camp at Hamilton for a few weeks, came back to fill up their regiment for three years' service, and returned within ten days. Captain Gunckel raised a company, which was ordered to Camp Dennison May 19. On the 22d of April, at Harrisburg, Lieutenant A. McD. McCook, of the Regular Army, was elected colonel of the First Ohio Regiment, E. A. Parrott lieutenant-colonel, and Captain J. S. Hughes major. On the evening of May 11 the people were listening to the farewell concert of the Regimental Band, who were to be thereafter musicians of the First Ohio Regiment.

Immediately after the departure of the three months' troops in April, militia companies were formed. Each ward had its company of home-guards. There was also the State Guard, composed of men over forty-five years of age.

Through the summer of 1861 Dayton was full of soldiers. Little else was thought of. Camp Corwin was located two and a half miles east of the city. On the 23d of August the first three companies of the First Ohio,—Dayton men,—and a little later the Dayton Cavalry, were ordered there. On August 20 a company marched in from the northern part of the county and camped in the Fair Grounds. In October the Government gave notice that it could not furnish blankets for the First Ohio. In a week they had been provided by the citizens of Dayton and the regiment was on its way to join General McCook's brigade and Camp Corwin was abandoned. During the month of August there were fourteen recruiting offices opened in Dayton. By the 29th of the month Dayton had sent one thousand two hundred and sixty-nine men to the front, out of an enrollment of three thousand one hundred and seventeen.

GENERAL ROBERT C. SCHENCK.

It is not possible in a few pages to follow all the Dayton soldiers through the war. Wherever brave men were needed they went gladly, and saw their share of service in Kentucky, Tennessee, and later on in the Shenandoah Valley and mountains of Virginia, with Grant before Richmond, with Thomas at Nashville, and marching through Georgia with Sherman.

The year 1862 was a dark one for the national cause. Recruiting for the Ninety-third began in July of that year. In it were four Dayton companies. Charles Anderson became the colonel and Hiram Strong lieutenant-colonel. Great interest was felt in this regiment in Dayton. Ten thousand dollars were raised at one meeting of the citizens in July as a fund for the families of volunteers. The rendezvous for the Ninety-third was Camp Dayton, afterwards located at the Fair Grounds. The regiment was ordered to Lexington, Kentucky, and left Dayton August 23. In September the camp rapidly filled up, and it was again necessary to supply the soldiers with blankets and clothing. There were also at that time five hundred families of volunteers dependent partly or entirely upon the public for means of support.

The advance of Kirby Smith towards Cincinnati thoroughly aroused Dayton. The Governor called out the militia of the river counties. All armed men who could be in readiness by the 4th of September would be accepted by General Wallace. Dayton was urged to send to Cincinnati by that day every man who could get away. In answer to these appeals, each ward raised at least one company for the defense of the State. Men came from all parts of the State, with all kinds of arms, and in all sorts of dress, so that they were called the "Squirrel-Hunters." Kirby Smith retreated southward, and these soldiers never knew what they *might* have done. One effect of this rush of citizen soldiers to the front was the postponement of the draft which had been ordered, first to the middle of September, then to the 1st of October, by which time Dayton had been able to fill up her quota.

The next excitement was over the election to Congress of General Robert C. Schenck from the Third Ohio District.

A Union League was formed in Dayton in March, 1863. Much had been done in Dayton since the war began for the support of the families of the soldiers. All sorts of entertainments were given and money was raised in every possible way. The various ladies' aid societies did noble work through the winters of 1862 and 1863. In April, 1863, there was an immense procession into Dayton of farm wagons loaded with wood and provisions brought by the farmers as their donation to the relief committee for the soldiers' families.

On the 5th of May, 1863, Mr. Vallandigham was arrested by order of General Burnside and taken to Cincinnati to be tried by a military commission for violation of "General Order No. 38," in which occurred this statement: "The habit of declaring sympathy for the enemy will no longer be tolerated in this department. Persons committing such offenses will at once be arrested with a view to being tried as above stated, or sent beyond our lines into the lines of their friends. It must be distinctly understood that treason, expressed or implied, will not be tolerated in this department." The arrest of Mr. Vallandigham ensued, and it was followed the next night by the burning of the *Journal* office by a mob. Dayton was at once placed under martial law by order of General Burnside, and remained so until the 21st of June.

Each ward of the city was divided on the 9th of July into three districts, each of which was obliged to organize a company of militia.

If there was a man in Dayton who had not felt a personal interest in the war, he must have come to his senses when told on July 13 that General Morgan was within a day's march of the city. Martial law was at once proclaimed by the Mayor. All of the original militia was called out by the Governor and ordered to Camp Dennison. Dayton sent two companies. Major Keith started at midnight for Hamilton with two companies of infantry. Such other citizens as had horses and guns organized as scouts to patrol the roads. The six months' cavalry recruits went in pursuit of and captured fifteen of the raiders. The men at home threw out pickets and patroled the surrounding country. As it happened, Morgan's men did not come near Dayton until the 27th of the month, when six car-loads of them passed through the city as prisoners.

Colonel King, a gallant soldier of two wars, who was killed while commanding a brigade in the second day's battle of Chickamauga, and whose body, lashed to a caisson, had been brought from the field by his soldiers, was buried from his home in Dayton with military honors on the last day of January, 1864.

During the early months of 1864 most of the regiments in which Dayton men had enlisted reënlisted for three years longer and were at home on furloughs. An incident about this time was the mobbing of the *Empire* office by a few soldiers at home on leave. On the 11th of May another draft occurred. Dayton had filled her quota excepting in one ward. Before the men were ordered to report, that ward also secured the requisite number of recruits.

There was another grand procession of wood-wagons in October, 1863. They brought in three hundred and twenty-five loads of wood and fifty-six wagons of farm produce. The boys of Dayton organized companies to saw and split the wood for the soldiers' families. In the fall of 1863 preparations began for a grand soldiers' fair by all the ladies' aid societies. It was opened the night before Christmas, and was a brilliant success, artistically, socially, and financially. The total receipts amounted to almost twenty thousand dollars.

In the first days of the war the women took up their task with cheerful enthusiasm. They were proud and smiling when the soldiers marched away carrying the banners they had fashioned. They made shirts and pretty pin-cushions, held fairs and bazaars, fed the hungry troops as they passed through the city, and unconsciously made out of the early days of impatient waiting and drilling in Camp Dayton bright memories for camp-fires and lonely marches. They learned to do without many a dear face and many a helping hand. But when the call came to be for bandages and lint—when the talk was more of hospital than of camp—the work went on, but it was often done in the shadow of a great terror, with brave, trembling hands. And when one soldier after another came home to die, or limping back on crutches, or with an empty sleeve,—when "killed" was written after names like Strong, King, Bruen, Forrer, and Birch, the tragedy of war stood revealed.

The professional and business men, who had organized as a home-guard, were surprised one fine morning in April (the 25th), 1864, to find themselves under orders from Governor Brough to take the field for one hundred days. Colonel Lowe at once summoned his regiment—the Second—to rendezvous at the Fair Grounds. The Twelfth Regiment was called to the same place. They left Dayton on the 11th and 12th of May for Camp Chase, where the two regiments were consolidated under Colonel

Lowe and ordered to Baltimore for garrison duty in the United States forts near that city. After three months of faithful service they were ordered back to Camp Chase, and mustered out on August 25.

The first veterans to return to Dayton after three years' service were Company A, Eleventh Ohio, and Company E, Twenty-fourth Ohio regiments. They came June 27, 1864,—a handful of men, but their welcome home was an ovation. In July the President called for five hundred thousand volunteers. On the 20th of the month Governor Brough called for twenty new regiments from the State of Ohio. It thus again became the duty of Dayton to raise her quota. Large bounties were offered, and every effort made to avoid a draft; still four wards failed to secure their proportion. After the draft (September 21), money was raised and substitutes enlisted. On the 19th of December the President called for three hundred thousand more men. The bounties offered were very high, and enlistments quite brisk from this time. The quota of some of the wards not being quite full, the last draft of the war was made March 30, 1865.

Those who had watched through dark days and long, stormy nights, saw the clouds beginning to break and the tide of victory setting in. With Farragut in Mobile Bay, Sherman in Atlanta, Grant before Richmond, and Sheridan dashing through the Shenandoah Valley, the country could but join in the "high hope for the future" which Mr. Lincoln guardedly expressed in his second inaugural address. It had been long years since Dayton had dared to be so happy as on the night of April 9, when the news of Lee's surrender was shouted through the streets by eager voices, and carried on the air as far as roaring cannon and ringing bells could take it. The war was over. Governor Brough set aside the 14th of the month as a day of thanksgiving. This was grandly celebrated in Dayton by services in the churches, a procession containing veterans with their tattered flags, and by fireworks and illuminations. The next morning brought the news that Lincoln was shot. The people were dumb with grief; the flags that had flaunted so proudly the day before now hung at half-mast, and festoons of black took the place of gay devices on public and private buildings. On the 19th of the month religious services were held in honor of the dead President.

Dayton enlisted very few men for the navy, but she has some

From a photograph by Appleton.

THE SOLDIERS' MONUMENT, AND APARTMENT HOUSE ON THE SITE OF NEWCOM'S TAVERN.

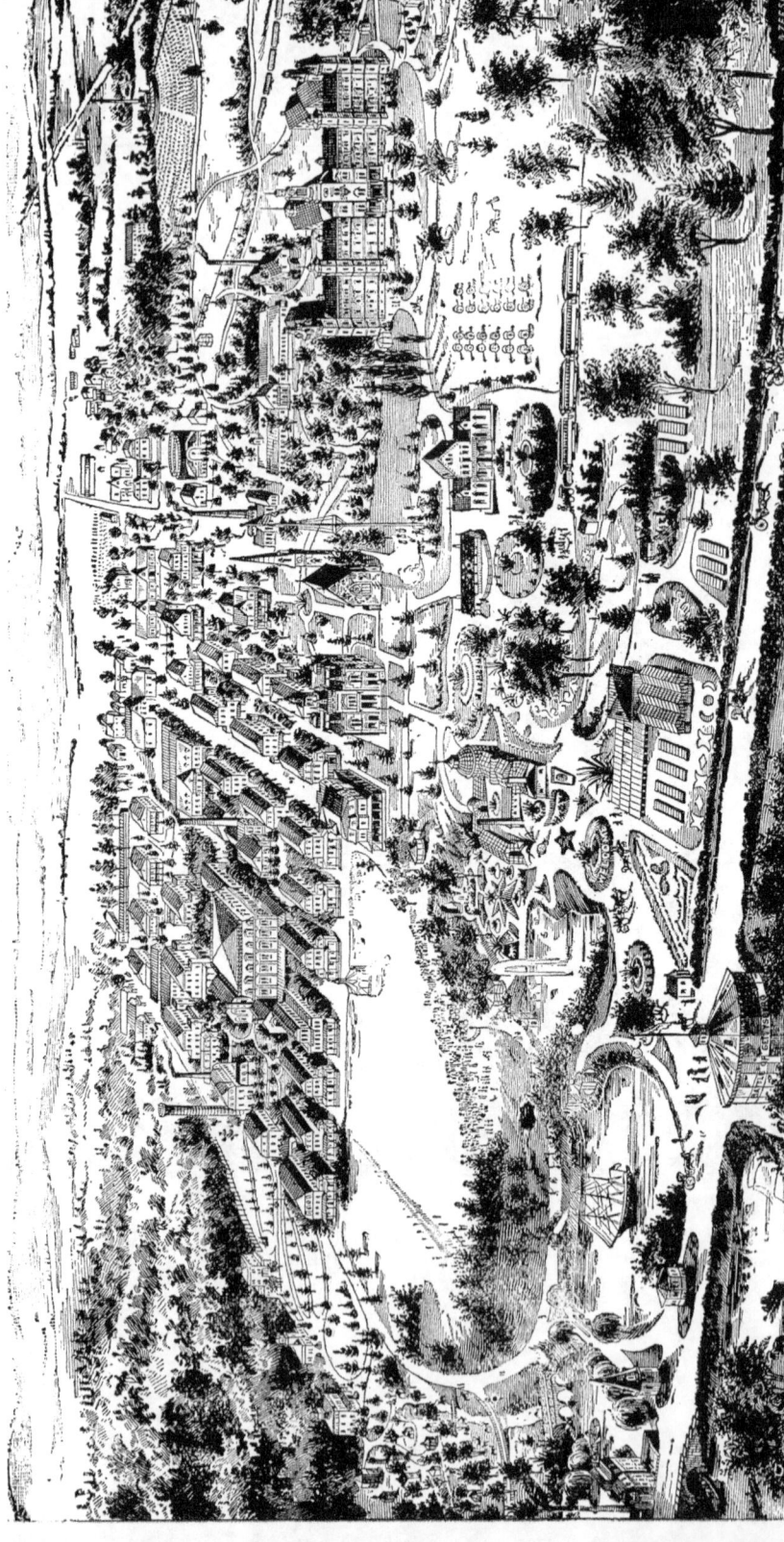

names in the register that cannot be forgotten. Admiral James F. Schenck—"the old Admiral," as he came to be called—was a unique character. He entered the United States Navy as midshipman in 1825. He came to Dayton in 1836, and bought a house for his family on the corner of First and Ludlow streets, an old-fashioned, comfortable home, where the children came to play in the shady garden, rolling down the hill at the side, or lying idle in the long grass, always undisturbed and quite welcome. When the owner came from a cruise in the West Indies, in the Mediterranean, or to the Sandwich Islands, the coast of Africa, China, Japan, or Brazil, the little front yard was scarcely large enough for the friends who loved to gather between the wide-open door and the gate that never shut and listen through long summer evenings to tales of other lands and people, seen with shrewd eyes and told with dry, caustic wit in original and characteristic language. In 1845 Lieutenant Schenck joined the *Congress*, on which he served at the capture of Los Angeles, Santa Barbara, and San Pedro, California. He also participated in the capture of Guaymas and Mazatlan, Mexico, and was commended for efficient service in the Mexican War. In 1862 Captain Schenck took command of the frigate *St. Lawrence*, and joined the blockading squadron at Key West. In 1864 Commodore Schenck hoisted his flag on board the *Powhatan* and led a division of the squadron at the bombardment of Fort Fisher. He was made rear-admiral in 1868, and placed upon the retired list in the following year. Admiral Schenck died at his home in Dayton on the 21st of December, 1882.

Rear-Admiral Greer, who retired at the head of the navy in February, 1895, was a Dayton man who sailed in many waters and saw many lands, from Africa to Greenland, from China to the Mediterranean. He fought through the war, assisting in the removal of Mason and Slidell from the *Trent*, commanding two ironclads and leading a division of Admiral Porter's squadron past Vicksburg, and also serving on the Red River expedition.

Paymaster Charles A. McDaniel died in Dayton in February, 1894. He left college to enter the army, in which he served through the early years of the war. Later he entered the navy, in which he had made an honorable record and many friends, when in the prime of life he faced suffering and death with the patience and quiet courage of a brave man.

At the close of the war there were hospitals in many of the

large cities where wounded soldiers received the tenderest and most skillful care. That these might be continued on a broader, more enduring basis, the soldiers' homes were devised and incorporated under an act of Congress. The committee appointed by the Board of Managers to select a site for the Central Branch reported April 11, 1867, recommending that offered by Dayton. Dayton was decided upon and four hundred acres bought about two miles west, on high ground overlooking the city, the citizens contributing twenty thousand dollars to the purchase. By December, 1867, the place was ready for occupation, General Ingraham being detailed as acting governor, and during the first year one thousand two hundred and fifty disabled soldiers were cared for. The first gift to the new home was that of a fine library and pictures given by Mrs. Mary Lowell Putnam in memory of her son, who fell at Ball's Bluff. After the barracks the first necessity was a hospital. Year by year handsome buildings were added, new land was bought, and the grounds artistically laid out, until now the Home is not only fulfilling its mission of grateful and loving protection of disabled soldiers, but has also become one of the most beautiful spots in the country. It is connected with Dayton by pleasant drives and by steam and electric roads. The Home was visited last year by over three hundred and fifty thousand people. The number of men cared for in the past year was six thousand seven hundred and thirty-nine.

The Home has been fortunate in its governors — Colonel Brown, whose occasional visits are hailed with delight by the men who were under his care for years; General Patrick, who died at his post, like the grand old soldier he was; and Colonel Thomas, whose administration is making its own record of wise and careful management.

The homes contain more inmates and are more needed every year, as the soldiers of thirty years ago grow to be old men; but the death-rate also increases, the ratio of deaths per thousand of number cared for being, in the past year, 47.65, and the sentinel on the beautiful monument in the cemetery watches over long rows of head-boards that must represent regiments.

Before the close of the war a monument in Dayton to her fallen heroes was talked of. Several committees were appointed, but it was not until after the organization of the Old Guard that much could be accomplished. This organization of veterans made a valiant effort. Finally, it was suggested that a law, raising the money by taxation, might be secured through the Legislature, subject to the approval of the people. General T. J. Wood, who was himself one of the bravest of soldiers, and had led his men through many bloody battles, who felt an interest in all soldiers and in his adopted city, was chairman of the trustees. He, assisted by Mr. D. B. Corwin, drafted a bill which, made more general, became a law on the 8th of April, 1881. This law was endorsed at the following October election. The contract was awarded in June, 1883, and the beautiful monument at the corner of Main and Water streets (now Monument Avenue) was dedicated with ceremony on the occasion of the soldiers' and sailors' reunion on the last day of July, 1884, as "the memorial of Montgomery County to her soldiers."

COLONEL ISRAEL LUDLOW [1]

ISRAEL LUDLOW was born at Long Hill, Morris County, New Jersey, in 1766. He was the youngest son of Cornelius Ludlow, who was a lieutenant-colonel in a New Jersey troop in the War of the Revolution. The family was of English descent, the ancestor coming from Hill Deverill, in Wilshire, England, to this country in the seventeenth century.

In 1787, when Mr. Ludlow was twenty-one or twenty-two years of age, he received the following letter from the Surveyor-General of the United States:

"*To Israel Ludlow, Esq.*

"DEAR SIR: I enclose to you an ordinance of Congress of the 20th inst., by which you will observe they have agreed to the sale of a large tract of land which the New Jersey Society have contracted to purchase. As it will be necessary to survey the boundary of this tract with all convenient speed, that the United States may receive the payment for the same, I propose to appoint you for that purpose, being assured of your abilities, diligence, and integrity. I hope you will accept it, and desire that you will furnish me with an estimate of the expense, and inform me what moneys will be necessary to advance to you to enable you to execute the same.

"I am, my dear sir,
"Yours,
"THO. HUTCHINS,
"*Surveyor-General, U. S.*"

He accepted his appointment, and received his instructions and an order on the frontier post for a sufficient escort to enable him to prosecute the survey; but the extreme weakness of the mili-

---

[1] Most of the material for the following sketch is taken from a memoir of Charlotte Chambers (Mrs. Israel Ludlow), written by her grandson Louis Garrard in 1856, and has been kindly furnished by Mr. William S. Ludlow, of Cincinnati, Ohio, a grandson of Colonel Ludlow. The greater portion of "Early Dayton" being already in type when the information was received, the insertion of this sketch near the end of the volume was made necessary. The prominence of Colonel Ludlow in the early history of the Miami region as well as in the founding of Dayton, renders the account here given especially valuable. It is regretted that no portrait of the Colonel is in existence.

tary force then in the Northwest, and the dangerous duty upon which he was employed, caused General Harmar to write that he regretted to be unable to comply with the directions, on account of the small force at his command; and, further, that if he were able to furnish the guards, it would be imprudent for Colonel Ludlow to go into the country which he was to survey, as at that time there were large numbers of Indians hunting there at that season, and that the survey would have to be deferred until the result of a treaty which was then being made was known. This reply was sent from Fort Harmar, August 28, 1788.

"The surveys prescribed by the instructions of Hutchins in 1787 were prosecuted notwithstanding the hostility of the savages and the deficiency of escort, but with the inevitable delay attending the movements of small parties where precautions from danger so materially engross the attention."

The following letter to General Hamilton explains the slow progress of the survey, and presents in a striking manner scenes of pioneer exposure and hardship:

"PHILADELPHIA, May 5, 1792.

"SIR: The unexpected delays that have attended my executing the surveys of the Ohio and Miami companies, together with your letters which I have received from time to time, urging my speedy exertions to effect the business, induces me to explain to you the cause of the delay.

"In November, 1790, I was honored with your letter of instruction at this place. I proceeded immediately to Fort Harmar, being possessed of General Knox's letter or order to the commandant for an escort. On my way, at Fort Pitt, I saw Major Doughty, who, after becoming acquainted with my business, informed me that there was no doubt but that an escort would be furnished on my arrival at Fort Harmar, upon which I supplied myself with chain-carriers and other hands necessary, packhorses, corn, provision, and camp equipage for the approaching cold season.

"On my arrival at Fort Harmar I found that no escort could be obtained. Major Zeigler, who commanded, gave me his answer in writing, which was that he did not consider the troops then under his command more than sufficient to guard the settlement of Marietta, the Indians having shortly before that defeated and broken up one of their frontier stations. Of course he could not comply with the order of General Knox and my request. (A copy of that letter I inclosed to you.) Upon that information, from necessity I gave up the pursuit at that time, and proceeded to Fort Washington, supposing I could execute the Miami survey.

"Discharging my hired men and packhorses, I applied to General Harmar who then commanded, for protection while surveying the Miami tract. He informed me he did not consider his whole command a sufficient escort for my purpose. (A copy of his answer I forwarded to you.) On the arrival of General St. Clair in May following, I made an official application for fifteen men or more, should it be convenient, to accompany me as an escort while surveying the Miami and Ohio tracts. He assured me that he considered the execution of this survey a matter of the highest interest and importance to the United States, and that he would make every effort to assist me with a sufficient guard, but that it was then impracticable. (His letter I will forward to you.) Thus the business was again put off until the 20th of October following, when I was favored with the services of fifteen men, commanded by a sergeant, with whom I proceeded to execute the Ohio Company's survey. I succeeded, and returned to Fort Washington, but with the loss of six of the escort, and leaving in the woods all my packhorses and their equipage, and being obliged to make a raft of logs to descend the Ohio as far as Limestone from opposite the mouth of the Great Sandy River.

"On my arrival at Fort Washington I again applied for protection to proceed in the Miami survey. That assistance was refused by Major Zeigler, who then commanded. (His letter I will produce.) My reputation, as well as the public good, being in some measure affected by the delay of the business, I was constrained to have recourse to an effort which my instruction did not advise, viz.: to attempt making the survey by the aid of three active woodsmen—to assist as spies and give notice of any approaching danger. My attempts proved unsuccessful. After extending the western boundary more than one hundred miles up the Miami River, the deep snows and cold weather rendered our situation too distressing, by reason of my men having their feet frozen and unfit to furnish game for supplies. In consequence, we returned to Fort Washington. The cold weather abating, I made another attempt, extending the east boundary as far as the line intersected the Little Miami River, where we discovered signs of the near approach of Indians, and having but three armed men in company, induced me to return again to Fort Washington, which I found commanded by General Wilkinson, to whom I applied for an escort, which was denied me. (His letter I have the honor to inclose to you with the others.)

"I now have the satisfaction to present to you the whole of the survey of the Ohio and part of the Miami purchases, executed agreeably to instructions. Any further information that may be required respecting the causes of delay of the above business, I presume may be had from Generals St. Clair and Harmar, who are now here present.

"I am, sir, yours respectfully,
"ISRAEL LUDLOW.

"HON. ALEX. HAMILTON, *Secretary of the Treasury.*"

In the winter of 1789 he became associated with Matthias Denham and Robert Patterson in the proprietorship of the future Cincinnati to the extent of one-third interest, and proceeded to lay out the town. In September, 1794, he surveyed the plat of a town adjacent to Fort Hamilton, and was sole owner. In August, 1795, Generals St. Clair, Wilkinson, and Dayton, and Colonel Ludlow purchased from John Cleves Symmes the seventh and eighth ranges of land between the two Miamis, including the site of Dayton, and in November of the same year Colonel Ludlow laid out the town of Dayton, naming it after one of his associates. He was also the owner of a large extent of land in the vicinity, on the banks of Mad and Miami rivers. He was commissioned to fix the boundary line between the United States and the Indians in accordance with the treaty of Greenville, made by General Wayne in 1795. This was done in 1797.

Colonel Ludlow was married in 1796, at Chambersburg, Pennsylvania, to Charlotte, daughter of General James Chambers. His death occurred at his residence, at that time a short distance outside of Cincinnati, but now included in the city, January 20, 1804, when he was but thirty-eight years of age. He was buried in the Presbyterian burying-ground at Public Square, Cincinnati, which was bounded by Fourth, Fifth, Main, and Walnut streets. Twice his remains were removed—for the second and last time in November, 1895, and were then interred in Spring Grove Cemetery, which had once been a part of his country residence.

"The shock created by the announcement of his death could be understood only in the new district, where the sparseness of population and community of interests and friendship rendered conspicuous a valuable man, and his loss deep-seated and seemingly irreparable. The inhabitants joined the Masonic Fraternity in paying a closing tribute of respect to his memory. An oration was pronounced by the Hon. T. Symmes."

Mr. Ludlow was not permitted to witness the wonderful results of the enterprise to the forwarding of which his untiring industry was directed. That he had a prescience of its importance is shown by his large entries of land, now noted for its great fertility and value. The selection of town sites when the territory was an unbroken forest, and where intimate knowledge of soil, timber, and natural outlet of country is necessary to eminent success, entitles him to no little credit for sound judgment and discriminating foresight. Modesty was a well-known trait of his character. With an eye quick to discern, and energy to have applied, every measure conducing to the prosperity of the territory and city whose early progress was the adumbration of speedy greatness, he was himself indifferent to his own political advancement, and willing to wait at least until the fulfillment of his present plans. Thus it is that, without legislative record of the facts, his name is not known in a manner commensurate with his services to the infant colony and the youthful State. His is not an anomalous case. The unwritten history of every community illustrates the point that the most valuable men are not always, and indeed but seldom, in office. Israel Ludlow was not a politician in the clamorous sense of the term. He was a man for the times in which he lived, and possessed a peculiar fitness for the extended sphere of his influence. The absence of such men in the necessitous condition of a struggling settlement explains the cause of premature decay and failure: their presence constitutes the mainspring of progress, the encouraging support of first puny effort, until accumulated strength affords the power of self-propulsion. He lived in a day when a citizen found in the extension of aid to the impoverished emigrant and his suffering family ample scope for the exercise of the most generous heart-impulses. To him they could turn as a safe adviser and a substantial friend without fear of neglect. His life was illustrated by a series of practical benevolences, free from ostentation and the laudation of scarcely other than the recipients of his disinterested kindness.

HISTORICAL AND STATISTICAL TABLES

COPYRIGHT, 1896
BY W. J. SHUEY, PUBLISHER
All rights reserved

HISTORICAL AND STATISTICAL TABLES

LOCATION AND AREA.

DAYTON, the county-seat of Montgomery County, Ohio, is located on both banks of the Great Miami River, at the confluence of Stillwater, Mad River, and Wolf Creek with the Miami, and on the line of the Miami and Erie Canal, sixty miles north-northeast of Cincinnati, and seventy-one miles west by south of Columbus. Its latitude is thirty-nine degrees forty-four minutes north, and its longitude is eighty-four degrees eleven minutes west from Greenwich, or seven degrees eleven minutes west from Washington. It is an important station on eleven railroads, which belong to four great systems, namely: The Pittsburgh, Cincinnati, Chicago & St. Louis and the Dayton & Western, of the Pennsylvania Lines; the Cleveland, Cincinnati, Chicago & St. Louis and the Dayton & Union, of the "Big Four" System; the Cincinnati, Hamilton & Dayton, the Dayton & Michigan, the Cincinnati, Dayton & Ironton, and the Cincinnati, Dayton & Chicago, of the C., H. & D. System; the New York, Pennsylvania & Ohio, of the Erie System; the Dayton, Lebanon & Cincinnati Railroad, and the Home Avenue Railroad. Thirty-six hard-graveled roads radiate in all directions from the city, with an aggregate length of over six hundred miles. The extreme dimensions of Dayton are: east and west, five and one-eighth miles; north and south, three and one-half miles. Its area is about ten and three-quarters square miles.

POPULATION.

1796....About 36.
1802....Five families.
1810....383.
1820....1,139.
1830....2,954.

1840....6,067.
1845....9,792.
1850....10,976.
1860....20,081.

1870....30,473.
1880....38,678.
1890....61,220.
1896....About 80,000.

CITY GOVERNMENT AND INSTITUTIONS.

(Compiled from latest reports.)

MAYOR.

Elected for two years; *ex officio* president of Board of Police Directors and Board of Health, and organizes the City Council; appoints the Board of City Affairs, the Tax Commission, Board of Work-House Directors, and Board of Elections.

BOARD OF CITY AFFAIRS.

Four members; term of office four years, one being appointed each year by the Mayor; powers executive.

CITY COUNCIL.

Sixteen members, elected from eight wards by the voters of the wards; term of office two years, half expiring each year; powers legislative.

Measures involving expenditure and public franchises must be approved by both City Council and Board of City Affairs.

BOARD OF ELECTIONS.

Four members, appointed by the Mayor, one secretary.

BOARD OF EQUALIZATION.

Six members, elected by the City Council.

MISCELLANEOUS.

City clerk, elected by the Council; treasurer, elected by the people; comptroller, solicitor, engineer, sealer of weights and measures, market-master, superintendent of levees, appointed by the Board of City Affairs; wood-measurer, elected by the people.

PUBLIC SCHOOLS.

Board of Education.—Sixteen members, elected for two years from eight wards by the voters of the wards, half being elected each year.

Officers and Teachers.—Clerk, superintendent of instruction, superintendent of buildings, truant officer, city board of examiners with three members, twenty principals, twenty-five High School teachers, three Normal School teachers, two Manual-Training School teachers, four special teachers, 251 district-school teachers; total number of teachers, 305.

Enumeration of School Youth (Between six and twenty-one years of age).—Public schools, 10,960; private schools, 240; church schools, 2,102; not attending, 7,276; grand total, 20,578.

Number of Pupils in Public Schools.—District schools, 5,143 boys, 5,037 girls, or a total of 10,180; High School, 297 boys, 474 girls, or a total of 771; Normal School, 31; grand total, 10,982. In Manual-Training School, 45 pupils from the High School and 76 pupils from the eighth grade of the district schools; total, 121.

Schools.—Nineteen district schools, one high school, one manual-training school, one normal school, two night grammar-schools, two night drawing-schools.

Buildings.—Twenty-nine district buildings, including annexes, one high-school building, one library building. Total value in 1895, $1,269,416.50; including personal property, $1,323,525.50. Value of High School: lot, $60,000; building, $255,000; personal property, $11,358; total, $326,358.

Finances.—Receipts, exclusive of temporary loans and bonds, for the year ending August 31, 1895, $314,878.14; expenses, exclusive of bonded debt and temporary loans, $355,700.81; bonded debt, August 31, 1895, $485,000.

PUBLIC LIBRARY.

Board of six members, elected by the Board of Education; librarian, cataloguer, five library assistants; occupies a fine stone library building, fireproof, erected in Cooper Park in 1886-87, and valued at $100,000; contains 35,325 volumes and 1,292 pamphlets; card and printed catalogues; museum attached; expenses, 1894-95, $10,830.50, of which $2,601.70 was spent for the purchase of books and periodicals, and $1,094.03 for the museum.

CITY GOVERNMENT AND INSTITUTIONS

POLICE DEPARTMENT.

Organization.—Mayor and four police directors, secretary, police judge, clerk of the police court, superintendent, captain, five sergeants, detective sergeant, surgeon, seventy-five patrolmen (eight mounted), two turnkeys, court bailiff, two telephone operators, one police matron.

Headquarters.—In City Building.

Equipment.—One central station, two substations, one patrol house, two patrol wagons, one ambulance, sixteen horses.

Finances.—1894: Receipts, $76,622.31; disbursements, $69,959.99; balance, January 1, 1895, $6,662.32.

A police benevolent association.

WORK-HOUSE.

Four directors, appointed by the Mayor, superintendent, matron; one work-house.

FIRE DEPARTMENT.

Organization.—Four fire commissioners, chief and secretary, first assistant chief, second assistant chief, seventy-six firemen.

Equipment.—Twelve engine, hose, and hook-and-ladder houses; a fire-alarm telegraph system, with over one hundred boxes; four steam fire-engines; two chemical engines; thirteen hose wagons; three hook-and-ladder wagons; two telegraph wagons; three buggies; thirty-six horses.

Finances.—1895: Cost of maintenance, $67,217.29; value of real estate, $90,500.

Service.—Number of alarms in 1895, 344; total loss, $21,978.05; total value of property where fires occurred, $2,012,675; total insurance, $1,011,557. The loss amounted to only about twenty-five cents *per capita* of the population.

A firemen's benevolent association.

WATER-WORKS.

Established, 1870.

Organization.—Three trustees, secretary, assistant secretary, chief engineer, first assistant engineer, second assistant engineer, superintendent of street department, two inspectors and collectors.

Equipment.—One pumping-house; three engines, with combined daily capacity of 29,000,000 gallons; eighty-five eight-inch tube-wells, driven to a depth of forty-five to fifty feet; over ninety-six miles of street mains, 937 fire-hydrants, 8,607 service connections, 1,300 meters.

Finances.—Total expenditures, 1870 to December 31, 1895, $1,792,560.39; total income to December 31, 1895, $938,872.77; net cost to December 31, 1895, $853,687.62; water-works bonded debt, November, 1895, $765,000, which is gradually being paid; cost of pipe, hydrants, etc., and laying of same, 1870-95, $700,000; received from sale of water, 1870-95, $860,926.83; net earnings, 1870-95, $342,000.

Quality of the Water.—The quality of the water, by recent analysis, has been found to be first-class. It is clear, cold, and remarkably free from injurious matter. In a recent analysis an average of only forty-eight germs to the cubic centimeter were found in the samples examined. The average temperature in the pipes is about 50°.

BOARD OF HEALTH.

Mayor and six members of the board, health officer, secretary, meat inspector, four sanitary policemen.

CITY INFIRMARY.

Three directors, superintendent, clerk, city physician.

MARKETS.

Two market-houses, with street markets adjoining; one market-master.

TAX COMMISSION

Six members, appointed by the Mayor.

TAXES.

City Expenses, 1894-95.

Board of Health and Sanitary	.10 mills	$4,104 82
Bridges	.25 mills	10,262 05
Elections	.15 mills	6,157 23
Fire Department	1.75 mills	71,834 37
General Expense	.60 mills	24,628 93
Hospitals (Deaconess and St. Elizabeth)	.05 mills	2,052 41
Infirmary	.05 mills	2,052 41
Lighting	.70 mills	28,733 75
Police Department	1.10 mills	45,153 03
Parks and Levees	.05 mills	2,052 41
Street Cleaning	.75 mills	30,786 16
Street Improvement	.35 mills	14,366 87
Sewers	.05 mills	2,052 41
Work-House	.05 mills	2,052 41
School Paving	.10 mills	4,104 82
	6.10 mills	$250,394 08
City Interest and Sinking Fund	5.45 mills	223,712 73
		$474,106 81

Board of Education, 1895-96.

Regular Levy	7.00 mills	$288,974 49
Manual-Training School	.20 mills	8,256 41
Public Library	.25 mills	10,320 52

Taxes for All Purposes, 1895-96.

City, County, and State	26.00 mills	$1,073,333 82

Tax Valuation, 1895-96.

Taxable Property	$41,282,070

BONDED DEBT.

General Bonds.

(Principal and interest payable from a direct tax upon the General Duplicate.)

Outstanding March 1, 1895—

Bridge	$68,000 00
City Hall	71,000 00
City Prison	10,000 00
Extending Indebtedness	150,000 00
Fire Department	24,000 00
Funded Debt	249,000 00

Outstanding March 1, 1895—

General Street and Improvement	$50,000 00
Levee	30,000 00
Park Street Sewer	126,000 00
Police Deficiency	36,000 00
Sewer	150,000 00
Street Paving	528,000 00
Southwestern Sewer	17,000 00
Street Improvement	150,000 00
Wolf Creek Improvement	50,000 00
Water-Works	505,000 00
Water-Works Enlargement	3,000 00
Water-Works Improvement	280,000 00
Total	$2,497,000 00

Improvement Bonds.

(Principal and interest payable from assessments upon abutting or benefited property.)

Outstanding March 1, 1895—

Street Paving	$1,178,000 00
Sewer	180,000 00
Special Assessment	36,165 00
Total	$1,394,165 00

PERIODICALS.

SECULAR.

Daily.—Six, one of which is German.
Weekly.—Nine, one of which is German.
Monthly.—Two.
    Total.—Seventeen.

RELIGIOUS.

Weekly.—Eleven, one of which is German.
Semimonthly.—Nine, one of which is German.
Monthly.—Three.
Quarterly.—Nine, one of which is German.
    Total.—Thirty-two.
    Grand Total.—Forty-nine.

CHURCHES.

Baptist, 11.
Baptist Brethren, 1.
Christian, 2.
Congregational, 1.
Disciples of Christ, 2.
Dunkards, 2.
Evangelical Association, 2.
Hebrew, 3.
Lutheran, 7.
Methodist Episcopal, 10.
Methodist Episcopal, African, 2.
Methodist Protestant, 1.
Methodist, Wesleyan, 1.
Presbyterian, 7.
Protestant Episcopal, 3.
Reformed, 5.
Roman Catholic, 7.
Salvation Army, 1.
United Brethren in Christ, 12.
United Presbyterian, 1.

    Total, 81.

CHURCH AND PRIVATE SCHOOLS.

PROTESTANT.

Union Biblical Seminary, the theological school of the Church of the United Brethren in Christ; four professors, one general manager, and forty-three students.

St. Paul's German Lutheran School, common branches.

ROMAN CATHOLIC.

Eight parochial schools and academies.

St. Mary's Institute; twenty-one officers and professors, 275 students in institute, and 120 students in normal department.

PRIVATE.

Miami Commercial College.	Young Ladies and Misses' School.
Dayton Commercial College.	Home School for Boys.
English Training School.	Conservatory of Music.
Deaver Collegiate Institute.	Dayton College of Music.

BENEVOLENT AND CHARITABLE INSTITUTIONS.

Young Men's Christian Association.—A Protestant institution, founded in 1870; occupies a fine stone-front building on the south side of Fourth Street, between Main and Jefferson; value of property, over $100,000; membership, over 2,500; conducts religious, educational, and physical departments, including manual training and industrial education; has reception-room, parlors, reading-room, junior room, educational rooms, shop, entertainment hall, gymnasium, bath-rooms, and athletic park; receipts in 1894-95, $19,386.95; expenses, $19,269.65.

Woman's Christian Association.—A Protestant institution, founded in 1870; occupies excellent brick buildings on the south side of Third Street, between Ludlow and Wilkinson; value of property, $60,000; membership, about 350; includes a young woman's department; conducts religious, charitable, educational, and physical departments, lunch-room, and exchange; has reception-room, parlors, reading-room, educational rooms, entertainment hall, industrial class-room, gymnasium, bath-rooms, etc.; receipts in 1894-95, $4,279.41; expenses, $4,242.92.

Young Women's League.—Founded in 1895; occupies a brick building on the west side of Jefferson Street, between Fifth and Sixth streets; membership, 450; conducts religious, educational, and physical departments, and lunch-room.

Young Men's Institute.—A Roman Catholic institution; occupies a brick building on the south side of Fourth Street, between Ludlow and Wilkinson.

St. Joseph's Institute.—Conducted by the Catholic Gesellen-Verein, for the benefit of young men; organized in 1868; furnishes reading-room, gymnasium, and free circulating library; building located on Montgomery Street.

Protestant Deaconess Home and Hospital.—Founded in 1890 by the Protestant Deaconess Society of Dayton; occupies an expensive pressed-brick building on south side of Apple Street, between Main and Brown, costing, with equipment, about $150,000; capacity, 175 patients.

St. Elizabeth Hospital.—A Roman Catholic institution, founded in 1878; conducted by the Sisters of the Poor of St. Francis; occupies a large brick building on the west side of Hopeland Street, between Washington and Albany, costing over $65,000; capacity, 242 patients.

Widows' Home.—Founded in 1875, by the Woman's Christian Association; occupies a brick building on the northeast corner of Findlay and May streets; capacity, twenty-eight inmates; endowment, $37,358.79; receipts, for year ending October 5, 1895, $3,124.99; expenses, $2,911.59.

Montgomery County Children's Home.—Founded in 1866; occupies a brick building on the east side of Summit Street, south of Home Avenue; number of inmates in February, 1895, fifty-one, of whom thirty-eight were boys and thirteen were girls; total received from the founding, 1,864.

Christian Deaconess Home.—Monument Avenue, West Side.

Children's Home.—116 South Ringgold Street.

Bethany Home.—For homeless girls and women; 159 East Park Street.

National Soldiers' Home (Central Branch).—Founded in 1867; located a short distance west of the city; grounds cover six hundred and twenty-five acres; number of inmates, about 6,000.

Southern Ohio Asylum for the Insane.—Founded in 1852; located at the south end of Wayne Avenue; capacity, 800 patients.

Humane Society.

Women's Christian Temperance Union, No. 1.

Women's Christian Temperance Union, No. 2.

St. Joseph's German Catholic Asylum.

Other Societies.—Numerous lodges of Masons, Knights of Pythias, Knights of St. John, Odd Fellows, Grand United Order of Odd Fellows, Grand Army of the Republic, Sons of Veterans, Woman's Veteran Relief Union, Order of United American Mechanics, Knights of Labor, trades unions, and other orders.

LITERARY AND MUSICAL SOCIETIES.

Present Day Club.
Woman's Literary Club.
"H. H." Club.
Emerson Club.
Friday Afternoon Club.

Shakespeare Club.
Philharmonic Society.
Mozart Club.
Harmonia Society.
Maennerchor.

POLITICAL CLUBS.

Garfield Club.
Jackson Club.
Gravel Hall Club.

Thurman Club.
Lincoln Club.

SOCIAL, CYCLING, GYMNASTIC, AND OTHER CLUBS.

Dayton Club.
Dayton Bicycle Club.
Y. M. C. A. Wheelmen.
Dayton Lawn Tennis Club.
Dayton Angling Club.

Dayton Gymnastic Club.
Dayton Turngemeinde.
Stillwater Canoe Club.
Ruckawa Canoe Club.
Dayton Camera Club.

MILITARY COMPANIES.

Phœnix Light Infantry, Company G, Third Regiment Infantry, Ohio National Guard.

Gem City Light Infantry, Company I, Third Regiment Infantry, Ohio National Guard.

STREET-RAILWAYS.

City Railway.—Third Street Line, from the east end of Third Street to the Soldiers' Home; electric; length of line, over six miles of double track and less than one-quarter mile of single track.

Fifth Street Line, from the east end of Huffman Avenue to the Soldiers' Home; electric; length of line, six and one-half miles of double track and about one-half mile of single track.

Green Line, from the east end of Richard Street to the corner of Fifth and Wilkinson; electric; length of line, over two miles of double track.

Authorized capital, $2,100,000; total length of lines operated, over fourteen and one-half miles of double track and about three-quarters of a mile of single track.

Oakwood Street-Railway.—From the north end of Salem Street in Dayton View to Oakwood, at the south end of Brown Street; electric; capital, $300,000; length of line, about four miles of double track.

White Line Street-Railway.—From the corner of Main Street and Forest Avenue in Riverdale, *via* Main, Third, Ludlow, Washington, and Germantown streets to the Soldiers' Home; electric; capital, $400,000; length of line, about six miles of double track.

Wayne Avenue and Fifth Street Railway.—From the south end of Wayne Avenue, *via* Wayne Avenue, Fifth, Jefferson, First, Keowee, and Valley streets to the east end of Valley Street in North Dayton; horse-cars; capital, $100,000; length of line, about three miles of double track and about one mile of single track.

Dayton Traction Company.—South Main Street, from the corner of Fifth and extending to Calvary Cemetery; electric; capital, $250,000; length of line, one and one-half miles of double track and one and one-half miles of single track.

Total length of street railways operated, over twenty-nine miles of double track and about three and one-quarter miles of single track. About two and one-half miles of double track being used jointly, the net length of double track is about twenty-six and one-half miles.

STREET IMPROVEMENTS.

Total length of streets in the city, one hundred and fifty-eight miles, of which nearly twenty-five miles are paved, as follows: asphalt, fourteen miles; brick, nearly nine miles; granite, over one mile; Medina stone, over one-half mile. Total cost of paving, $1,800,000. Eighty-three miles of streets are graded and graveled, and fifty miles are unimproved.

Thirty-nine miles of sanitary sewers and forty miles of storm sewers have been laid, at a cost of $495,000.

COMMERCIAL AND INDUSTRIAL.

Board of Trade.—Officers: president, first vice-president, second vice-president, secretary, treasurer, fifteen directors.

National Banks.—Seven, with combined capital of $2,500,000, and cash assets of over $3,000,000; a clearing-house.

Building and Loan Associations.—Seventeen, with combined capital amounting to $43,350,000.

Fire-Insurance Companies (Home).—Seven, with investment of $700,000, and net assets amounting to $1,213,204; one underwriters' association.

Incorporated Companies.—One hundred and seventy, with capital stock of over $25,000,000.

Builders' Exchange.—Officers: president, first vice-president, second vice-president, secretary, treasurer.
Gas Company.
Natural Gas Company.
Electric Light Company.
Telegraph and Cable Companies.—Two.
District Telegraph Company.
Telephone Exchange.
Railways.—Eleven, with sixty-four passenger trains daily.
Manufacturing Establishments.—Number, about one thousand; capital invested in 1894, $11,650,043; value of manufactured products, 1894, $10,163,913.60; wages paid, 1894, $2,176,156.15. In number of factories, in capital invested in manufacturing industries, and in wages paid, Dayton ranks as the third city in the State; in value of manufactured products, fourth.

POSTOFFICE STATISTICS, 1895.

Postage Receipts	$178,451.08
Expenses of Office	$74,648.98
Number of Money Orders Issued	19,852
Value of Money Orders Issued	$154,367.35
Number of Money Orders Paid	60,058
Value of Money Orders Paid	$333,093.77
Pieces of First-Class Mail Received	4,480,000
Pieces of All Other Classes Received	3,948,800
Special Letters Received	9,831
Pieces of First-Class Mail Dispatched	7,620,907
Pieces of All Other Classes Dispatched	7,054,850
Special Letters Dispatched	6,257
Registered Letters and Parcels Received	40,920
Registered Letters and Parcels Dispatched	19,742
Total Number Pieces Received and Dispatched	23,120,645
Weight in Pounds of Second-Class Matter Mailed by Publishers	47,441
Number of Carriers	40
Mail Trains Arriving Daily	39
Mail Trains Departing Daily	42

PARTIAL ENUMERATION OF MERCANTILE, MANUFACTURING, AND OTHER BUSINESS CONCERNS.

Abstracters of Titles	4	Auctioneers	6
Agricultural Implements, Dealers	10	Autographic Registers, Manufs.	2
		Awnings, Manufs	4
Agricultural Implements, Mfs.	6	Bakeries	50
Architects	10	Bakers' Supplies	1
Architectural Iron, Manuf	1	Baking-Powder, Munufs	6
Art Glass	1	Banks, National	7
Artificial Flowers	1	Barber Shops	120
Artificial Stone Pavements	2	Barbers' Supplies	1
Artists	22	Baskets, Manufs	9
Asbestos Packing and Mill Boards	1	Bicycles, Dealers	13
		Bicycles, Manuf	1
Asphalt Pavements	2	Blackboards, Slate Stone, Mf.	1
Asphalt Roofing	2	Blacking, Manuf	1
Attorneys-at-Law	123	Blacksmith Shops	36

Blank Books, Manufs	5
Boarding-Houses	72
Boat-Houses	3
Boats, Manuf	1
Boilers, Steam, Manufs	4
Bolt and Screw Cases	1
Bookbinders	6
Bookbinders' Machinery, Mf	1
Book-Cover Dies and Tools	1
Book Publishers	4
Booksellers and Stationers	10
Boot- and Shoe-Makers	113
Boots and Shoes, Retail	46
Boots and Shoes, Wholesale	1
Boxes, Manuf	1
Brass-Founders	3
Brass Goods	2
Brass Stamps	2
Breweries	17
Brick, Manufs	11
Bricklayers	17
Brickmaking Machinery	1
Brokers	18
Brooms, Manufs	11
Brushes, Manufs	2
Building and Loan Associations	17
Candy, Manufs	4
Candy-Molds, Manuf	1
Canning Factory	1
Carbon, Manuf	1
Car-Furnishings, Manuf	1
Carpenters and Builders	118
Carpet Cleaners	7
Carpet Dealers	14
Carpet Weavers	11
Carriages and Buggies, Dealers	4
Carriages and Buggies, Manufs	9
Cars, Railroad, Manuf	1
Cash Registers, Manuf	1
Caterers	2
Cement Pavements	13
Chain, Manufs	2
Chairs, Manuf	1
China and Queensware Dealers	10
Church Furniture	1
Cigar-Boxes, Manufs	3
Cigar Dealers	53
Cigars, Manufs	58
Cistern Builders	5
Civil Engineers	6
Clearing-House	1
Clergymen	135
Clothing Dealers	27
Clothing Renovators	19
Coal Dealers	40
Coal Miners	4
Cold Storage	1
Commercial Colleges	2
Commission Merchants	11
Confectioners, Retail	55
Confectioners, Wholesale	10
Cooper Shops	7
Coppersmith	1
Corsets, Manufs	3
Cotton Batting	1
Daily Markets	112
Dairies	25
Dental Electrical Specialties	1
Dentists	31
Detective Agency	1
Dressmakers	300
Druggist, Wholesale	1
Druggists and Apothecaries	55
Dry Goods, Retail	44
Dry Goods, Wholesale	4
Dye Houses	2
Electric Construction and Supplies	5
Electric Light Company	1
Electric Supplies, Dealer	1
Electrical Engineers	2
Electrical Goods, Manuf	1
Electrotypers	2
Employment Agency	1
Engravers	6
Express Companies	7
Fancy Goods	8
Fans, Ventilating	1
Feed Stores	32
Fences, Manufs	4
File-Cases, Manuf	1
Files, Manufs	2
Fire-Alarm Operators	1
Fire-Brick and Clay	4
Flavoring Extracts	2
Flax-Mill	1
Florists	18
Flour-Mills	9
Freight Lines	9
Fresco Artists	2
Fruit-Growers	11
Fruits, Retail	10
Fruits, Wholesale	6
Furnaces, Warm Air	7
Furniture, Dealers	16
Furniture, Manufs	5

COMMERCIAL AND INDUSTRIAL

Furniture-Cars	12
Galvanized Iron Cornices	6
Gas-Burners and Appliances	1
Gas Company	1
Gas Company, Natural	1
Gas-Engine, Manufs	3
Gas-Fitters and Fixtures	15
Gas-Machine, Manuf	1
Gas Range and Heater, Manuf.	1
Gasoline Stove, Manuf	1
Grain Dealers	5
Grain Elevator	1
Grocers, Retail	307
Grocers, Wholesale	9
Guns, Pistols, etc	2
Gunsmiths	3
Hardware and Cutlery	12
Hardware, Wholesale	4
Harness and Saddles	17
Hats and Caps	20
Hedges	1
Hotels	19
House-Furnishing Goods	8
House-Movers and Raisers	2
Hubs, Spokes, etc	2
Hydraulic Machinery	2
Ice, Dealers	3
Ice, Manufs	2
Ice Cream	13
Ice and Refrigerator Machinery, Manuf	1
Ink, Manuf	1
Insurance Agents	38
Insurance Companies, Fire	9
Insurance Companies, Life	2
Iron-Founders	10
Iron Posts, Manuf	1
Iron- and Wood-Working Machinery	1
Jewelers	26
Justices of the Peace	4
Kindergartens	3
Lamps and Lamp Goods	1
Lasts, Manufs	2
Laundries	17
Leather and Findings	2
Lime, Plaster, and Cement	11
Linseed- and Cotton-Oil Machinery	2
Linseed Oil, Manufs	4
Lithographers	3
Livery-Stables	36
Loan Agents	6
Loan Offices	5
Locksmiths	2
Lumber Dealers	15
Machine Knives, Manuf	1
Machine Tools	2
Machinists	15
Machinists' Tools	1
Malleable Iron Works	1
Mantels and Grates	4
Marble Dust	1
Marble Quarry	1
Marble Works	8
Mattresses, Manufs	4
Meats, Wholesale	2
Mechanics' Tools	3
Medicines, Patent	19
Men's Furnishing Goods	32
Mercantile Agencies	3
Milk Depots	8
Mill Supplies	4
Milliners, Retail	41
Milliners, Wholesale	2
Mineral Water, Manufs	2
Mittens, Manuf	1
Model Makers	2
Motor, Water, Manuf	1
Music Colleges	2
Music Publisher	1
Music Teachers	80
Musical Instruments, Dealers	5
News Depots	8
Notaries Public	114
Notions, Retail	20
Notions, Wholesale	5
Novelties, Manufs	2
Nozzles, Manufs	2
Nurseries	6
Nurses	37
Oculists and Aurists	3
Oils	15
Opticians	5
Overalls, Manufs	3
Oysters, Fish, and Game	7
Pails, Manuf	1
Paint, Manuf	1
Painters, House and Sign	73
Paints, Oils, etc	7
Pants, Manufs	3
Paper, Dealers	3
Paper, Manufs	7
Paper Bags	1
Paper-Box Makers' Machinery	1
Paper Boxes, Manufs	2

Paper Hangers	27
Paper Hangings	17
Paper-Mill Machinery	1
Paper and Wooden Plate, Mf	1
Parquetry Floors	1
Patent Attorneys	3
Patent Solicitors	2
Pattern-Makers	11
Pension Attorneys	2
Pension Claim Agents	3
Perfumery, Manuf	1
Photographers	17
Photographers' Supplies	2
Physicians	147
Pianos and Organs	7
Pictures and Picture Frames	9
Planing-Mills	8
Plasterers	21
Plows, Manufs	2
Plumbers	15
Pork Packers	4
Potteries	2
Poultry Dealers	2
Printers, Book and Job	26
Pumps	8
Putty, Manuf	1
Rags, Metals, etc	7
Railroad Ticket Brokers	3
Railway Cars, Manuf	1
Railway Supplies, Manuf	1
Real Estate	62
Restaurants	23
Ropes and Cordage	1
Rubber Goods	1
Rubber Stamps	3
Safe Deposit Companies	2
Saloons	399
Sash, Doors, and Blinds, Manufs	9
Sawmills	2
Saws, Manufs	2
Scales, Computing, Manuf	1
School Furniture, Manuf	1
Screws, Manuf	1
Sculptors	2
Sealing-Wax, Manuf	1
Second-Hand Stores	2
Seeds	4
Sewer Pipe	7
Sewing-Machines, Dealers	15
Sewing-Machines, Manuf	1
Sheet-Iron Workers	3
Shirts, Manufs	6
Shoes, Manuf	1
Showcase Dealers	2
Sign Painters	10
Soap, Manufs	6
Spice-Mills	5
Spraying-Machines, Manufs	2
Stained Glass	1
Stair-Builder	1
Stationers	12
Steam-Engine Builders	3
Steam-Fitters	7
Steamship Agents	3
Stencils	2
Stenographers	6
Stock Yard	1
Stockings, Manuf	1
Stone-Cutters' Tools, Manufs	3
Stonemasons	22
Stone-Quarries	3
Stoneware	2
Stone-Yards	5
Storage	4
Stove-Polish, Manuf	1
Stoves, Manufs	3
Stoves and Tinware, Dealers	35
Straw-Boards, Manuf	1
Street-Cars, Manuf	1
Street Contractors	16
Street-Paving Contractors	2
Street Sprinklers	7
Subscription Books	3
Sweeping-Machines, Manuf	1
Switch and Car Locks, Manuf	1
Table-Slides, Manuf	1
Tablets, Manuf	1
Tags, Manuf	1
Tailors, Merchant	38
Teas and Coffees, Retail	10
Teas and Coffees, Wholesale	1
Telegraph Companies	3
Telephone Company	1
Telephone Construction	1
Theaters	2
Tinware	10
Tobacco, Leaf	22
Tobacco, Manufs	3
Tobacco Machinery	1
Toilet Articles, Manuf	1
Toys	3
Transfer Companies	2
Trunk Materials	1
Trunks, Valises, etc	4
Twines and Cordage	2
Typewriters	3

Umbrellas, Manuf.	1	Wheels, Manuf.	1
Undertakers.	10	White Lead, Manuf.	1
United States Commissioner	1	Wind Engines	1
Upholsterers.	10	Window Glass.	2
Varnish, Manufs.	2	Window Shades.	3
Veterinary Hospital.	1	Wood Dealers.	11
Veterinary Surgeons.	4	Wood- and Iron-Working Machinery	1
Wagon-Makers.	26	Wood Mantels, Manuf.	1
Washing-Machines, Manuf.	1	Wood and Willow Ware.	2
Water-Supply.	2	Yeast, Manufs.	3
Water-Wheels, Manufs.	2		

CHRONOLOGICAL RECORD.

1749—French Major Celoron de Bienville ascended the La Roche or Big Miami River.

1751—Gist visited the Twightwee or Miami villages.

1780—General George Rogers Clark led an expedition against the Indians of the Miami region, one of his officers being Colonel Robert Patterson.

1782—November 9, A skirmish between American soldiers under General Clark and the Indians on the site of Dayton, in which the Americans were victorious.

1786—Americans under Colonel Logan again defeated the Indians on the site of Dayton, one of the brigades being commanded by Colonel Robert Patterson.

1789—Plans formed for a town named Venice on the site of Dayton.

1795—August 3, A treaty of peace made with the Indians at Greenville, Ohio, by General Wayne—August 20, The site of Dayton purchased by Generals St. Clair, Dayton, and Wilkinson, and Colonel Ludlow—November, The town laid out by Colonel Israel Ludlow.

1796—April 1, Arrival of first settlers, by the Miami River, landing at the head of St. Clair Street; two other parties coming a few days later by land—Newcom's first log cabin built.

1798—First sermon preached in Dayton by Rev. John Kobler, of the Methodist Episcopal Church—First Methodist Episcopal class, now Grace Church, organized, with eight members—Newcom's Tavern built—Taxes paid, $29.74.

1799—First Presbyterian Church organized—Blockhouse built—First school opened—First industries established, consisting of distillery, saw-mill, and corn-cracker mill—First lime made—First flatboat left for New Orleans—Dayton three years old and contained nine cabins—Only two houses on Main Street—D. C. Cooper appointed justice of the peace.

1800—Presbyterian meeting-house, eighteen by twenty feet in size, built of logs, on northeast corner of Main and Third streets—August 28, First wedding in Dayton, that of Benjamin Van Cleve and Mary Whitten—April 14, First child born in Dayton, Jane Newcom—First store opened, in Newcom's Tavern.

1801—First male child born in Dayton, John W. Van Cleve.

1802—Only five families in Dayton—Ohio admitted into the Union.

1803—D. C. Cooper resuscitated the town—Montgomery County organized—Dayton made the county-seat—First court held in Dayton—Newcom's Tavern used as court-house, jail, church, and country store.

1804—Postoffice and mail-route established—Benjamin Van Cleve, first postmaster—Mail every two weeks, between Cincinnati and Detroit, via Dayton—Letter postage twenty to twenty-five cents—Log jail built on Court-house lot—First grist-mill erected—Taxes for the year, $458.40.

1805—The town of Dayton incorporated—First town election held—Presbyterian log meeting-house sold for twenty-two dollars and services continued in log tavern—Dayton Social Library Society incorporated—First brick building erected—First disastrous flood.

1806—First Court-house built, of brick, on present Court-house lot—Two brick stores erected—First newspaper published.

1807—Dayton Academy incorporated.

1808—First brick residence built—196 votes cast—*Repertory* first published.

1809—Freight line of keel-boats established between Dayton, Laramie, and St. Mary's—Fourth of July celebrated with a procession—First drug-store opened—First political convention in the county.

1810—Population, 383—New sidewalks ordered by Select Council—*Ohio Centinel* first published.

1811—Nine flatboats left for New Orleans, with products of the surrounding country—A comet visible, and severe earthquake shocks felt.

1812—A company enlisted for the War of 1812—Ohio militia encamped in Dayton.

1813—First society of mechanics organized—First Dayton bank chartered—August 13, Present Grand Opera House lot, on southeast corner of Main and First streets, purchased by James Steele and Joseph Peirce for twenty dollars.

1814—First Methodist church completed—Ferry began to operate at Ludlow Street—*Ohio Republican* first published—First Dayton bank opened for business—A flood.

1815—Dayton Female Charitable and Bible Society organized—First market-house opened—About one hundred dwellings in Dayton, chiefly log cabins—Moral Society and Society of Associated Bachelors formed—First school for girls opened.

1816—First theater held in Dayton—*Ohio Watchman* first published.

1817—New Court-house finished—Presbyterians erected a brick church—St. Thomas Episcopal Parish organized—Bridge across Mad River built—Bridge Street Bridge Company incorporated—First Sabbath-School Association organized—Only two carriages owned in Dayton.

1818—Stage-coach line began to run between Dayton and Cincinnati.

1819—A keel-boat arrived from Cincinnati—St. Thomas Episcopal Church organized—An African lion exhibited at Reid's Inn—Bridge at Bridge Street completed.

1820—Cooper's Mills burned—Population, 1,000.

1822—Montgomery County Bible Society organized—Lancasterian method of instruction introduced—The *Gridiron* published—Seven flatboats and one keel-boat left for New Orleans.

1823—*Miami Republican and Dayton Advertiser* first published.

1824—First Baptist Church organized—First cotton factory erected, by Thomas Clegg.

1825—Law passed authorizing the construction of a canal from Dayton to Cincinnati—Stage-line established between Columbus, Dayton, and Cincinnati—497 passengers by stage passed through Dayton during the year.

CHRONOLOGICAL RECORD 235

1826—The *Watchman* and *Miami Republican* consolidated, and named the *Ohio National Journal and Montgomery and Dayton Advertiser*, afterward becoming the Dayton *Journal*.

1827—First volunteer fire company organized—Baptist society built a church.

1828—Water first turned into the canal—First canal-boat launched—Twenty stage-coaches arrived every week—First iron foundry established, now the Globe Iron Works—A flood.

1829—First arrival of canal-boats from Cincinnati—First temperance society formed—A new market-house built—Last factory established, now Crawford, McGregor & Canby's Dayton Last Works—Steele's dam constructed—A majority of the First Baptist Church established a Campbellite church, now the Church of Christ.

1830—Population, 2,954—*Dayton Republican* first published.

1831—First public school opened—Christ Church Parish organized—First Catholic family arrived in Dayton—R. C. Schenck began practice of law in Dayton.

1832—A fugitive slave captured in Dayton—First Board of Health appointed—Fifty-one brick and sixty-two wooden houses built—A silk manufactory established—Dayton Lyceum organized—First parochial school opened—A flood—Mad River & Lake Erie Railroad Company incorporated.

1833—First Reformed Church organized—Mechanics' Institute organized—Population, 4,000—Thirty-three deaths from cholera.

1834—*Democratic Herald* first published—Police Department organized.

1835—Firemen's Insurance Company chartered.

1836—Main Street bridge opened for travel—First book published.

1837—Emmanuel Catholic Church dedicated.

1838—The "public square," now Cooper Park, prepared for and planted with trees—Convention held in the interest of free schools—Dayton and Springfield turnpike constructed—Montgomery County Agricultural Society organized—Erection of public school-houses ordered.

1839—Dayton Township first divided into election precincts—First county agricultural fair held—Dayton Silk Company organized, with capital of $100,000—First English Lutheran Church organized.

1840—Harrison campaign—General Harrison visited Dayton—Dayton *Journal* began to issue first daily paper—Emmanuel Church of the Evangelical Association organized—Population, 6,067—Paper-mill established—Montgomery County Mutual Fire Insurance Company organized.

1841—Dayton incorporated as a city—The works of W. P. Callahan & Company established.

1842—*Western Empire*, now Dayton *Times*, established.

1843—Woodland Cemetery opened—John Quincy Adams entertained—Bank of Dayton chartered by the State Legislature.

1844—St. Henry's Cemetery opened.

1845—Bank of Dayton (a State bank), now the Dayton National Bank, organized—Dayton Bank, to which the Winters National Bank traces its origin, organized.

1846—Dayton furnished soldiers for the Mexican War.

1847—Disastrous flood—Dayton Library Association organized—First United Brethren Church organized—First telegraph message received.

1849—Two hundred and twenty-five deaths from cholera—The Barney & Smith Car Works established—Dayton lighted by gas—St. Mary's Institute founded—W. C. Howells purchased the Dayton *Transcript*.

1850—Central High School established—Present old Court-house completed—City Bank and Farmers' Bank opened—D. L. Rike, now the Rike Dry Goods Company, began business—First Hebrew Congregation organized—Population, 10,976.

1851—First railroad, from Dayton to Springfield completed—Cincinnati, Hamilton & Dayton Railway completed to Dayton—First passenger station located at northeast corner of Jefferson and Sixth streets—Miami Valley Bank established—Dayton Insurance Company organized—Hebrew cemetery opened.

1852—Probate Court of Montgomery County first opened—Southern Ohio Insane Asylum located at Dayton—Exchange Bank, successor of the Dayton Bank, opened—Dayton & Union Railroad opened for traffic.

1853—United Brethren Publishing House, established in 1834 at Circleville, Ohio, removed to Dayton—Dayton & Western Railroad opened.

1854—First Orthodox Congregational Society organized.

1855—Public Library established—The works of Pinneo & Daniels established.

1856—Union Passenger Station erected.

1857—Old Central High School building erected.

1859—Stomps-Burkhardt chair factory established.

1860—Miami Commercial College established—Population, 20,081.

1861-65—Dayton furnished to the United States service 2,699 soldiers; under special calls of the State, 965; grand total of Dayton men in the service, 3,664.

1862—Lowe Brothers' paint factory founded.

1863—First National Bank, now the City National Bank, established—Second National Bank chartered—Miami Valley Insurance Company organized—First steam fire-engine purchased—Vallandigham arrested—*Journal* office burned—Dayton & Michigan Railroad opened.

1864—*Empire* office mobbed—The Brownell Company began business.

1865—Miami Valley Boiler Works established—Teutonia Insurance Company organized—Ohio Insurance Company began business—Atlantic & Great Western Railway, now the New York, Pennsylvania & Ohio, formed by the consolidation of several roads.

1866—Great destruction by flood—National Soldiers' Home located near Dayton—Stilwell & Bierce Manufacturing Company began business—*Volks-Zeitung* established—Christian Publishing Association, established in 1843, reincorporated and located in Dayton.

1867—Central Branch National Military Home established near Dayton—Dayton Building Association No. 1 organized—Montgomery County Children's Home founded—Cooper Insurance Company incorporated.

1868—McHose & Lyon Architectural Iron Works established—John Dodds began to manufacture agricultural implements.

1869—First street-railway constructed, on Third Street—Normal School opened—Dayton Malleable Iron Company incorporated—Thresher & Company began to manufacture varnish—Sunday, May 16, 1 A.M., Turner's Opera House and adjoining buildings burned; loss, $500,000; insurance, $128,000.

1870—Holly Water-Works established—Young Men's Christian Association organized—Woman's Christian Association organized—Population, 30,473—Cincinnati "Short Line" Railroad, now a part of the Cleveland, Cincinnati, Chicago & St. Louis Railroad, incorporated.

CHRONOLOGICAL RECORD 237

1871—Union Biblical Seminary opened—Merchants National Bank incorporated—Wayne and Fifth Street Railway and Dayton View Street-Railway chartered.

1872—Calvary Cemetery opened.

1873—Metropolitan police force organized—Mutual Home and Savings Association organized.

1874—Philharmonic Society organized—New jail completed—Smith & Vaile Company began business.

1875—J. W. Stoddard & Company began business.

1877—Free night schools established—Crume & Sefton Manufacturing Company established—Dayton & Southeastern Railroad, now the Cincinnati, Dayton & Ironton, opened.

1878—St. Elizabeth Hospital founded—Woodhull's carriage and buggy works established.

1879—Dayton *Daily Herald* first published.

1880—Fifth Street Railway Company incorporated—Population, 38,678.

1881—St. Elizabeth Hospital erected.

1882—Third National Bank chartered—Columbia Insurance Company organized—Reformed Publishing Company organized.

1883—Serious flood—Montgomery County Bar Association organized—Electric light introduced—Dayton Manufacturing Company incorporated—Historical Publishing Company incorporated.

1884—New Court-house completed—National Cash Register Company organized—Montgomery County Soldiers' Monument dedicated—Ohio Rake Company incorporated.

1886—A destructive flood, damaging West Dayton.

1887—White Line Street-Railway, the first operated by electricity, constructed—Union Safe Deposit and Trust Company incorporated—Pasteur-Chamberland Filter Company incorporated—Board of Trade organized.

1888—New Public Library building occupied—Fourth National Bank incorporated—Davis Sewing-Machine Company removed to Dayton—First street-paving laid, on East Fifth Street.

1889—Woman's Literary Club organized—Natural gas introduced—Teutonia National Bank chartered.

1890—Protestant Deaconess Society organized—First sanitary sewers laid—Lorenz & Company, music publishers, began business—Population, 61,220.

1891—Dayton Computing Scale Company incorporated—Dayton Underwriters' Association incorporated—Deaconess Society opened a temporary hospital—Dayton *Press* established.

1892—Columbian Centennial celebrated—Seybold Machine Company incorporated.

1893—New High School building completed—Thresher Electrical Company began business.

1894—Deaconess Hospital completed and dedicated—Police matron appointed.

1895—All street railways except one operated by electricity—Dayton Traction Company began to operate its line—Present Day Club organized—Young Women's League organized.

1896—Manual-training school opened—Population, about 80,000—Sixty-four passenger trains daily—April 1, Centennial celebration begun.

BIBLIOGRAPHY.

BLACK, ALEXANDER. *Story of Ohio.* Boston. 1888.

BROWN, ASHLEY. History of Dayton in the *History of Montgomery County, Ohio.* Chicago. 1882.

CURWEN, MASKELL E. *A Sketch of the History of Dayton.* 1850.

HOWE, HENRY. *Historical Collections of Ohio.* 1847.
—— *The Same.* Revised and enlarged. 2 vols. Columbus. 1889.

KING, RUFUS. *History of Ohio.* Boston. 1888.

Newspapers from 1808 to 1896, on file in Dayton Public Library.

Records of the Dayton Academy. 1808-1047. MS.

STEELE, ROBERT W. *Historical Sketch of the Dayton Schools.*
—— *Historical Sketch of the Woodland Cemetery Association.* 1875.

STEELE, ROBERT W., AND STEELE, MARY DAVIES. *Early Dayton.* 300 pp., 12mo. Dayton, Ohio: W. J. Shuey, United Brethren Publishing House. 1896.

STEELE, ROBERT W., WOOLDRIDGE, J., AND OTHERS. *History of Dayton, Ohio.* 728 pp., quarto. Dayton, Ohio: W. J. Shuey, United Brethren Publishing House. 1889.

VAN CLEVE, BENJAMIN. *Memoranda.* MS.

VAN CLEVE, JOHN W. *Brief History of the Settlement of the Town of Dayton.* Published in Journal of Historical and Philosophical Society of Ohio, page 73.

Note.—For a more complete bibliography see *Catalogue of the Dayton Public Library.*

INDEX

INDEX

ABOLITIONISTS mobbed, 94, 95.
Academy, Dayton, 92, 145.
Adams, John Quincy, 183.
Anderson, Governor Charles, 186, 205.
Antislavery society, 94.
Asbury, Bishop, 127.
Associated Bachelors' Society, 132, 133.
Asylum, 227.

BACON, HENRY, 93.
Bacon, Richard, 108.
Baker, Aaron, 93, 94, 127, 128, 133.
Banks, 90, 126, 185, 199, 228, 234 *et seq.*
Baptist Church, First, 149, 191.
Bar of Dayton, 186, 187.
Barney, E. E., 90, 92, 165, 184, 199.
Bartholomew, Jean, 184.
Battles on site of Dayton, 19, 20.
Benevolent and charitable institutions, 130, 194, 195, 226, 227.
Benham, Captain, 40, 41, 45.
Bibliography, 238.
Bickham, Major W. D., 197.
Bienville, Major Celoron de, 17.
"Black Ben," 94.
Blockhouse, 34.
Board of City Affairs, 221.
Board of Education, 222.
Board of Elections, 222.
Board of Equalization, 222.
Board of Health, 159, 223.
Board of Trade, 228.
Bomberger, Mrs. Sarah, 136, 137.
Bonded debt, 224, 225.
Bridges, 88, 89, 136, 161.
Brown, Ashley, 67, 238.
Brown, Henry, 32, 96.
Brown, Henry L., 32, 160.
Brown, Thomas, 109, 189.
Bruen, Luther, 93, 94, 207.
Builders' Exchange, 229.

Building and loan associations, 197, 228.
Burnet, Isaac G., 110, 128.
Business men in "the thirties," 165.

CABINS, 24, 33, 51, 52.
Cabintown, 154.
Calvary Cemetery, 186.
Campbell, James, 184.
Canal, Miami and Erie, 150 *et seq.*, 221.
Canal-boat, first, built in Dayton, 151.
    first to arrive, 152.
Carpet manufacture, 173.
Cass, General, 119.
Catholic church, Franklin Street, 191.
Catholic family, first, 191.
Cemeteries, 61, 71, 72, 183, 186.
Centennial of Dayton, 29.
Centinel, Ohio, 109, 110, 126.
Central High School, 184.
Charitable and benevolent institutions, 130, 194, 195, 226, 227.
Chase, Governor, 193.
Children's Home, 194, 227.
Chillicothe, 78.
Cholera, 159, 192.
Chronological record, 233 *et seq.*
Churches, 191, 225.
Cincinnati, 21, 22, 23, 25, 54, 138, 139, 216, 221.
City government and institutions, 221 *et seq.*
City Infirmary, 224.
Civil War, Dayton in the, 202 *et seq.*
Clark, General George Rogers, 19.
Clay, Henry, 178, 183.
Clegg, Thomas, 108, 234.
Cleveland, 139.
Clinton, Governor DeWitt, 150.
Clubs, 196, 227.
Colonization society formed, 94.

INDEX

Colored people left for Hayti, 94.
Columbian Centennial, 196.
Columbus, 139, 221.
Comet of 1811, 110.
Comly, R. N., 75, 148.
Comly, W. F., 75, 148.
Commercial and industrial, 228 et seq.
Commercial colleges, 226.
Compton's Tavern, 150.
Conestoga wagons, 103.
Congregational Church, First, 236.
Conover, Obadiah B., 93, 94, 114, 133.
Cooper, D. C., 20, 21, 29, 30, 65, 79, 87, 92, 111, 133.
    becomes titular proprietor of Dayton, 30, 63.
    his improvements and liberality, 30, 31.
Cooper, David Zeigler, 163, 164.
Cooper Female Seminary, 184.
Cooper Hydraulic, 172.
Cooper Park, 26, 30, 119, 164, 190, 196.
Corwin, Thomas, 179.
Council, Town, 109, 163, 164.
    City, 222.
Court-house, 89, 135, 185.
Cox, Miss, 184.
Crane, Judge Joseph H., 70, 78, 80, 81, 106, 108, 109, 121, 133, 179, 186, 187.
    quoted, 90.
Curwen, quoted, 27, 55, 59, 61, 67, 104, 176, 193, 194.
    History of Dayton, 67, 68, 238.
Cut money, 60.

DARST, ABRAM, 100, 141, 165.
Davies, Edward W., 98, 108, 162.
Davis, Dr. John, 190.
Dayton, site purchased, 20.
    laid out, 21.
    named, 21.
    settled, 21-25.
    in 1800-1805, 25.
    made county-seat, 55, 64.
    incorporated, as a town, 83.
    as a city, 235.
    location and area, 221.
    population, 221.
    government and institutions, 221 et seq.
    from 1840 to 1896, 183 et seq.
    in the Civil War, 202 et seq.
Dayton, General Jonathan, 20, 29, 216.

Dayton Academy, 92, 145.
Dayton bank, first, 90, 126.
Dayton Female Charitable and Bible Society, 130.
Dayton Foreign Missionary Society, 144.
Dayton Library Association, 190.
Dayton Lyceum, 160.
Dayton Social Library Society, 84.
Dayton Temperance Society, 153.
Dayton View Hydraulic, 157.
De Bienville, 17.
Deaconess Hospital, 195, 196, 226.
Debt, bonded, 224, 225.
Detroit, 78.
Dickson, Miss Mary G., 184.
Disbrow, Henry, 99, 105, 106.
Doddridge, quoted, 33.
Dover, Mrs. Thomas, 35.
Doyle, Major, 46.
Drake, Dr., quoted, 25.
Dunlevy, Hon. Francis, 55.

EAKER, WILLIAM, 101, 102, 109.
Earthquakes, 110.
Edgar, Robert, 31, 100.
Election, first town, 64.
Electric light, 193.
Elliott, Dr. John, 25, 84, 97.
Emerson Club, 196, 227.
Empire office mobbed, 207.
Engle, George, 108.
Episcopal Church, St. Thomas, 140.
    Christ, 140.
Este, Dr. Charles, 107.
Evangelical Association, Emmanuel Church, 235.

FALES, STEPHEN, 108.
Ferries, 88, 89, 128.
Findlay, Rev. James B., 92.
Fire Department, 140-144, 194, 223.
Fire-hunting, 59.
Fire-insurance companies, 197, 228.
Fires, 133, 140, 141, 142, 143.
First book published, 235.
First brick building, 84.
First brick residence erected, 96.
First bridge, 136.
First business house erected, 32.
First canal-boat built, 151.
First child born, 53.
First county court, 55, 64.

INDEX

First county fair, 173.
First court-house, 54, 55.
First court-house built, 89.
First drug-store, 109.
First flatboat to New Orleans, 33.
First flood, 86.
First graveyard, 61.
First industries established, 61, 233.
First jail, 54.
First jail built, 66.
First justice of the peace, 61.
First library in Ohio, 84.
First lime made, 53.
First male child born, 67.
First market-house, 131.
First mayor, 92.
First mechanics' society, 125.
First meeting-house, 61.
First mill built, 61.
First minister, 26.
First musical society, 71.
First newspaper, 89.
First passenger station, 236.
First postmaster, 34, 78.
First postoffice, 78.
First railroad company organized, 168.
First school, 34.
First school-teacher, 34.
First sermon, 26, 233.
First settlers, 21.
First store opened, 32.
First street-railway, 194.
First telegraph message, 193.
First temperance society, 153.
First theater, 133, 134.
First town election, 64.
First wedding, 57.
Fish, 138.
Flatboating, 104.
Flint, Rev. Timothy, quoted, 132.
Floods, 86, 158, 192.
Folkerth, John, 84, 92, 109.
Forrer, Samuel, 99, 170, 171.
    quoted, 99, 127, 137, 177.
Fort Greenville, 48.
Fort Hamilton, 25, 30, 32, 40, 42, 54, 216.
Fort Jefferson, 40, 42.
Fort Washington, 40, 42, 214, 215.
Fort Wayne, 78.
Fourth of July celebrations, 106-109, 146.

Franklin, 78, 139.
Friday Afternoon Club, 196, 227.

GAME, 138.
Gano, General, 119.
Gano, John Stites, 20.
Gas, 193.
Gas, natural, 197.
Gebhart, Frederick, 199, 200.
Gebhart, George, 199.
Gebhart, Herman, 199.
George, William, 78, 79.
Gist, 17, 18.
    quoted, 18.
Glass, Francis, 146.
Glassmire, Abraham, 21, 22, 33.
Goforth, William, 20.
Greene, Charles Russell, 87, 88, 109, 112.
Greenville, Fort, 48.
Greenville, treaty of, 20.
Greer, Rear-Admiral, 209.
Gridiron, 146.
Grimes, Alexander, 98, 149.
Grimes, Colonel John, 98.
Grimes's Tavern, 98, 107.
Gunckel, Hon. Lewis B., 187.

"H. H." CLUB, 196, 227.
Haines, Dr. Job, 93, 130, 141, 190.
Hamer, William, 21, 128.
Hamilton, Alexander, 214, 215.
Hamilton, Fort, 25, 30, 32, 40, 42, 54, 216.
Hamilton County, 61.
Hanna, James, 92.
Harmar, Fort, 214.
Harmar, General, 214, 215.
Harmonia Society, 196, 227.
Harries, John, 139.
Harrison, General W. H., 122, 174, 175, 176, 177, 179.
Harrison campaign, 174 *et seq.*
Harshman, Jonathan, 93, 95, 96, 168, 175.
Haynes, Judge Daniel A., 165, 179, 186, 189.
Hebrew cemetery, 186.
Hebrew congregation, first, 191.
Herald, 198.
High School, 184, 222.
Hildreth, cited, 24.
Historical and statistical tables, 221.

History of Dayton, material for, 67, 68, 238.
Hogs introduced, 33.
Holt, Colonel Jerome, 64, 109, 123, 124.
Holt, Judge George B., 147, 149, 165.
Hospitality, early, 178.
Hospitals, 115, 195, 196, 226, 227.
Houk, Adam, 108.
Houston, George S., 80, 126, 129, 133.
Howells, W. C., quoted, 51, 52, 59.
Howells, W. D., quoted, 59, 60.
Howe's "Historical Collections of Ohio," quoted, 170, 171.
Huffman, William, 110, 111, 133, 134.
Huffman, William P., 111.
Hull, General, 120, 121.
Hunting, 60, 138.
Hunting-grounds, Indian, 18, 19.
Hydraulics, 157, 172.

IMPROVING the town, 163.
Incorporated companies, 228.
Incorporation, as a town, 83.
 as a city, 235.
Indian villages, 17.
Indians, early experiences with, 27, 28, 31, 38, 39, 56.
Indians, wars with, 19, 20.
Industrial and commercial, 228 *et seq.*
Infirmary, 224.

JACKSON, ANDREW, 185.
Jail, 54, 126, 127, 185.
Jefferson, Fort, 40, 42.
Jennison, William, 167.
Jewett, Dr. Adams, 190.
Jewett, Dr. Hibberd, 95, 190.
Journal, 197.
 office burned, 206.
Jubilee of the United States, 108, 109.

KEEL-BOATS, 105.
Kentucky, incursions from, 18.
King, Colonel Edward A., 193, 203, 206.
King, Rufus, quoted, 125.
King, William, 76, 77, 78.
Knox, General, 43, 214.
Kobler, Rev. John, 26, 127, 233.

LA ROCHE RIVER, 17.
Lafayette, death of, 162.
Lancasterian instruction, 145.
Latitude and longitude, 221.

Levees, 72, 86.
Libraries, 74, 84, 85, 160, 190, 222.
Lime first made in Dayton, 53.
Lincoln, Abraham, 187, 202, 208.
Literary societies, 196, 227.
Location and area, 221.
Log cabin described, 52.
Log Cabin, 75, 174.
Logan, Colonel, 19.
Lowe, Colonel John G., 109, 207.
Lowe, Mrs. John G., 113, 114.
Lowe, Peter P., 108, 147.
Lowry, David, 33, 102.
Ludlow, Colonel Israel, 20, 21, 29, 49, 63, 213 *et seq.*
Lutheran Church, First English, 191.

MAD RIVER, 18, 19, 20, 22, 30, 48, 49, 54, 62, 172, 173, 221.
Maennerchor Society, 196, 227.
Mails, 78, 79, 80.
Manual-labor school, 155.
Manual-training school, 184, 222.
Manufacturing interests, 196, 197, 229 *et seq.*
Marietta, 24.
Market-house, 131, 153, 154, 224.
Markets, 171, 172, 224.
Marriages, early, 62.
Mayor, 221.
 first, 92.
McClure, William, 78, 79, 99.
McCullum's Tavern, 65, 84, 119, 125.
McDaniel, Charles A., 209.
McDaniel, James, 165.
McDermont, Dr. Clarke, 190.
McGuffey, Rev. W. H., 165.
McMahon, Hon. John A., 186.
McMillan, Gideon, 146.
McMullin, Captain John, 146.
Mechanics' Institute, 160.
Mechanics' society, first, 125.
Medical profession, 190.
Medical societies, 129, 130.
Meigs, Governor, 118 *et seq.*
Mercantile interests, 197, 228 *et seq.*
Merchants, early, 165.
Methodist church, first, 127, 128.
Mexican War, 192, 193.
Miami City, 185.
Miami Republican and Dayton Advertiser, 147.

Miami River, Big, or Great, 17, 18, 22, 62, 104, 105, 221.
navigable, 104.
Miami River, Little, 18, 20, 215.
Miami Valley, its beauty and fertility, 18.
Miami villages, 17.
Military companies, 227.
Military history, 19, 111, 112, 116 et seq., 192, 193, 202 et seq.
Mitchell, James H., 92.
Mobs, 94, 95, 206, 207.
Money, 60.
Montgomery County Agricultural Fair, first, 173.
Montgomery County Agricultural Society organized, 173.
Montgomery County Bible Society organized, 144.
Montgomery separated from Hamilton County, 64.
Moral Society, 132, 133.
Morgan's raid, 206.
Morrison, Thomas, 166, 167, 174.
Morus multicaulis, 173.
Mozart Musical and Literary Society, 196, 227.
Mt. Vernon, 139.
Munger, General, 118, 119, 121.
Munger, Warren, 139.
Musical societies, 196, 227.

NATIONAL GUARD, 227.
National Hotel, 153.
National Military Home, 209, 210, 227.
Natural advantages of the Miami region, 18.
Natural gas, 197.
Navigation of Miami River, 104, 105.
New Orleans a market for Dayton produce, 104, 105.
Newcom, Colonel George, 21, 53-57, 126, 133.
Newcom, Mrs. George, 56.
Newcom's Tavern, 27, 30, 32, 53, 54, 55, 64.
News, 197.
Newspapers, 89, 99, 109, 110, 128, 129, 146, 147, 148, 197, 198, 225.
Night schools, 222.
Normal school, 184, 222.

ODLIN, PETER, 109, 168.
Ohio admitted into the Union, 64.

Ohio Centinel, 109, 110, 126.
Ohio Land Company, 17, 20, 87, 88.
Ohio National Journal, 147.
Ohio Republican, 128.
Ohio Watchman, 128, 129.
Oregon, 185.
Original settlers, 21, 23, 24.
Orphans' Home, 194.
Osborn, Cyrus, 78.

PARROTT, COLONEL E. A., 204.
Passenger trains, 229, 237.
Patterson, Colonel Robert, 19, 82, 83, 108, 216.
Patterson, Jefferson, 108.
Patton, Matthew, 99, 133, 141.
Peirce, Joseph, 80, 106, 111, 133.
Periodicals, 198, 225.
Perrine, James, 148.
Perrine, Johnson V., 109.
Petition to Congress, 62, 63.
Philharmonic Society, 196, 227.
Phillips, Horatio G., 108, 111, 112, 137.
Phillips, J. D., 112, 113, 178, 179.
Phillips, Mrs. Horatio G., 113.
Physicians, 190.
Pioneer life, 33, 51 et seq.
Piqua, 17.
Plats of the town, 64, 75.
Pleyel Society organized, 71.
Police Department, 161, 185, 223.
Police matron appointed, 237.
Political clubs, 227.
Political excitement, 158, 159, 161, 192, 202.
Population, 221.
Postage, early, 79, 80.
Postoffice, 78.
Postoffice statistics, 229.
Presbyterian Church, First, 61, 65, 107, 108, 174, 191.
Presbyterian meeting-house, 61, 65.
Present Day Club, 196, 227.
Press, see Newspapers.
Press, 198.
Probate Court opened, 236.
Processions of school-children, 146, 196.
Protestant Deaconess Home and Hospital, 195, 196, 226.
Protestant Deaconess Society, 195.
Public Library, 190, 222.
Public schools, 157, 183, 184, 222.

RAILROADS, steam, 193, 194, 221, 236, 237.
  street, 194, 228, 236, 237.
Rebellion, War of the, 202 et seq.
Reeve, Dr. J. C., 190.
Reformed Church, First, 191.
Regans, Jephtha, 147.
Reid, Colonel, 98, 99.
Reid, Major David, 109, 118.
Reid's Inn, 98, 99, 107, 109, 122, 140.
Repertory, 99.
Rike, D. L., 200, 236.
Roads, 102, 103, 221.
Robert, Prof. J. A., 196.

SABBATH-SCHOOL ASSOCIATION, 136.
Sandusky, 139, 194.
Schenck, Admiral James F., 209.
Schenck, General Robert C., 108, 157, 160, 165, 168, 179, 187, 188, 205.
Schenck, General W. C., 34, 49.
School convention, 165.
School enumeration, 222.
School-houses, public, 169, 222.
Schools, public, 157, 183, 184, 222.
  church, 184, 226.
  private, 34, 154, 155, 184, 226.
  manual-labor, 155.
Settlement, the, 21–25.
Settlers, original, 21, 23, 24.
Sewers, 197, 228.
Sheep first brought to Dayton, 33, 34.
Sherman, Senator John, quoted, 189.
Shows, 140.
Shuey, Rev. W. J., 238.
Silk manufactory, 160.
Silkworms, culture of, 173.
Site of Dayton purchased, 20.
Slave captured in Dayton, 93, 94.
Smith, George W., 101, 102, 107.
Smith, William M., 92, 106.
Social, cycling, and other clubs, 227.
Society of Associated Bachelors, 132, 133.
Soldiers' Home, 209, 210, 227.
Soldiers' Monument, 210, 211.
Soule, Charles, 161, 179.
Southern Ohio Asylum, 227.
Spining, Judge Isaac, 76, 77, 107, 108.
Springfield, 19, 168, 236.
Squier, David, 66, 109.
St. Clair, Governor Arthur, 20, 29, 40, 215, 216.
St. Elizabeth Hospital, 195, 226, 227.
St. Henry's Cemetery, 186.
St. Joseph's Institute, 226.
St. Mary's Institute, 226.
Stage-coaches, 138, 139.
Stebbins, Colonel, 108.
Steele, Dr. John, 95, 107, 115, 116, 129, 190.
Steele, Judge James, 79, 89, 90, 91, 93, 106, 107, 108, 121, 122, 126, 141.
Steele, Miss Mary D., 91.
  History of Dayton, 238.
Steele, Robert W., 67, 68, 91, 184, 186.
  quoted, 69.
  biographical sketch, 91, 200.
  History of Dayton, 238.
Steele High School, 184, 222.
Steele's Dam, 157.
Stillwater, 221.
Stites, Major Benjamin, 20.
Stoddard, Henry, 85, 94, 139.
Stores, early, 104.
Stout, David, 135, 228.
Strain, Robert, 131.
Street improvements, 197, 228.
Street-paving, 197, 228.
Street-railways, 194, 228, 236, 237.
Strong, Lieutenant-Colonel Hiram, 205, 207.
Sun Inn, 137.
Swaynie's Tavern, 153, 173.
Symmes, John Cleves, 20, 63, 216.

TAX COMMISSION, 224.
Taxes, early, 62, 64, 233, 234.
  1894–96, 224.
Tecumseh, 19, 109.
Temperance society, 153.
Tennery, George T., 92.
Theater, first, 133, 134.
Thespian Society, 85.
Thomas, Rev. Thomas E., 76.
Thompson, Mrs. Samuel, 23, 27.
Thompson, Samuel, 21, 23, 27.
Thresher, Ebenezer, 198, 199.
Thruston, Robert A., 108, 162.
Times, 197.
Trains, passenger, 229, 237.
Transportation, early, 102, 103, 104, 105.
Turnpikes, 168, 169, 170.
Turpin, James, 75, 76, 184.
Twightwee villages, 17.

UNION BIBLICAL SEMINARY, 226.
Union Passenger Station, 236.
United Brethren Church, First, 191.
Urbana, 78, 79.

VALLANDIGHAM, CLEMENT L., 188, 189, 206.
Van Cleve, Benjamin, 21, 25, 34 et seq., 55, 57, 58, 62, 67, 68, 78, 79, 83, 84, 92, 106, 107, 109, 126.
 quoted, 34, 49, 63, 69.
 "Memoranda," 35, 36.
 biography of, 35 et seq.
 historian of Dayton from 1795 to 1821, 36.
Van Cleve, Captain William, 21, 22, 119, 120.
Van Cleve, John, 27, 36, 37, 38, 39.
Van Cleve, John W., 58, 67 et seq., 85, 93, 108, 141, 142, 148, 174, 186.
 quoted, 25, 85, 86, 87.
 biography of, 67 et seq.
 historian of Dayton, 67.
Van Cleve, Mary, 27, 28.
Venice, plans for a town named, 20.
Volks-Zeitung, 198.

WAR OF 1812, 111, 112, 116 et seq.
Washington, Fort, 40, 42, 214, 215.
Water-works, 194, 223.
Wayne, General Anthony, 20, 44.
Welsh, Dr. James, 92, 97, 106.

West Dayton, 185.
Westfall, Cornelius, 83.
Wheelock, Major Daniel W., 164.
Whig Glee Club, 76.
Whiting, Swansey, 83.
Whitten, Mary, 57, 58.
Widows' Home, 195, 227.
Wight, Collins, 93, 114.
Wilbur, Rev. Backus, 136.
Wilkinson, General James, 20, 29, 216.
Williams, John H., 76, 78.
Williams, Milo G., 93, 165, 184.
Wilson, Mrs. Jane Newcom, 53, 56.
Winters, J. H., 186.
Winters, Mrs. J. H., 196.
Winters, Valentine, 199.
Wolf Creek, 221.
Woman's Christian Association, 195, 226.
Woman's Literary Club, 196, 227.
Women's literary clubs, 196, 227.
Wood, General T. J., 211.
Woodland Cemetery, 71, 72, 186.
Work-house, 223.

XENIA, 19.

YOUNG MEN'S CHRISTIAN ASSOCIATION, 195, 226.
Young Men's Institute, 226.
Young Women's League, 195, 226.

ZANESVILLE, 78.

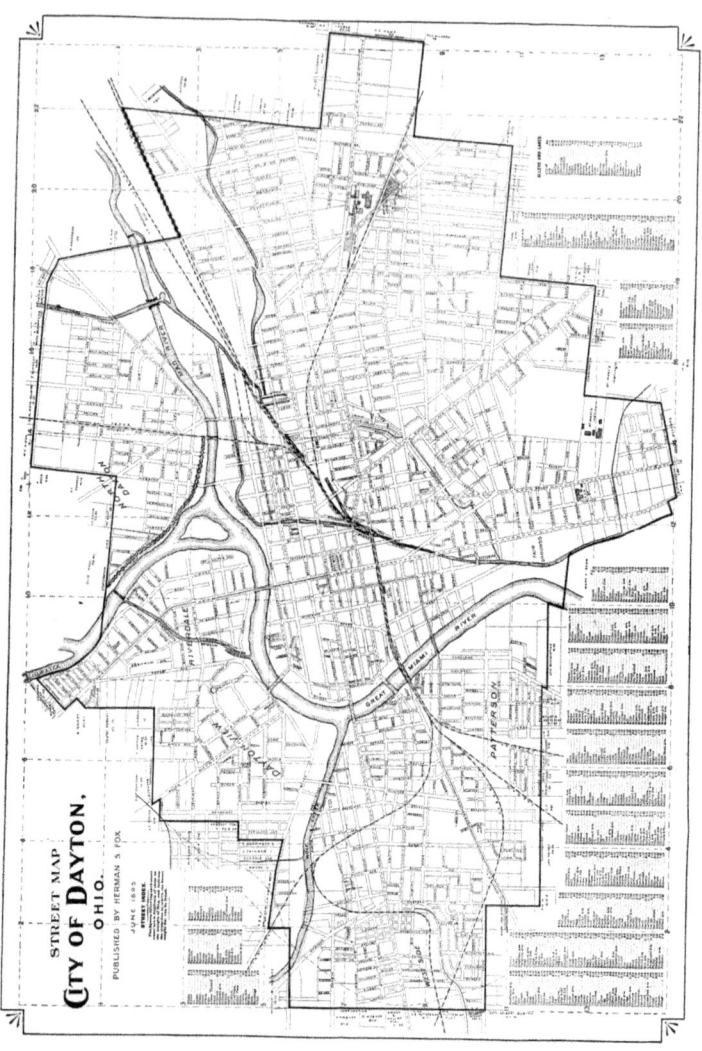